MYTHS AND MYTH MAKERS

JOHN FISKE

SENATE

Myths and Myth Makers

First published in 1873 by James R. Osgood & Company,
Boston, USA

This edition first published in 1996 by Senate, an imprint of
Random House UK Ltd, Random House, 20 Vauxhall Bridge
Road, London SW1V 2SA

ISBN 1 85958 202 8

Printed and bound in Guernsey by The Guernsey Press Co. Ltd

CONTENTS.

MYTHS AND MYTH-MAKERS.

I.

THE ORIGINS OF FOLK–LORE.

FEW mediæval heroes are so widely known as William Tell. His exploits have been celebrated by one of the greatest poets and one of the most popular musicians of modern times. They are doubtless familiar to many who have never heard of Stauffacher or Winkelried, who are quite ignorant of the prowess of Roland, and to whom Arthur and Lancelot, nay, even Charlemagne, are but empty names.

Nevertheless, in spite of his vast reputation, it is very likely that no such person as William Tell ever existed, and it is certain that the story of his shooting the apple from his son's head has no historical value whatever. In spite of the wrath of unlearned but patriotic Swiss, especially of those of the *cicerone* class, this conclusion is forced upon us as soon as we begin to study the legend in accordance with the canons of modern historical criticism. It is useless to point to Tell's lime-tree, standing to-day in the centre of the market-place at Altdorf, or to quote for our confusion his crossbow preserved in the arsenal at Zurich, as unimpeachable witnesses to the truth of the story. It is in vain that we are told, " The bricks are alive to this day to testify to it;

1

therefore, deny it not." These proofs are not more valid
than the handkerchief of St. Veronica, or the fragments
of the true cross. For if relics are to be received as
evidence, we must needs admit the truth of every miracle
narrated by the Bollandists.

The earliest work which makes any allusion to the
adventures of William Tell is the chronicle of the
younger Melchior Russ, written in 1482. As the shooting of the apple was supposed to have taken place in
1296, this leaves an interval of one hundred and eighty-
six years, during which neither a Tell, nor a William,
nor the apple, nor the cruelty of Gessler, received any
mention. It may also be observed, parenthetically, that
the charters of Küssenach, when examined, show that
no man by the name of Gessler ever ruled there. The
chroniclers of the fifteenth century, Faber and Hammer-
lin, who minutely describe the tyrannical acts by which
the Duke of Austria goaded the Swiss to rebellion, do
not once mention Tell's name, or betray the slightest
acquaintance with his exploits or with his existence. In
the Zurich chronicle of 1479 he is not alluded to. But
we have still better negative evidence. John of Winter-
thür, one of the best chroniclers of the Middle Ages, was
living at the time of the battle of Morgarten (1315), at
which his father was present. He tells us how, on the
evening of that dreadful day, he saw Duke Leopold himself in his flight from the fatal field, half dead with fear.
He describes, with the loving minuteness of a contemporary, all the incidents of the Swiss revolution, but
nowhere does he say a word about William Tell. This
is sufficiently conclusive. These mediæval chroniclers,
who never failed to go out of their way after a bit of the
epigrammatic and marvellous, who thought far more of a
pointed story than of historical credibility, would never

have kept silent about the adventures of Tell, if they had known anything about them.

After this, it is not surprising to find that no two authors who describe the deeds of William Tell agree in the details of topography and chronology. Such discrepancies never fail to confront us when we leave the solid ground of history and begin to deal with floating legends. Yet, if the story be not historical, what could have been its origin? To answer this question we must considerably expand the discussion.

The first author of any celebrity who doubted the story of William Tell was Guillimann, in his work on Swiss Antiquities, published in 1598. He calls the story a pure fable, but, nevertheless, eating his words, concludes by proclaiming his belief in it, because the tale is so popular! Undoubtedly he acted a wise part; for, in 1760, as we are told, Uriel Freudenberger was condemned by the canton of Uri to be burnt alive, for publishing his opinion that the legend of Tell had a Danish origin.*

The bold heretic was substantially right, however, like so many other heretics, earlier and later. The Danish account of Tell is given as follows, by Saxo Grammaticus: —

"A certain Palnatoki, for some time among King Harold's body-guard, had made his bravery odious to very many of his fellow-soldiers by the zeal with which he surpassed them in the discharge of his duty. This man once, when talking tipsily over his cups, had boasted that he was so skilled an archer that he could hit the smallest apple placed a long way off on a wand at the first shot; which talk, caught up at first by the ears of backbiters, soon came to the hearing of the king. Now, mark how the wickedness of the king turned the confidence of the

---

* See Delepierre, Historical Difficulties, p. 75.

sire to the peril of the son, by commanding that this dearest pledge of his life should be placed instead of the wand, with a threat that, unless the author of this promise could strike off the apple at the first flight of the arrow, he should pay the penalty of his empty boasting by the loss of his head. The king's command forced the soldier to perform more than he had promised, and what he *had* said, reported by the tongues of slanderers, bound him to accomplish what he had *not* said. Yet did not his sterling courage, though caught in the snare of slander, suffer him to lay aside his firmness of heart; nay, he accepted the trial the more readily because it was hard. So Palnatoki warned the boy urgently when he took his stand to await the coming of the hurtling arrow with calm ears and unbent head, lest, by a slight turn of his body, he should defeat the practised skill of the bowman; and, taking further counsel to prevent his fear, he turned away his face, lest he should be scared at the sight of the weapon. Then, taking three arrows from the quiver, he struck the mark given him with the first he fitted to the string. . . . . But Palnatoki, when asked by the king why he had taken more arrows from the quiver, when it had been settled that he should only try the fortune of the bow *once*, made answer, 'That I might avenge on thee the swerving of the first by the points of the rest, lest perchance my innocence might have been punished, while your violence escaped scot-free.' " *

This ruthless king is none other than the famous Harold Blue-tooth, and the occurrence is placed by Saxo in the year 950. But the story appears not only in Denmark, but in England, in Norway, in Finland and Russia, and in Persia, and there is some reason for supposing that it was known in India. In Norway we have the adven-

* Saxo Grammaticus. Bk. X. p. 166, ed. Frankf. 1576.

tures of Pansa the Splay-footed, and of Hemingr, a
vassal of Harold Hardrada, who invaded England in
1066. In Iceland there is the kindred legend of Egil,
brother of Wayland Smith, the Norse Vulcan. In England there is the ballad of William of Cloudeslee, which
supplied Scott with many details of the archery scene
in "Ivanhoe." Here, says the dauntless bowman,

> " I have a sonne seven years old ;
>   Hee is to me full deere ;
> I will tye him to a stake —
>   All shall see him that bee here —
> And lay an apple upon his head,
>   And goe six paces him froe,
> And I myself with a broad arrowe
>   Shall cleave the apple in towe."

In the *Malleus Maleficarum* a similar story is told of
Puncher, a famous magician on the Upper Rhine. The
great ethnologist Castrén dug up the same legend in Finland. It is common, as Dr. Dasent observes, to the Turks
and Mongolians; "and a legend of the wild Samoyeds,
who never heard of Tell or saw a book in their lives,
relates it, chapter and verse, of one of their marksmen."
Finally, in the Persian poem of Farid-Uddin Attar, born
in 1119, we read a story of a prince who shoots an apple
from the head of a beloved page. In all these stories,
names and motives of course differ ; but all contain the
same essential incidents. It is always an unerring archer
who, at the capricious command of a tyrant, shoots from
the head of some one dear to him a small object, be it an
apple, a nut, or a piece of coin. The archer always pro-
vides himself with a second arrow, and, when questioned
as to the use he intended to make of his extra weapon,
the invariable reply is, " To kill thee, tyrant, had I slain
my son." Now, when a marvellous occurrence is said to
have happened everywhere, we may feel sure that it

never happened anywhere. Popular fancies propagate themselves indefinitely, but historical events, especially the striking and dramatic ones, are rarely repeated. The facts here collected lead inevitably to the conclusion that the Tell myth was known, in its general features, to our Aryan ancestors, before ever they left their primitive dwelling-place in Central Asia.

It may, indeed, be urged that some one of these wonderful marksmen may really have existed and have performed the feat recorded in the legend ; and that his true story, carried about by hearsay tradition from one country to another and from age to age, may have formed the theme for all the variations above mentioned, just as the fables of La Fontaine were patterned after those of Æsop and Phædrus, and just as many of Chaucer's tales were consciously adopted from Boccaccio. No doubt there has been a good deal of borrowing and lending among the legends of different peoples, as well as among the words of different languages ; and possibly even some picturesque fragment of early history may have now and then been carried about the world in this manner. But as the philologist can with almost unerring certainty distinguish between the native and the imported words in any Aryan language, by examining their phonetic peculiarities, so the student of popular traditions, though working with far less perfect instruments, can safely assert, with reference to a vast number of legends, that they cannot have been obtained by any process of conscious borrowing. The difficulties inseparable from any such hypothesis will become more and more apparent as we proceed to examine a few other stories current in different portions of the Aryan domain.

As the Swiss must give up his Tell, so must the Welshman be deprived of his brave dog Gellert, over whose

cruel fate I confess to having shed more tears than I
should regard as well bestowed upon the misfortunes of
many a human hero of romance. Every one knows how
the dear old brute killed the wolf which had come to
devour Llewellyn's child, and how the prince, returning
home and finding the cradle upset and the dog's mouth
dripping blood, hastily slew his benefactor, before the cry
of the child from behind the cradle and the sight of the
wolf's body had rectified his error. To this day the vis-
itor to Snowdon is told the touching story, and shown
the place, called Beth-Gellert,* where the dog's grave is
still to be seen. Nevertheless, the story occurs in the
fireside lore of nearly every Aryan people. Under the
Gellert-form it started in the Panchatantra, a collection
of Sanskrit fables; and it has even been discovered in a
Chinese work which dates from A. D. 668. Usually the
hero is a dog, but sometimes a falcon, an ichneumon, an
insect, or even a man. In Egypt it takes the following
comical shape: " A Wali once smashed a pot full of herbs
which a cook had prepared. The exasperated cook
thrashed the well-intentioned but unfortunate Wali within
an inch of his life, and when he returned, exhausted with
his efforts at belabouring the man, to examine the broken
pot, he discovered amongst the herbs a poisonous snake."†
Now this story of the Wali is as manifestly identical
with the legend of Gellert as the English word *father* is
with the Latin *pater;* but as no one would maintain

---

* According to Mr. Isaac Taylor, the name is really derived from "St.
Celert, a Welsh saint of the fifth century, to whom the church of Llan-
geller is consecrated." (Words and Places, p. 339.)

† Compare Krilof's story of the Gnat and the Shepherd, in Mr. Ralston's excellent version, Krilof and his Fables, p. 170. Many parallel
examples are cited by Mr. Baring-Gould, Curious Myths, Vol. I. pp.
126 - 136. See also the story of Folliculus, — Swan, Gesta Romanorum,
ed. Wright, Vol. I. p. lxxxii.

that the word *father* is in any sense derived from *pater*, so it would be impossible to represent either the Welsh or the Egyptian legend as a copy of the other. Obviously the conclusion is forced upon us that the stories, like the words, are related collaterally, having descended from a common ancestral legend, or having been suggested by one and the same primeval idea.

Closely connected with the Gellert myth are the stories of Faithful John and of Rama and Luxman. In the German story, Faithful John accompanies the prince, his master, on a journey in quest of a beautiful maiden, whom he wishes to make his bride. As they are carrying her home across the seas, Faithful John hears some crows, whose language he understands, foretelling three dangers impending over the prince, from which his friend can save him only by sacrificing his own life. As soon as they land, a horse will spring toward the king, which, if he mounts it, will bear him away from his bride forever; but whoever shoots the horse, and tells the king the reason, will be turned into stone from toe to knee. Then, before the wedding a bridal garment will lie before the king, which, if he puts it on, will burn him like the Nessos-shirt of Herakles; but whoever throws the shirt into the fire and tells the king the reason, will be turned into stone from knee to heart. Finally, during the wedding-festivities, the queen will suddenly fall in a swoon, and "unless some one takes three drops of blood from her right breast she will die"; but whoever does so, and tells the king the reason, will be turned into stone from head to foot. Thus forewarned, Faithful John saves his master from all these dangers; but the king misinterprets his motive in bleeding his wife, and orders him to be hanged. On the scaffold he tells his story, and while the king humbles himself in an agony of remorse, his noble friend is turned into stone.

In the South Indian tale Luxman accompanies Rama, who is carrying home his bride. Luxman overhears two owls talking about the perils that await his master and mistress. First he saves them from being crushed by the falling limb of a banyan-tree, and then he drags them away from an arch which immediately after gives way. By and by, as they rest under a tree, the king falls asleep. A cobra creeps up to the queen, and Luxman kills it with his sword; but, as the owls had foretold, a drop of the cobra's blood falls on the queen's forehead. As Luxman licks off the blood, the king starts up, and, thinking that his vizier is kissing his wife, upbraids him with his ingratitude, whereupon Luxman, through grief at this unkind interpretation of his conduct, is turned into stone.*

For further illustration we may refer to the Norse tale of the "Giant who had no Heart in his Body," as related by Dr. Dasent. This burly magician having turned six brothers with their wives into stone, the seventh brother — the crafty Boots or many-witted Odysseus of European folk-lore — sets out to obtain vengeance if not reparation for the evil done to his kith and kin. On the way he shows the kindness of his nature by rescuing from destruction a raven, a salmon, and a wolf. The grateful wolf carries him on his back to the giant's castle, where the lovely princess whom the monster keeps in irksome bondage promises to act, in behalf of Boots, the part of Delilah, and to find out, if possible, where her lord keeps his heart. The giant, like the Jewish hero, finally succumbs to feminine blandishments. "Far, far away in a lake lies an island; on that island stands a church; in that church is a well; in that well swims a duck; in that duck there is an egg; and in that egg there lies my

---

* See Cox, Mythology of the Aryan Nations, Vol. I. pp. 145–149.

heart, you darling." Boots, thus instructed, rides on the
wolf's back to the island; the raven flies to the top of the
steeple and gets the church-keys; the salmon dives to
the bottom of the well, and brings up the egg from the
place where the duck had dropped it; and so Boots
becomes master of the situation. As he squeezes the
egg, the giant, in mortal terror, begs and prays for his
life, which Boots promises to spare on condition that his
brothers and their brides should be released from their
enchantment. But when all has been duly effected, the
treacherous youth squeezes the egg in two, and the giant
instantly bursts.

The same story has lately been found in Southern
India, and is published in Miss Frere's remarkable collection of tales entitled "Old Deccan Days." In the Hindu
version the seven daughters of a rajah, with their husbands, are transformed into stone by the great magician
Punchkin, — all save the youngest daughter, whom
Punchkin keeps shut up in a tower until by threats
or coaxing he may prevail upon her to marry him. But
the captive princess leaves a son at home in the cradle,
who grows up to manhood unmolested, and finally under-
takes the rescue of his family. After long and weary
wanderings he finds his mother shut up in Punchkin's
tower, and persuades her to play the part of the princess
in the Norse legend. The trick is equally successful.
"Hundreds of thousands of miles away there lies a deso-
late country covered with thick jungle. In the midst of
the jungle grows a circle of palm-trees, and in the centre
of the circle stand six jars full of water, piled one above
another; below the sixth jar is a small cage which contains a little green parrot; on the life of the parrot depends my life, and if the parrot is killed I must die." *

---

* The same incident occurs in the Arabian story of Seyf-el-Mulook

The young prince finds the place guarded by a host of dragons, but some eaglets whom he has saved from a devouring serpent in the course of his journey take him on their crossed wings and carry him to the place where the jars are standing. He instantly overturns the jars, and seizing the parrôt, obtains from the terrified magician full reparation. As soon as his own friends and a stately procession of other royal or noble victims have been set at liberty, he proceeds to pull the parrot to pieces. As the wings and legs come away, so tumble off the arms and legs of the magician; and finally as the prince wrings the bird's neck, Punchkin twists his own head round and dies.

The story is also told in the highlands of Scotland, and some portions of it will be recognized by the reader as incidents in the Arabian tale of the Princess Parizade. The union of close correspondence in conception with manifest independence in the management of the details of these stories is striking enough, but it is a phenomenon with which we become quite familiar as we proceed in the study of Aryan popular literature. The legend of the Master Thief is no less remarkable than that of Punchkin. In the Scandinavian tale the Thief, wishing to get possession of a farmer's ox, carefully hangs himself to a tree by the roadside. The farmer, passing by with his ox, is indeed struck by the sight of the dangling

and Bedeea-el-Jemál, where the Jinni's soul is enclosed in the crop of a sparrow, and the sparrrow imprisoned in a small box, and this enclosed in another small box, and this again in seven other boxes, which are put into seven chests, contained in a coffer of marble, which is sunk in the ocean that surrounds the world. Seyf-el-Mulook raises the coffer by the aid of Suleymán's seal-ring, and having extricated the sparrow, strangles it, whereupon the Jinni's body is converted into a heap of black ashes, and Seyf-el-Mulook escapes with the maiden Dólet-Khátoon. See Lane's Arabian Nights, Vol. III. p. 316.

body, but thinks it none of his business, and does not stop
to interfere. No sooner has he passed than the Thief lets
himself down, and running swiftly along a by-path, hangs
himself with equal precaution to a second tree. This
time the farmer is astonished and puzzled; but when for
the third time he meets the same unwonted spectacle,
thinking that three suicides in one morning are too much
for easy credence, he leaves his ox and runs back to see
whether the other two bodies are really where he thought
he saw them. While he is framing hypotheses of witchcraft by which to explain the phenomenon, the Thief gets
away with the ox. In the Hitopadesa the story receives
a finer point. "A Brahman, who had vowed a sacrifice,
went to the market to buy a goat. Three thieves saw
him, and wanted to get hold of the goat. They stationed
themselves at intervals on the high road. When the
Brahman, who carried the goat on his back, approached
the first thief, the thief said, 'Brahman, why do you carry
a dog on your back?' The Brahman replied, 'It is not
a dog, it is a goat.' A little while after he was accosted
by the second thief, who said, 'Brahman, why do you
carry a dog on your back?' The Brahman felt per-
plexed, put the goat down, examined it, took it up again,
and walked on. Soon after he was stopped by the third
thief, who said, 'Brahman, why do you carry a dog on
your back?' Then the Brahman was frightened, threw
down the goat, and walked home to perform his ablutions
for having touched an unclean animal. The thieves took
the goat and ate it." The adroitness of the Norse King
in "The Three Princesses of Whiteland" shows but poor-
ly in comparison with the keen psychological insight and
cynical sarcasm of these Hindu sharpers. In the course
of his travels this prince met three brothers fighting on
a lonely moor. They had been fighting for a hundred

years about the possession of a hat, a cloak, and a pair
of boots, which would make the wearer invisible, and
convey him instantly whithersoever he might wish to
go. The King consents to act as umpire, provided he
may once try the virtue of the magic garments; but once
clothed in them, of course he disappears, leaving the
combatants to sit down and suck their thumbs. Now in
the "Sea of Streams of Story," written in the twelfth
century by Somadeva of Cashmere, the Indian King
Putraka, wandering in the Vindhya Mountains, similarly
discomfits two brothers who are quarrelling over a pair
of shoes, which are like the sandals of Hermes, and a
bowl which has the same virtue as Aladdin's lamp.
"Why don't you run a race for them?" suggests Putraka;
and, as the two blockheads start furiously off, he quietly
picks up the bowl, ties on the shoes, and flies away!*

It is unnecessary to cite further illustrations. The
tales here quoted are fair samples of the remarkable correspondence which holds good through all the various
sections of Aryan folk-lore. The hypothesis of lateral
diffusion, as we may call it, manifestly fails to explain
coincidences which are maintained on such an immense
scale. It is quite credible that one nation may have
borrowed from another a solitary legend of an archer who
performs the feats of Tell and Palnatoki; but it is utterly
incredible that ten thousand stories, constituting the entire mass of household mythology throughout a dozen
separate nations, should have been handed from one to
another in this way. No one would venture to suggest
that the old grannies of Iceland and Norway, to whom
we owe such stories as the Master Thief and the Princesses
of Whiteland, had ever read Somadeva or heard of the

---

* The same incident is repeated in the story of Hassan of El-Basrah.
See Lane's Arabian Nights, Vol. III. p. 452.

treasures of Rhampsinitos. A large proportion of the
tales with which we are dealing were utterly unknown
to literature until they were taken down by Grimm and
Frere and Castrén and Campbell, from the lips of ignorant peasants, nurses, or house-servants, in Germany and
Hindustan, in Siberia and Scotland. Yet, as Mr. Cox
observes, these old men and women, sitting by the chim-
ney-corner and somewhat timidly recounting to the literary explorer the stories which they had learned in childhood from their own nurses and grandmas, " reproduce the
most subtle turns of thought and expression, and an endless series of complicated narratives, in which the order
of incidents and the words of the speakers are preserved
with a fidelity nowhere paralleled in the oral tradition
of historical events. It may safely be said that no series
of stories introduced in the form of translations from
other languages could ever thus have filtered down into
the lowest strata of society, and thence have sprung up
again, like Antaios, with greater energy and heightened
beauty." There is indeed no alternative for us but to
admit that these fireside tales have been handed down
from parent to child for more than a hundred generations; that the primitive Aryan cottager, as he took his
evening meal of *yava* and sipped his fermented mead,
listened with his children to the stories of Boots and
Cinderella and the Master Thief, in the days when the
squat Laplander was master of Europe and the dark-
skinned Sudra was as yet unmolested in the Punjab.
Only such community of origin can explain the community in character between the stories told by the Aryan's
descendants, from the jungles of Ceylon to the highlands
of Scotland.

This conclusion essentially modifies our view of the
origin and growth of a legend like that of William Tell.

The case of the Tell legend is radically different from the case of the blindness of Belisarius or the burning of the Alexandrian library by order of Omar. The latter are isolated stories or beliefs; the former is one of a family of stories or beliefs. The latter are untrustworthy traditions of doubtful events; but in dealing with the former, we are face to face with a *myth*.

What, then, is a myth? The theory of Euhemeros, which was so fashionable a century ago, in the days of the Abbé Banier, has long since been so utterly abandoned that to refute it now is but to slay the slain. The peculiarity of this theory was that it cut away all the extraordinary features of a given myth, wherein dwelt its inmost significance, and to the dull and useless residuum accorded the dignity of primeval history. In this way the myth was lost without compensation, and the student, in seeking good digestible bread, found but the hardest of pebbles. Considered merely as a pretty story, the legend of the golden fruit watched by the dragon in the garden of the Hesperides is not without its value. But what merit can there be in the gratuitous statement which, degrading the grand Doric hero to a level with any vulgar fruit-stealer, makes Herakles break a close with force and arms, and carry off a crop of oranges which had been guarded by mastiffs? It is still worse when we come to the more homely folk-lore with which the student of mythology now has to deal. The theories of Banier, which limped and stumbled awkwardly enough when it was only a question of Hermes and Minos and Odin, have fallen never to rise again since the problems of Punchkin and Cinderella and the Blue Belt have begun to demand solution. The conclusion has been gradually forced upon the student, that the marvellous portion of these old stories is no illegitimate excrescence, but was rather the pith and centre of the whole,* in days when there was no supernatural, because it had not yet been discovered that there was such a thing as nature. The religious myths of antiquity and the fireside legends of ancient and modern times have their common root in the mental habits of primeval humanity. They are the earliest recorded utterances of men concerning the visible phenomena of the world into which they were born.

That prosaic and coldly rational temper with which modern men are wont to regard natural phenomena was in early times unknown. We have come to regard all events as taking place regularly, in strict conformity to law : whatever our official theories may be, we instinctively take this view of things. But our primitive ancestors knew nothing about laws of nature, nothing about physical forces, nothing about the relations of cause and effect, nothing about the necessary regularity of things. There was a time in the history of mankind when these things had never been inquired into, and when no generalizations about them had been framed, tested, or established. There was no conception of an order of nature, and therefore no distinct conception of a supernatural order of things. There was no belief in miracles as infractions of natural laws, but there was a belief in the occurrence of wonderful events too mighty to have been brought about by ordinary means. There was an unlimited capacity for believing and fancying, because fancy and belief had not yet been checked and headed off in various directions by established rules of experience. Physical science is a very late acquisition of the human mind, but we are already sufficiently imbued with it to

---

* "Retrancher le merveilleux d'un mythe, c'est le supprimer." — Bréal, *Hercule et Cacus*, p. 50.

be almost completely disabled from comprehending the thoughts of our ancestors. "How Finn cosmogonists could have believed the earth and heaven to be made out of a severed egg, the upper concave shell representing heaven, the yolk being earth, and the crystal surrounding fluid the circumambient ocean, is to us incomprehensible; and yet it remains a fact that they did so regard them. How the Scandinavians could have supposed the mountains to be the mouldering bones of a mighty Jötun, and the earth to be his festering flesh, we cannot conceive; yet such a theory was solemnly taught and accepted. How the ancient Indians could regard the rain-clouds as cows with full udders milked by the winds of heaven is beyond our comprehension, and yet their Veda contains indisputable testimony to the fact that they were so regarded." We have only to read Mr. Baring-Gould's book of "Curious Myths," from which I have just quoted, or to dip into Mr. Thorpe's treatise on "Northern Mythology," to realize how vast is the difference between our stand-point and that from which, in the later Middle Ages, our immediate forefathers regarded things. The frightful superstition of werewolves is a good instance. In those days it was firmly believed that men could be, and were in the habit of being, transformed into wolves. It was believed that women might bring forth snakes or poodle-dogs. It was believed that if a man had his side pierced in battle, you could cure him by nursing the sword which inflicted the wound. "As late as 1600 a German writer would illustrate a thunder-storm destroying a crop of corn by a picture of a dragon devouring the produce of the field with his flaming tongue and iron teeth."

Now if such was the condition of the human intellect only three or four centuries ago, what must it have been

in that dark antiquity when not even the crudest generalizations of Greek or of Oriental science had been
reached ?   The same mighty power of imagination which
now, restrained and guided by scientific principles, leads
us to discoveries and inventions, must then have wildly
run riot in mythologic fictions whereby to explain the
phenomena of nature.   Knowing nothing whatever of
physical forces, of the blind steadiness with which a
given effect invariably follows its cause, the men of primeval antiquity could interpret the actions of nature
only after the analogy of their own actions.   The only
force they knew was the force of which they were directly
conscious, — the force of will.   Accordingly, they imagined all the outward world to be endowed with volition,
and to be directed by it.   They personified everything,
— sky, clouds, thunder, sun, moon, ocean, earthquake,
whirlwind.*   The comparatively enlightened Athenians
of the age of Perikles addressed the sky as a person, and
prayed to it to rain upon their gardens.†   And for calling
the moon a mass of dead matter, Anaxagoras came near
losing his life.   To the ancients the moon was not a lifeless ball of stones and clods : it was the horned huntress,
Artemis, coursing through the upper ether, or bathing
herself in the clear lake ; or it was Aphrodite, protectress
of lovers, born of the sea-foam in the East near Cyprus.
The clouds were no bodies of vaporized water : they were

---

* "No distinction between the animate and inanimate is made in the
languages of the Esquimaux, the Choctaws, the Muskoghee, and the
Caddo.   Only the Iroquois, Cherokee, and the Algonquin-Lenape have
it, so far as is known, and with them it is partial."   According to the
Fijians, "vegetables and stones, nay, even tools and weapons, pots and
canoes, have *souls* that are immortal, and that, like the souls of men,
pass on at last to *Mbulu*, the abode of departed spirits." — M'Lennan,
The Worship of Animals and Plants, Fortnightly Review, Vol. XII. p.
416.

† Marcus Aurelius, V. 7.

cows with swelling udders, driven to the milking by Hermes, the summer wind; or great sheep with moist fleeces, slain by the unerring arrows of Bellerophon, the sun; or swan-maidens, flitting across the firmament, Valkyries hovering over the battle-field to receive the souls of falling heroes; or, again, they were mighty mountains piled one above another, in whose cavernous recesses the divining-wand of the storm-god Thor revealed hidden treasures. The yellow-haired sun, Phoibos, drove westerly all day in his flaming chariot; or perhaps, as Meleagros, retired for a while in disgust from the sight of men; wedded at eventide the violet light (Oinone, Iole), which he had forsaken in the morning; sank, as Herakles, upon a blazing funeral-pyre, or, like Agamemnon, perished in a blood-stained bath; or, as the fish-god, Dagon, swam nightly through the subterranean waters, to appear eastward again at daybreak. Sometimes Phaëthon, his rash, inexperienced son, would take the reins and drive the solar chariot too near the earth, causing the fruits to perish, and the grass to wither, and the wells to dry up. Sometimes, too, the great all-seeing divinity, in his wrath at the impiety of men, would shoot down his scorching arrows, causing pestilence to spread over the land. Still other conceptions clustered around the sun. Now it was the wonderful treasure-house, into which no one could look and live; and again it was Ixion himself, bound on the fiery wheel in punishment for violence offered to Here, the queen of the blue air.

This theory of ancient mythology is not only beautiful and plausible, it is, in its essential points, demonstrated. It stands on as firm a foundation as Grimm's law in philology, or the undulatory theory in molecular physics. It is philology which has here enabled us to read the primitive thoughts of mankind. A large number of the

names of Greek gods and heroes have no meaning in the
Greek language; but these names occur also in Sanskrit,
with plain physical meanings. In the Veda we find
Zeus or Jupiter (Dyaus-pitar) meaning the sky, and
Sarameias or Hermes, meaning the breeze of a summer
morning. We find .Athene (Ahana), meaning the light
of daybreak; and we are thus enabled to understand why
the Greek described her as sprung from the forehead of
Zeus. There too we find Helena (Sarama), the fickle
twilight, whom the Panis, or night-demons, who serve as
the prototypes of the Hellenic Paris, strive to seduce
from her allegiance to the solar monarch. Even Achilleus
(Aharyu) again confronts us, with his captive Briseis (Brisaya's offspring); and the fierce Kerberos (Çarvara) barks
on Vedic ground in strict conformity to the laws of phonetics.* Now, when the Hindu talked about Father
Dyaus, or the sleek kine of Siva, he thought of the personified sky and clouds; he had not outgrown the primitive mental habits of the race. But the Greek, in whose
language these physical meanings were lost, had long
before the Homeric epoch come to regard Zeus and
Hermes, Athene, Helena, Paris, and Achilleus, as mere
persons, and in most cases the originals of his myths were
completely forgotten. In the Vedas the Trojan War is
carried on in the sky, between the bright deities and the
demons of night; but the Greek poet, influenced perhaps
by some dim historical tradition, has located the contest
on the shore of the Hellespont, and in his mind the

---

* Some of these etymologies are attacked by Mr. Mahaffy in his Prolegomena to Ancient History, p. 49. After long consideration I am
still disposed to follow Max Müller in adopting them, with the possible
exception of *Achilleus*. With Mr. Mahaffy's suggestion (p. 52) that
many of the Homeric legends may have "clustered around some historical basis," I fully agree; as will appear, further on, from my paper
on "Juventus Mundi."

actors, though superhuman, are still completely anthropomorphic. Of the true origin of his epic story he knew
as little as Euhemeros, or Lord Bacon, or the Abbé
Banier.

After these illustrations, we shall run no risk of being
misunderstood when we define a *myth* as, in its origin,
an explanation, by the uncivilized mind, of some natural
phenomenon; not an allegory, not an esoteric symbol, —
for the ingenuity is wasted which strives to detect in
myths the remnants of a refined primeval science, — but
an explanation. Primitive men had no profound science
to perpetuate by means of allegory, nor were they such
sorry pedants as to talk in riddles when plain language
would serve their purpose. Their minds, we may be sure,
worked like our own, and when they spoke of the far-
darting sun-god, they meant just what they said, save
that where we propound a scientific theorem, they constructed a myth.* A thing is said to be explained when
it is classified with other things with which we are already acquainted. That is the only kind of explanation
of which the highest science is capable. We explain the
origin, progress, and ending of a thunder-storm, when we
classify the phenomena presented by it along with other
more familiar phenomena of vaporization and condensa-
tion. But the primitive man explained the same thing
to his own satisfaction when he had classified it along
with the well-known phenomena of human volition, by
constructing a theory of a great black dragon pierced by

* "Les facultés qui engendrent la mythologie sont les mêmes que
celles qui engendront la philosophie, et ce n'est pas sans raison que
l'Inde et la Grèce nous présentent le phénomène de la plus riche mythologie à côté de la plus profonde métaphysique." "La conception de
la multiplicité dans l'univers, c'est le polythéisme chez les peuples en-
fants ; c'est la science chez les peuples arrivés à l'âge mûr." — Renan,
Hist. des Langues Sémitiques, Tom. I. p. 9.

the unerring·arrows of a heavenly archer. We consider
the nature of the stars to a certain extent explained when
they are classified as suns; but the Mohammedan com-
piler of the "Mishkat-ul-Ma'sábih" was content to explain them as missiles useful for stoning the Devil! Now,
as soon as the old Greek, forgetting the source of his
conception, began to talk of a human Oidipous slaying a
leonine Sphinx, and as soon as the Mussulman began, if
he ever did, to tell his children how the Devil once got
a good pelting with golden bullets, then both the one and
the other were talking pure mythology.

We are justified, accordingly, in distinguishing between
a myth and a legend. Though the words are etymologically parallel, and though in ordinary discourse we may
use them interchangeably, yet when strict accuracy is
required, it is well to keep them separate. And it is
perhaps needless, save for the sake of completeness, to
say that both are to be distinguished from stories which
have been designedly fabricated. The distinction may
occasionally be subtle, but is usually broad enough.
Thus, the story that Philip II. murdered his wife Elizabeth, is a misrepresentation; but the story that the same
Elizabeth was culpably enamoured of her step-son Don
Carlos, is a legend. The story that Queen Eleanor saved
the life of her husband, Edward I., by sucking a wound
made in his arm by a poisoned arrow, is a legend; but
the story that Hercules killed a great robber, Cacus, who
had stolen his cattle, conceals a physical meaning, and is
a myth. While a legend is usually confined to one or
two localities, and is told of not more than one or two
persons, it is characteristic of a myth that it is spread, in
one form or another, over a large part of the earth, the
leading incidents remaining constant, while the names
and often the motives vary with each locality. This is

partly due to the immense antiquity of myths, dating as
they do from a period when many nations, now widely
separated, had not yet ceased to form one people. Thus,
many elements of the myth of the Trojan War are to be
found in the Rig-Veda; and the myth of St. George and
the Dragon is found in all the Aryan nations. But we
must not always infer that myths have a common descent,
merely because they resemble each other. We must remember that the proceedings of the uncultivated mind
are more or less alike in all latitudes, and that the same
phenomenon might in various places independently give
rise to similar stories.* The myth of Jack and the Bean-
Stalk is found not only among people of Aryan descent,
but also among the Zulus of South Africa, and again
among the American Indians. Whenever we can trace
a story in this way from one end of the world to the
other, or through a whole family of kindred nations, we
are pretty safe in assuming that we are dealing with a
true myth, and not with a mere legend.

Applying these considerations to the Tell myth, we at
once obtain a valid explanation of its origin. The conception of infallible skill in archery, which underlies such
a great variety of myths and popular fairy-tales, is originally derived from the inevitable victory of the sun over
his enemies, the demons of night, winter, and tempest.
Arrows and spears which never miss their mark, swords
from whose blow no armour can protect, are invariably
the weapons of solar divinities or heroes. The shafts of
Bellerophon never fail to slay the black demon of the
rain-cloud, and the bolt of Phoibos Chrysaor deals sure
destruction to the serpent of winter. Odysseus, warring
against the impious night-heroes, who have endeavoured

---

* Cases coming under this head are discussed further on, in my paper
on "Myths of the Barbaric World."

throughout ten long years or hours of darkness to seduce
from her allegiance his twilight-bride, the weaver of the
never-finished web of violet clouds, — Odysseus, stripped
of his beggar's raiment and endowed with fresh youth
and beauty by the dawn-goddess, Athene, engages in
no doubtful conflict as he raises the bow which none but
himself can bend. Nor is there less virtue in the spear
of Achilleus, in the swords of Perseus and Sigurd, in
Roland's stout blade Durandal, or in the brand Excali-
bur, with which Sir Bedivere was so loath to part. All
these are solar weapons, and so, too, are the arrows of
Tell and Palnatoki, Egil and Hemingr, and William of
Cloudeslee, whose surname proclaims him an inhabitant
of the Phaiakian land. William Tell, whether of Cloudland or of Altdorf, is the last reflection of the beneficent
divinity of daytime and summer, constrained for a while
to obey the caprice of the powers of cold and darkness,
as Apollo served Laomedon, and Herakles did the bidding of Eurystheus. His solar character is well preserved, even in the sequel of the Swiss legend, in which
he appears no less skilful as a steersman than as an
archer, and in which, after traversing, like Dagon, the
tempestuous sea of night, he leaps at daybreak in re-
gained freedom upon the land, and strikes down the
oppressor who has held him in bondage.

But the sun, though ever victorious in open contest
with his enemies, is nevertheless not invulnerable. At
times he succumbs to treachery, is bound by the frost-
giants, or slain by the demons of darkness. The poisoned
shirt of the cloud-fiend Nessos is fatal even to the mighty
Herakles, and the prowess of Siegfried at last fails to
save him from the craft of Hagen. In Achilleus and
Meleagros we see the unhappy solar hero doomed to toil
for the profit of others, and to be cut off by an untimely

death. The more fortunate Odysseus, who lives to a ripe
old age, and triumphs again and again over all the powers
of darkness, must nevertheless yield to the craving desire
to visit new cities and look upon new works of strange
men, until at last he is swallowed up in the western sea.
That the unrivalled navigator of the celestial ocean should
disappear beneath the western waves is as intelligible as
it is that the horned Venus or Astarte should rise from
the sea in the far east. It is perhaps less obvious that
winter should be so frequently symbolized as a thorn or
sharp instrument. Achilleus dies by an arrow-wound in
the heel; the thigh of Adonis is pierced by the boar's
tusk, while Odysseus escapes with an ugly scar, which
afterwards secures his recognition by his old servant, the
dawn-nymph Eurykleia; Sigurd is slain by a thorn, and
Balder by a sharp sprig of mistletoe; and in the myth
of the Sleeping Beauty, the earth-goddess sinks into her
long winter sleep when pricked by the point of the spin-
dle. In her cosmic palace, all is locked in icy repose,
naught thriving save the ivy which defies the cold, until
the kiss of the golden-haired sun-god reawakens life and
activity.

The wintry sleep of nature is symbolized in innumerable stories of spell-bound maidens and fair-featured
youths, saints, martyrs, and heroes. Sometimes it is the
sun, sometimes the earth, that is supposed to slumber.
Among the American Indians the sun-god Michabo is
said to sleep through the winter months; and at the
time of the falling leaves, by way of composing himself
for his nap, he fills his great pipe and divinely smokes;
the blue clouds, gently floating over the landscape, fill
the air with the haze of Indian summer. In the Greek
myth the shepherd Endymion preserves his freshness in
a perennial slumber. The German Siegfried, pierced by

2

the thorn of winter, is sleeping until he shall be again called forth to fight. In Switzerland, by the Vierwald-stättersee, three Tells are awaiting the hour when their country shall again need to be delivered from the oppressor. Charlemagne is reposing in the Untersberg, sword in hand, waiting for the coming of Antichrist; Olger Danske similarly dreams away his time in Avallon; and in a lofty mountain in Thuringia, the great Emperor Frederic Barbarossa slumbers with his knights around him, until the time comes for him to sally forth and raise Germany to the first rank among the kingdoms of the world. The same story is told of Olaf Tryggvesson, of Don Sebastian of Portugal, and of the Moorish King Boabdil. The Seven Sleepers of Ephesus, having taken refuge in a cave from the persecutions of the heathen Decius, slept one hundred and sixty-four years, and awoke to find a Christian emperor on the throne. The monk of Hildesheim, in the legend so beautifully rendered by Longfellow, doubting how with God a thousand years ago could be as yesterday, listened three minutes entranced by the singing of a bird in the forest, and found, on waking from his revery, that a thousand years had flown. To the same family of legends belong the notion that St. John is sleeping at Ephesus until the last days of the world; the myth of the enchanter Merlin, spell-bound by Vivien; the story of the Cretan philosopher Epimenides, who dozed away fifty-seven years in a cave; and Rip Van Winkle's nap in the Catskills.*

We might go on almost indefinitely citing household tales of wonderful sleepers; but, on the principle of the

---

* A collection of these interesting legends may be found in Baring-Gould's "Curious Myths of the Middle Ages," of which work this paper was originally a review.

association of opposites, we are here reminded of sundry
cases of marvellous life and wakefulness, illustrated in
the Wandering Jew; the dancers of Kolbeck; Joseph of
Arimathæa with the Holy Grail; the Wild Huntsman,
who to all eternity chases the red deer; the Captain of
the Phantom Ship; the classic Tithonos; and the Man in
the Moon.

The lunar spots have afforded a rich subject for the
play of human fancy. Plutarch wrote a treatise on
them, but the myth-makers had been before him.
"Every one," says Mr. Baring-Gould, "knows that
the moon is inhabited by a man with a bundle of
sticks on his back, who has been exiled thither for
many centuries, and who is so far off that he is beyond
the reach of death. He has once visited this earth, if
the nursery rhyme is to be credited when it asserts that

> ' The Man in the Moon
> Came down too soon
> And asked his way to Norwich ';

but whether he ever reached that city the same authority
does not state." Dante calls him Cain; Chaucer has him
put up there as a punishment for theft, and gives him a
thorn-bush to carry; Shakespeare also loads him with
the thorns, but by way of compensation gives him a dog
for a companion. Ordinarily, however, his offence is
stated to have been, not stealing, but Sabbath-breaking,
— an idea derived from the Old Testament. Like the
man mentioned in the Book of Numbers, he is caught
gathering sticks on the Sabbath; and, as an example to
mankind, he is condemned to stand forever in the moon,
with his bundle on his back. Instead of a dog, one German version places with him a woman, whose crime was
churning butter on Sunday. She carries her butter-tub;
and this brings us to Mother Goose again: —

"Jack and Jill went up the hill
　　To get a pail of water.
　Jack fell down and broke his crown,
　　And Jill came tumbling after."

This may read like mere nonsense ; but there is a point
of view from which it may be safely said that there is
very little absolute nonsense in the world. The story of
Jack and Jill is a venerable one. In Icelandic mythology
we read that Jack and Jill were two children whom the
moon once kidnapped and carried up to heaven. They
had been drawing water in a bucket, which they were
carrying by means of a pole placed across their shoulders ;
and in this attitude they have stood to the present day
in the moon. Even now this explanation of the moon-
spots is to be heard from the mouths of Swedish peasants.
They fall away one after the other, as the moon wanes,
and their water-pail symbolizes the supposed connection
of the moon with rain-storms. Other forms of the myth
occur in Sanskrit.

The moon-goddess, or Aphrodite, of the ancient Germans, was called Hörsel, or Ursula, who figures in
Christian mediæval mythology as a persecuted saint,
attended by a troop of eleven thousand virgins, who all
suffer martyrdom as they journey from England to Co-
logne. The meaning of the myth is obvious. In German
mythology, England is the Phaiakian land of clouds and
phantoms; the *succubus*, leaving her lover before daybreak, excuses herself on the plea that "her mother is
calling her in England." * The companions of Ursula
are the pure stars, who leave the cloudland and suffer
martyrdom as they approach the regions of day. In the
Christian tradition, Ursula is the pure Artemis; but, in

---

* See Procopius, De Bello Gothico, IV. 20 ; Villemarqué, Barzas
Breiz, I. 136. As a child I was instructed by an old nurse that Van
Diemen's Land is the home of ghosts and departed spirits.

accordance with her ancient character, she is likewise the
sensual Aphrodite, who haunts the Venusberg; and this
brings us to the story of Tannhäuser.

The Hörselberg, or mountain of Venus, lies in Thuringia, between Eisenach and Gotha. High up on its
slope yawns a cavern, the Hörselloch, or cave of Venus,
within which is heard a muffled roar, as of subterranean
water. From this cave, in old times, the frightened in-
habitants of the neighbouring valley would hear at night
wild moans and cries issuing, mingled with peals of
demon-like laughter. Here it was believed that Venus
held her court; "and there were not a few who declared
that they had seen fair forms of female beauty beckoning
them from the mouth of the chasm."* Tannhäuser was
a French knight, and a renowned troubadour, who, travelling at twilight past the Hörselberg, " saw a white glim-
mering figure of matchless beauty standing before him
and beckoning him to her." Leaving his horse, he went
up to meet her, whom he knew to be none other than
Venus. He descended to her palace in the heart of the
mountain, and there passed seven years in careless revelry. Then, stricken with remorse and yearning for
another glimpse of the pure light of day, he called in
agony upon the Virgin Mother, who took compassion on
him and released him. He sought a village church, and
to priest after priest confessed his sin, without obtaining
absolution, until finally he had recourse to the Pope. But
the holy father, horrified at the enormity of his misdoing,
declared that guilt such as his could never be remitted:
sooner should the staff in his hand grow green and blos-
som. "Then Tannhäuser, full of despair and with his
soul darkened, went away, and returned to the only
asylum open to him, the Venusberg. But lo! three days

---

* Baring-Gould, Curious Myths, Vol. I. p. 197.

after he had gone, Pope Urban discovered that his pastoral staff had put forth buds and had burst into flower. Then he sent messengers after Tannhäuser, and they reached the Hörsel vale to hear that a wayworn man, with haggard brow and bowed head, had just entered the Hörselloch. Since then Tannhäuser has not been seen." (p. 201.)

As Mr. Baring-Gould rightly observes, this sad legend, in its Christianized form, is doubtless descriptive of the struggle between the new and the old faiths. The knightly Tannhäuser, satiated with pagan sensuality, turns to Christianity for relief, but, repelled by the hypocrisy, pride, and lack of sympathy of its ministers, gives up in despair, and returns to drown his anxieties in his old debauchery.

But this is not the primitive form of the myth, which recurs in the folk-lore of every people of Aryan descent. Who, indeed, can read it without being at once reminded of Thomas of Erceldoune (or Hörsel-hill), entranced by the sorceress of the Eilden; of the nightly visits of Numa to the grove of the nymph Egeria; of Odysseus held captive by the Lady Kalypso; and, last but not least, of the delightful Arabian tale of Prince Ahmed and the Peri Banou? On his westward journey, Odysseus is ensnared and kept in temporary bondage by the amorous nymph of darkness, Kalypso ($\kappa\alpha\lambda\acute{u}\pi\tau\omega$, to veil or cover). So the zone of the moon-goddess Aphrodite inveigles all-seeing Zeus to treacherous slumber on Mount Ida; and by a similar sorcery Tasso's great hero is lulled in unseemly idleness in Armida's golden paradise, at the western verge of the world. The disappearance of Tannhäuser behind the moonlit cliff, lured by Venus Ursula, the pale goddess of night, is a precisely parallel circumstance.

But solar and lunar phenomena are by no means the

only sources of popular mythology. Opposite my writ-
ing-table hangs a quaint German picture, illustrating
Goethe's ballad of the Erlking, in which the whole
wild pathos of the story is compressed into one supreme
moment; we see the fearful, half-gliding rush of the Erlking, his long, spectral arms outstretched to grasp the
child, the frantic gallop of the horse, the alarmed fathei
clasping his darling to his bosom in convulsive embrace,
the siren-like elves hovering overhead, to lure the little
soul with their weird harps. There can be no better
illustration than is furnished by this terrible scene of the
magic power of mythology to invest the simplest physical
phenomena with the most intense human interest; for
the true significance of the whole picture is contained in
the father's address to his child,

> "Sei ruhig, bleibe ruhig, mein Kind ;
> In dürren Blättern säuselt der Wind."

The story of the Piper of Hamelin, well known in the
version of Robert Browning, leads to the same conclusion.
In 1284 the good people of Hamelin could obtain no rest,
night or day, by reason of the direful host of rats which
infested their town. One day came a strange man in a
bunting-suit, and offered for five hundred guilders to rid
the town of the vermin. The people agreed : whereupon
the man took out a pipe and piped, and instantly all the
rats in town, in an army which blackened the face of the
earth, came forth from their haunts, and followed the
piper until he piped them to the river Weser, where they
all jumped in and were drowned. But as soon as the
torment was gone, the townsfolk refused to pay the piper,
on the ground that he was evidently a wizard. He went
away, vowing vengeance, and on St. John's day reappeared, and putting his pipe to his mouth blew a different air. Whereat all the little, plump, rosy-cheeked,

golden-haired children came merrily running after him, their parents standing aghast, not knowing what to do, while he led them up a hill in the neighbourhood. A door opened in the mountain-side, through which he led them in, and they never were seen again; save one lame boy, who hobbled not fast enough to get in before the door shut, and who lamented for the rest of his life that he had not been able to share the rare luck of his comrades. In the street through which this procession passed no music was ever afterwards allowed to be played. For a long time the town dated its public documents from this fearful calamity, and many authorities have treated it as an historical event.* Similar stories are told of other towns in Germany, and, strange to say, in remote Abyssinia also. Wesleyan peasants in England believe that angels pipe to children who are about to die; and in Scandinavia, youths are said to have been enticed away by the songs of elf-maidens. In Greece, the sirens by their magic lay allured voyagers to destruction; and Orpheus caused the trees and dumb beasts to follow him. Here we reach the explanation. For Orpheus is the wind sighing through untold acres of pine forest. "The piper is no other than the wind, and the ancients held that in the wind were the souls of the dead." To this day the English peasantry believe that they hear the wail of the spirits of unbaptized children, as the gale sweeps past their cottage doors. The Greek Hermes resulted from the fusion of two deities. He is the sun and also the wind; and in the latter capacity he bears away the souls of the dead. So the Norse Odin, who like Hermes fulfils a double function, is supposed to rush at night over the tree-tops, "accompanied by the scudding train of brave men's spirits." And readers of recent French

---

* Hence perhaps the adage, "Always remember to pay the piper."

literature cannot fail to remember Erckmann-Chatrian's terrible story of the wild huntsman Vittikab, and how he sped through the forest, carrying away a young girl's soul.

Thus, as Tannhäuser is the Northern Ulysses, so is Goethe's Erlking none other than the Piper of Hamelin. And the piper, in turn, is the classic Hermes or Orpheus, the counterpart of the Finnish Wainamoinen and the Sanskrit Gunadhya. His wonderful pipe is the horn of Oberon, the lyre of Apollo (who, like the piper, was a rat-killer), the harp stolen by Jack when he climbed the bean-stalk to the ogre's castle.* And the father, in Goethe's ballad, is no more than right when he assures his child that the siren voice which tempts him is but the rustle of the wind among the dried leaves; for from such a simple class of phenomena arose this entire family of charming legends.

But why does the piper, who is a leader of souls (*Psychopompos*), also draw rats after him? In answering this we shall have occasion to note that the ancients by no means shared that curious prejudice against the brute creation which is indulged in by modern anti-Darwinians. In many countries, rats and mice have been regarded as sacred animals; but in Germany they were thought to represent the human soul. One story out of a hundred must suffice to illustrate this. "In Thuringia, at Saalfeld, a servant-girl fell asleep whilst her companions were shelling nuts. They observed a little red mouse creep from her mouth and run out of the window.

---

* And it reappears as the mysterious lyre of the Gaelic musician, who

> " Could harp a fish out o' the water,
>   Or bluid out of a stane,
>   Or milk out of a maiden's breast,
>   That bairns had never nane."

2 *

One of the fellows present shook the sleeper, but could not wake her, so he moved her to another place. Presently the mouse ran back to the former place and dashed about, seeking the girl; not finding her, it vanished; at the same moment the girl died."* This completes the explanation of the piper, and it also furnishes the key to the horrible story of Bishop Hatto.

This wicked prelate lived on the bank of the Rhine, in the middle of which stream he possessed a tower, now pointed out to travellers as the Mouse Tower. In the year 970 there was a dreadful famine, and people came from far and near craving sustenance out of the Bishop's ample and well-filled granaries. Well, he told them all to go into the barn, and when they had got in there, as many as could stand, he set fire to the barn and burnt them all up, and went home to eat a merry supper. But when he arose next morning, he heard that an army of rats had eaten all the corn in his granaries, and was now advancing to storm the palace. Looking from his window, he saw the roads and fields dark with them, as they came with fell purpose straight toward his mansion. In frenzied terror he took his boat and rowed out to the tower in the river. But it was of no use : down into the water marched the rats, and swam across, and scaled the walls, and gnawed through the stones, and came swarming in about the shrieking Bishop, and ate him up, flesh, bones, and all. Now, bearing in mind what was said above, there can be no doubt that these rats were the souls of those whom the Bishop had murdered. There are many versions of the story in different Teutonic countries, and in some of them the avenging rats or mice issue directly, by a strange metamorphosis, from the corpses of the victims. St. Gertrude, moreover, the

* Baring-Gould, Curious Myths, Vol. II. p. 159.

heathen Holda, was symbolized as a mouse, and was said to lead an army of mice; she was the receiver of children's souls. Odin, also, in his character of a Psychopompos, was followed by a host of rats.*

As the souls of the departed are symbolized as rats, so is the psychopomp himself often figured as a dog. Sarameias, the Vedic counterpart of Hermes and Odin, sometimes appears invested with canine attributes; and countless other examples go to show that by the early Aryan mind the howling wind was conceived as a great dog or wolf. As the fearful beast was heard speeding by the windows or over the house-top, the inmates trembled, for none knew but his own soul might forthwith be required of him. Hence, to this day, among ignorant people, the howling of a dog under the window is supposed to portend a death in the family. It is the fleet greyhound of Hermes, come to escort the soul to the river Styx.†

But the wind-god is not always so terrible. Nothing can be more transparent than the phraseology of the Homeric Hymn, in which Hermes is described as acquiring the strength of a giant while yet a babe in the cradle, as sallying out and stealing the cattle (clouds) of Apollo, and driving them helter-skelter in various directions, then as crawling through the keyhole, and with a mocking laugh shrinking into his cradle. He is the Master Thief, who can steal the burgomaster's horse from under him and his wife's mantle from off her back, the prototype not only of the crafty architect of Rhampsinitos, but even of the ungrateful slave who robs Sancho of his mule in the Sierra Morena. He furnishes in part the conceptions

* Perhaps we may trace back to this source the frantic terror which Irish servant-girls often manifest at sight of a mouse.

† In Persia a dog is brought to the bedside of the person who is dying, in order that the soul may be sure of a prompt escort. The same custom exists in India. Breal, Hercule et Cacus, p. 123.

of Boots and Reynard; he is the prototype of Paul Pry
and peeping Tom of Coventry; and in virtue of his
ability to contract or expand himself at pleasure, he is
both the Devil in the Norse Tale,* whom the lad persuades to enter a walnut, and the Arabian Efreet, whom
the fisherman releases from the bottle.

The very interesting series of myths and popular superstitions suggested by the storm-cloud and the lightning
must be reserved for a future occasion. When carefully
examined, they will richly illustrate the conclusion which
is the result of the present inquiry, that the marvellous
tales and quaint superstitions current in every Aryan
household have a common origin with the classic legends
of gods and heroes, which formerly were alone thought
worthy of the student's serious attention. These stories
— some of them familiar to us in infancy, others the
delight of our maturer years — constitute the *débris*, or
alluvium, brought down by the stream of tradition from
the distant highlands of ancient mythology.

* The Devil, who is proverbially "active in a gale of wind," is none
other than Hermes.

September, 1870.

II.

THE DESCENT OF FIRE.

IN the course of my last summer's vacation, which was
spent at a small inland village, I came upon an un-
expected illustration of the tenacity with which conceptions descended from prehistoric antiquity have
now and then kept their hold upon life. While sitting one evening under the trees by the roadside, my
attention was called to the unusual conduct of half a
dozen men and boys who were standing opposite. An
elderly man was moving slowly up and down the road,
holding with both hands a forked twig of hazel, shaped
like the letter Y inverted. With his palms turned upward, he held in each hand a branch of the twig in such
a way that the shank pointed upward; but every few
moments, as he halted over a certain spot, the twig would
gradually bend downwards until it had assumed the likeness of a Y in its natural position, where it would remain
pointing to something in the ground beneath. One by
one the bystanders proceeded to try the experiment, but
with no variation in the result. Something in the ground
seemed to fascinate the bit of hazel, for it could not pass
over that spot without bending down and pointing to it.

My thoughts reverted at once to Jacques Aymar and
Dousterswivel, as I perceived that these men were
engaged in sorcery. During the long drought more than
half the wells in the village had become dry, and here
was an attempt to make good the loss by the aid of the

god Thor. These men were seeking water with a divining-rod. Here, alive before my eyes, was a superstitious observance, which I had supposed long since dead and forgotten by all men except students interested in mythology.

As I crossed the road to take part in the ceremony a farmer's boy came up, stoutly affirming his incredulity,

and offering to show the company how he could carry the rod motionless across the charmed spot. But when he came to take the weird twig he trembled with an ill-defined feeling of insecurity as to the soundness of his conclusions, and when he stood over the supposed rivulet the rod bent in spite of him, — as was not so very strange. For, with all his vague scepticism, the honest lad had not, and could not be supposed to have, the *foi scientifique* of which Littré speaks.*

* "Il faut que la cœur devienne ancien parmi les anciennes choses, et la plénitude de l'histoire ne se dévoile qu'à celui qui descend, ainsi disposé, dans le passé. Mais il faut que l'esprit demeure moderne, et n'oublie jamais qu'il n'y a pour lui d'autre foi que la foi scientifique.' — Littré.

Hereupon I requested leave to try the rod; but something in my manner seemed at once to excite the suspicion and scorn of the sorcerer. "Yes, take it," said he, with uncalled-for vehemence, "but you can't stop it; there's water below here, and you can't help its bending, if you break your back trying to hold it." So he gave me the twig, and awaited, with a smile which was meant to express withering sarcasm, the discomfiture of the supposed scoffer. But when I proceeded to walk four or five times across the mysterious place, the rod pointing steadfastly toward the zenith all the while, our friend became grave and began to philosophize. "Well," said he, "you see, your temperament is peculiar; the conditions ain't favourable in your case; there are some people who never can work these things. But there's water below here, for all that, as you'll find, if you dig for it; there's nothing like a hazel-rod for finding out water."

Very true: there are some persons who never can make such things work; who somehow always encounter "unfavourable conditions" when they wish to test the marvellous powers of a clairvoyant; who never can make "Planchette" move in conformity to the requirements of any known alphabet; who never see ghosts, and never have "presentiments," save such as are obviously due to association of ideas. The ill-success of these persons is commonly ascribed to their lack of faith; but, in the majority of cases, it might be more truly referred to the strength of their faith, — faith in the constancy of nature, and in the adequacy of ordinary human experience as interpreted by science.* *La foi scientifique* is an excellent preventive against that obscure, though not uncommon,

---

* For an admirable example of scientific self-analysis tracing one of these illusions to its psychological sources, see the account of Dr. Lazarus, in Taine, De l'Intelligence, Vol. I. pp. 121 – 125.

kind of self-deception which enables wooden tripods to
write and tables to tip and hazel-twigs to twist upside-
down, without the conscious intervention of the per-
former. It was this kind of faith, no doubt, which caused
the discomfiture of Jacques Aymar on his visit to Paris,*
and which has in late years prevented persons from obtaining the handsome prize offered by the French Acad-
emy for the first authentic case of clairvoyance.

But our village friend, though perhaps constructively
right in his philosophizing, was certainly very defective
in his acquaintance with the time-honoured art of rhab-
domancy. Had he extended his inquiries so as to cover
the field of Indo-European tradition, he would have
learned that the mountain-ash, the mistletoe, the white
and black thorn, the Hindu *asvattha,* and several other
woods, are quite as efficient as the hazel for the purpose
of detecting water in times of drought; and in due course
of time he would have perceived that the divining-rod
itself is but one among a large class of things to which
popular belief has ascribed, along with other talismanic
properties, the power of opening the ground or cleaving
rocks, in order to reveal hidden treasures. Leaving him
in peace, then, with his bit of forked hazel, to seek for
cooling springs in some future thirsty season, let us en-
deavour to elucidate the origin of this curious superstition.

The detection of subterranean water is by no means
the only use to which the divining-rod has been put.
Among the ancient Frisians it was regularly used for the
detection of criminals; and the reputation of Jacques

---

* See the story of Aymar in Baring-Gould, Curious Myths, Vol. I.
pp. 57–77. The learned author attributes the discomfiture to the un-
congenial Parisian environment; which is a style of reasoning much like
that of my village sorcerer, I fear.

Aymar was won by his discovery of the perpetrator of a horrible murder at Lyons. Throughout Europe it has been used from time immemorial by miners for ascertaining the position of veins of metal; and in the days when talents were wrapped in napkins and buried in the field, instead of being exposed to the risks of financial speculation, the divining-rod was employed by persons covetous of their neighbours' wealth. If Boulatruelle had lived in the sixteenth century, he would have taken a forked stick of hazel when he went to search for the buried treasures of Jean Valjean. It has also been applied to the cure of disease, and has been kept in households, like a wizard's charm, to insure general good-fortune and immunity from disaster.

As we follow the conception further into the elf-land of popular tradition, we come upon a rod which not only points out the situation of hidden treasure, but even splits open the ground and reveals the mineral wealth contained therein. In German legend, "a shepherd, who was driving his flock over the Ilsenstein, having stopped to rest, leaning on his staff, the mountain suddenly opened, for there was a springwort in his staff without his knowing it, and the princess [Ilse] stood before him. She bade him follow her, and when he was inside the mountain she told him to take as much gold as he pleased. The shepherd filled all his pockets, and was going away, when the princess called after him, 'Forget not the best.' So, thinking she meant that he had not taken enough, he filled his hat also; but what she meant was his staff with the springwort, which he had laid against the wall as soon as he stepped in. But now, just as he was going out at the opening, the rock suddenly slammed together and cut him in two." *

* Kelly, Indo-European Folk-Lore, p. 177.

Here the rod derives its marvellous properties from the enclosed springwort, but in many cases a leaf or flower is itself competent to open the hillside. The little blue flower, forget-me-not, about which so many sentimental associations have clustered, owes its name to the legends told of its talismanic virtues.† A man, travelling on a lonely mountain, picks up a little blue flower and sticks it in his hat. Forthwith an iron door opens, showing up a lighted passage-way, through which the man advances into a magnificent hall, where rubies and diamonds and all other kinds of gems are lying piled in great heaps on the floor. As he eagerly fills his pockets his hat drops from his head, and when he turns to go out the little flower calls after him, "Forget me not!" He turns back and looks around, but is too bewildered with his good fortune to think of his bare head or of the luck-flower which he has let fall. He selects several more of the finest jewels he can find, and again starts to go out; but as he passes through the door the mountain closes amid the crashing of thunder, and cuts off one of his heels. Alone, in the gloom of the forest, he searches in vain for the mysterious door: it has disappeared forever, and the traveller goes on his way, thankful, let us hope, that he has fared no worse.

Sometimes it is a white lady, like the Princess Ilse, who invites the finder of the luck-flower to help himself to her treasures, and who utters the enigmatical warning. The mountain where the event occurred may be found almost anywhere in Germany, and one just like it stood in Persia, in the golden prime of Haroun Alraschid. In the story of the Forty Thieves, the mere name of the plant *sesame* serves as a talisman to open and shut the

† The story of the luck-flower is well told in verse by Mr. Baring-Gould, in his Silver Store, p. 115, *seq.*

secret door which leads into the robbers' cavern; and when the avaricious Cassim Baba, absorbed in the contemplation of the bags of gold and bales of rich merchandise, forgets the magic formula, he meets no better fate than the shepherd of the Ilsenstein. In the story of Prince Ahmed, it is an enchanted arrow which guides the young adventurer through the hillside to the grotto of the Peri Banou. In the tale of Baba Abdallah, it is an ointment rubbed on the eyelid which reveals at a single glance all the treasures hidden in the bowels of the earth.

The ancient Romans also had their rock-breaking plant, called *Saxifraga*, or "sassafras." And the further we penetrate into this charmed circle of traditions the more evident does it appear that the power of cleaving rocks or shattering hard substances enters, as a primitive element, into the conception of these treasure-showing talismans. Mr. Baring-Gould has given an excellent account of the rabbinical legends concerning the wonderful schamir, by the aid of which Solomon was said to have built his temple. From Asmodeus, prince of the Jann, Benaiah, the son of Jehoiada, wrested the secret of a worm no bigger than a barley-corn, which could split the hardest substance. This worm was called schamir. "If Solomon desired to possess himself of the worm, he must find the nest of the moor-hen, and cover it with a plate of glass, so that the mother bird could not get at her young without breaking the glass. She would seek schamir for the purpose, and the worm must be obtained from her." As the Jewish king did need the worm in order to hew the stones for that temple which was to be built without sound of hammer, or axe, or any tool of iron,* he sent Benaiah to obtain it. According to another account, schamir was a mystic stone which enabled Solomon to

* 1 Kings vi. 7.

penetrate the earth in search of mineral wealth. Directed by a Jinni, the wise king covered a raven's eggs
with a plate of crystal, and thus obtained schamir which
the bird brought in order to break the plate.*

In these traditions, which may possibly be of Aryan
descent, due to the prolonged intercourse between the
Jews and the Persians, a new feature is added to those
before enumerated : the rock-splitting talisman is always
found in the possession of a bird. The same feature in
the myth reappears on Aryan soil. The springwort,
whose marvellous powers we have noticed in the case of
the Ilsenstein shepherd, is obtained, according to Pliny,
by stopping up the hole in a tree where a woodpecker
keeps its young. The bird flies away, and presently returns with the springwort, which it applies to the plug,
causing it to shoot out with a loud explosion. The same
account is given in German folk-lore. Elsewhere, as in
Iceland, Normandy, and ancient Greece, the bird is an
eagle, a swallow, an ostrich, or a hoopoe.

In the Icelandic and Pomeranian myths the schamir,
or "raven-stone," also renders its possessor invisible, —
a property which it shares with one of the treasure-find-
ing plants, the fern.† In this respect it resembles the
ring of Gyges, as in its divining and rock-splitting qualities it resembles that other ring which the African magi-

---

* Compare the Mussulman account of the building of the temple, in
Baring-Gould, Legends of the Patriarchs and Prophets, pp. 337, 338.
And see the story of Diocletian's ostrich, Swan, Gesta Romanorum, ed.
Wright, Vol. I. p. lxiv. See also the pretty story of the knight un-
justly imprisoned, id. p. cii.

† "We have the receipt of fern-seed. We walk invisible." —
Shakespeare, Henry IV. See Ralston, Songs of the Russian People,
p. 98.

According to one North German tradition, the luck-flower also will
make its finder invisible at pleasure. But, as the myth shrewdly adds,
it is absolutely essential that the flower be found by accident : he who

cian gave to Aladdin, to enable him to descend into the
cavern where stood the wonderful lamp.

In the North of Europe schamir appears strangely and
grotesquely metamorphosed. The hand of a man that
has been hanged, when dried and prepared with certain
weird unguents and set on fire, is known as the Hand
of Glory; and as it not only bursts open all safe-locks,
but also lulls to sleep all persons within the circle of its
influence, it is of course invaluable to thieves and burg-
lars. I quote the following story from Thorpe's "Northern Mythology": "Two fellows once came to Huy, who
pretended to be exceedingly fatigued, and when they had
supped would not retire to a sleeping-room, but begged
their host would allow them to take a nap on the hearth.
But the maid-servant, who did not like the looks of the
two guests, remained by the kitchen door and peeped
through a chink, when she saw that one of them drew a
thief's hand from his pocket, the fingers of which, after
having rubbed them with an ointment, he lighted, and
they all burned except one. Again they held this finger
to the fire, but still it would not burn, at which they
appeared much surprised, and one said, 'There must
surely be some one in the house who is not yet asleep.'
They then hung the hand with its four burning fingers by
the chimney, and went out to call their associates. But
the maid followed them instantly and made the door
fast, then ran up stairs, where the landlord slept, that
she might wake him, but was unable, notwithstanding
all her shaking and calling. In the mean time the
thieves had returned and were endeavouring to enter the

seeks for it never finds it! Thus all cavils are skilfully forestalled, even
if not satisfactorily disposed of. The same kind of reasoning is favoured
by our modern dealers in mystery : somehow the "conditions" always
are askew whenever a scientific observer wishes to test their pretensions.

house by a window, but the maid cast them down from the ladder. They then took a different course, and would have forced an entrance, had it not occurred to the maid that the burning fingers might probably be the cause of her master's profound sleep. Impressed with this idea she ran to the kitchen and blew them out, when the master and his men-servants instantly awoke, and soon drove away the robbers." The same event is said to have occurred at Stainmore in England; and Torquemada relates of Mexican thieves that they carry with them the left hand of a woman who has died in her first childbed, before which talisman all bolts yield and all opposition is benumbed. In 1831 " some Irish thieves attempted to commit a robbery on the estate of Mr. Naper, of Loughcrew, county Meath. They entered the house armed with a dead man's hand with a lighted candle in it, believing in the superstitious notion that a candle placed in a dead man's hand will not be seen by any but those by whom it is used; and also that if a candle in a dead hand be introduced into a house, it will prevent those who may be asleep from awaking. The inmates, however, were alarmed, and the robbers fled, leaving the hand behind them." *

In the Middle Ages the hand of glory was used, just like the divining-rod, for the detection of buried treasures.

Here, then, we have a large and motley group of objects — the forked rod of ash or hazel, the springwort and the luck-flower, leaves, worms, stones, rings, and dead men's hands — which are for the most part competent to open the way into cavernous rocks, and which all agree in pointing out hidden wealth. We find, moreover, that many of these charmed objects are carried about by birds, and that some of them possess, in addi-

* Henderson, Folk-Lore of the Northern Counties of England, p. 202.

tion to their generic properties, the specific power of benumbing people's senses. What, now, is the common origin of this whole group of superstitions? And since mythology has been shown to be the result of primeval attempts to explain the phenomena of nature, what natural phenomenon could ever have given rise to so many seemingly wanton conceptions? Hopeless as the problem may at first sight seem, it has nevertheless been solved. In his great treatise on "The Descent of Fire," Dr. Kuhn has shown that all these legends and traditions are descended from primitive myths explanatory of the lightning and the storm-cloud.*

To us, who are nourished from childhood on the truths revealed by science, the sky is known to be merely an optical appearance due to the partial absorption of the solar rays in passing through a thick stratum of atmospheric air; the clouds are known to be large masses of watery vapour, which descend in rain-drops when sufficiently condensed; and the lightning is known to be a flash of light accompanying an electric discharge. But these conceptions are extremely recondite, and have been attained only through centuries of philosophizing and after careful observation and laborious experiment. To the untaught mind of a child or of an uncivilized man, it seems far more natural and plausible to regard the sky as a solid dome of blue crystal, the clouds as snowy mountains, or perhaps even as giants or angels, the lightning as a flashing dart or a fiery serpent. In point of fact, we find that the conceptions actually entertained are often far more grotesque than these. I can recollect once framing the hypothesis that the flaming clouds of sunset were transient apparitions, vouchsafed us by way of warn-

* Kuhn, Die Herabkunft des Feuers und des Göttertranks. Berlin, 1859.

ing, of that burning Calvinistic hell with which my
childish imagination had been unwisely terrified ; * and I
have known of a four-year-old boy who thought that the
snowy clouds of noonday were the white robes of the
angels hung out to dry in the sun.† My little daughter
is anxious to know whether it is necessary to take a bal-
loon in order to get to the place where God lives, or
whether the same end can be accomplished by going to
the horizon and crawling up the sky ; ‡ the Mohammedan of old was working at the same problem when he
called the rainbow the bridge Es-Sirat, over which souls
must pass on their way to heaven. According to the
ancient Jew, the sky was a solid plate, hammered out by
the gods, and spread over the earth in order to keep up
the ocean overhead ; § but the plate was full of little
windows, which were opened whenever it became necessary to let the rain come through. ‖ With equal plausi-
bility the Greek represented the rainy sky as a sieve in
which the daughters of Danaos were vainly trying to draw

---

* " Saga me forwhan byth seo sunne read on æfen ? Ic the secge,
forthon heo locath on helle. — Tell me, why is the sun red at even ?
I tell thee, because she looketh on hell." Thorpe, Analecta Anglo-
Saxonica, p. 115, *apud* Tylor, Primitive Culture, Vol. II. p. 63. Barbaric thought had partly anticipated my childish theory.

† "Still in North Germany does the peasant say of thunder, that the
angels are playing skittles aloft. and of the snow, that they are shaking
up the feather-beds in heaven." — Baring-Gould, Book of Werewolves,
p. 172.

‡ "The Polynesians imagine that the sky descends at the horizon
and encloses the earth. Hence they call foreigners *papalangi*, or 'heav-
en-bursters,' as having broken in from another world outside." — Max
Müller, Chips, II. 268.

§ " Way-yo'hmer 'helohim yᵉhi raquiaⁿh bᵉ-thok ham-mayim wihi
mavdil beyn mayim la-mayim. — And said the gods, let there be a hammered plate in the midst of the waters, and let it be dividing between
waters and waters." Genesis i. 6.

‖ Genesis vii. 11.

water ; while to the Hindu the rain-clouds were celestial cattle milkèd by the wind-god. In primitive Aryan lore, the sky itself was a blue sea, and the clouds were ships sailing over it ; and an English legend tells how one of these ships once caught its anchor on a gravestone in the churchyard, to the great astonishment of the peop'e who were coming out of church. Charon's ferry-boat was one of these vessels, and another was Odin's golden ship, in which the souls of slain heroes were conveyed to Valhalla. Hence it was once the Scandinavian practice to bury the dead in boats ; and in Altmark a penny is still placed in the mouth of the corpse, that it may have the means of paying its fare to the ghostly ferryman.* In such a vessel drifted the Lady of Shalott on her fatal voyage ; and of similar nature was the dusky barge, " dark as a funeral-scarf from stem to stern," in which Arthur was received by the black-hooded queens.†

But the fact that a natural phenomenon was explained in one way did not hinder it from being explained in a dozen other ways. The fact that the sun was generally regarded as an all-conquering hero did not prevent its

---

* See Kelly, Indo-European Folk-Lore, p. 120 ; who states also that in Bengal the Garrows burn their dead in a small boat, placed on top of the funeral-pile.

In their character of cows, also, the clouds were regarded as psychopomps ; and hence it is still a popular superstition that a cow breaking into the yard foretokens a death in the family.

† The sun-god Freyr had a cloud-ship called Skithblathnir, which is thus described in Dasent's Prose Edda : " She is so great, that all the Æsir, with their weapons and war-gear, may find room on board her " ; but " when there is no need of faring on the sea in her, she is made . . . . with so much craft that Freyr may fold her together like a cloth, and keep her in his bag." This same virtue was possessed by the fairy pavilion which the Peri Banou gave to Ahmed ; the cloud which is no bigger than a man's hand may soon overspread the whole heaven, and shade the Sultan's army from the solar rays.

being called an egg, an apple, or a frog squatting on the
waters, or Ixion's wheel, or the eye of Polyphemos, or
the stone of Sisyphos, which was no sooner pushed up to
the zenith than it rolled down to the horizon. So the
sky was not only a crystal dome, or a celestial ocean, but
it was also the Aleian land through which Bellerophon
wandered, the country of the Lotos-eaters, or again the
realm of the Graiai beyond the twilight; and finally it
was personified and worshipped as Dyaus or Varuna,
the Vedic prototypes of the Greek Zeus and Ouranos.
The clouds, too, had many other representatives besides
ships and cows. In a future paper it will be shown that
they were sometimes regarded as angels or houris; at
present it more nearly concerns us to know that they
appear, throughout all Aryan mythology, under the form
of birds. It used to be a matter of hopeless wonder to
me that Aladdin's innocent request for a roc's egg to
hang in the dome of his palace should have been regarded as a crime worthy of punishment by the loss of
the wonderful lamp; the obscurest part of the whole
affair being perhaps the Jinni's passionate allusion to the
egg as his master: " Wretch! dost thou command me to
bring thee my master, and hang him up in the midst of
this vaulted dome?" But the incident is to some extent
cleared of its mystery when we learn that the roc's egg is
the bright sun, and that the roc itself is the rushing storm-
cloud which, in the tale of Sindbad, haunts the sparkling
starry firmament, symbolized as a valley of diamonds.*

---

* Euhemerism has done its best with this bird, representing it as an
immense vulture or condor or as a reminiscence of the extinct dodo.
But a Chinese myth, cited by Klaproth, well preserves its true character
when it describes it as " a bird which in flying *obscures the sun*, and of
whose quills are made *water-tuns*." See Nouveau Journal Asiatique,
Tom. XII. p. 235. The big bird in the Norse tale of the " Blue Belt "
belongs to the same species.

According to one Arabic authority, the length of its wings is ten thousand fathoms. But in European tradition it dwindles from these huge dimensions to the size of an eagle, a raven, or a woodpecker. Among the birds enumerated by Kuhn and others as representing the storm-cloud are likewise the wren or "kinglet" (French *roitelet*); the owl, sacred to Athene; the cuckoo, stork, and sparrow; and the red-breasted robin, whose name Robert was originally an epithet of the lightning-god Thor. In certain parts of France it is still believed that the robbing of a wren's nest will render the culprit liable to be struck by lightning. The same belief was formerly entertained in Teutonic countries with respect to the robin; and I suppose that from this superstition is descended the prevalent notion, which I often encountered in childhood, that there is something peculiarly wicked in killing robins.

Now, as the raven or woodpecker, in the various myths of schamir, is the dark storm-cloud, so the rock-splitting worm or plant or pebble which the bird carries in its beak and lets fall to the ground is nothing more or less than the flash of lightning carried and dropped by the cloud. "If the cloud was supposed to be a great bird, the lightnings were regarded as writhing worms or serpents in its beak. These fiery serpents, ἑλικίαι γραμμοειδῶς φερομενοι, are believed in to this day by the Canadian Indians, who call the thunder their hissing."*

But these are not the only mythical conceptions which are to be found wrapped up in the various myths of schamir and the divining-rod. The persons who told these stories were not weaving ingenious allegories about thunder-storms; they were telling stories, or giving utter-

* Baring-Gould, Curious Myths, Vol. II. p. 146. Compare Tylor, Primitive Culture, Vol. II. p. 237, seq.

ance to superstitions, of which the original meaning was
forgotten. The old grannies who, along with a stoical
indifference to the fate of quails and partridges, used to
impress upon me the wickedness of killing robins, did
not add that I should be struck by lightning if I failed
to heed their admonitions. They had never heard that
the robin was the bird of Thor; they merely rehearsed
the remnant of the superstition which had survived to
their own times, while the essential part of it had long
since faded from recollection. The reason for regarding
a robin's life as more sacred than a partridge's had been
forgotten; but it left behind, as was natural, a vague
recognition of that mythical sanctity. The primitive
meaning of a myth fades away as inevitably as the
primitive meaning of a word or phrase; and the rabbins
who told of a worm which shatters rocks no more
thought of the writhing thunderbolts than the modern
reader thinks of oyster-shells when he sees the word
ostracism, or consciously breathes a prayer as he writes
the phrase *good bye*. It is only in its callow infancy that
the full force of a myth is felt, and its period of luxuriant
development dates from the time when its physical significance is lost or obscured. It was because the Greek
had forgotten that Zeus meant the bright sky, that he
could make him king over an anthropomorphic Olympos.
The Hindu Dyaus, who carried his significance in his
name as plainly as the Greek Helios, never attained such
an exalted position; he yielded to deities of less obvious
pedigree, such as Brahma and Vishnu.

Since, therefore, the myth-tellers recounted merely the
wonderful stories which their own nurses and grandmas
had told them, and had no intention of weaving subtle
allegories or wrapping up a physical truth in mystic
emblems, it follows that they were not bound to avoid

incongruities or to preserve a philosophical symmetry in their narratives. In the great majority of complex myths, no such symmetry is to be found. A score of different mythical conceptions would get wrought into the same story, and the attempt to pull them apart and construct a single harmonious system of conceptions out of the pieces must often end in ingenious absurdity. If Odysseus is unquestionably the sun, so is the eye of Polyphemos, which Odysseus puts out.[*] But the Greek poet knew nothing of the incongruity, for he was thinking only of a superhuman hero freeing himself from a giant cannibal; he knew nothing of Sanskrit, or of comparative mythology, and the sources of his myths were as completely hidden from his view as the sources of the Nile.

We need not be surprised, then, to find that in one version of the schamir-myth the cloud is the bird which carries the worm, while in another version the cloud is the rock or mountain which the talisman cleaves open; nor need we wonder at it, if we find stories in which the two conceptions are mingled together without regard to an incongruity which in the mind of the myth-teller no longer exists.[†]

In early Aryan mythology there is nothing by which

[*] "If Polyphemos's eye be the sun, then Odysseus, the solar hero, extinguishes himself, a very primitive instance of suicide." Mahaffy, Prolegomena, p. 57. See also Brown, Poseidon, pp. 39, 40. This objection would be relevant only in case Homer were supposed to be constructing an *allegory* with entire knowledge of its meaning. It has no validity whatever when we recollect that Homer could have known nothing of the incongruity.

[†] The Sanskrit myth-teller indeed mixes up his materials in a way which seems ludicrous to a Western reader. He describes Indra (the sun-god) as not only cleaving the cloud-mountains with his sword, but also *cutting off their wings* and hurling them from the sky. See Burnouf, Bhâgavata Purâna, VI. 12, 26.

the clouds are more frequently represented than by rocks or mountains. Such were the Symplegades, which, charmed by the harp of the wind-god Orpheus, parted to make way for the talking ship Argo, with its crew of solar heroes.* Such, too, were the mountains Ossa and Pelion, which the giants piled up one upon another in their impious assault upon Zeus, the lord of the bright sky. As Mr. Baring-Gould observes : " The ancient Aryan had the same name for cloud and mountain. To him the piles of vapour on the horizon were so like Alpine ranges, that he had but one word whereby to designate both.† These great mountains of heaven were opened by the lightning. In the sudden flash he beheld the dazzling splendour within, but only for a moment, and then, with a crash, the celestial rocks closed again. Believing these vaporous piles to contain resplendent treasures of which partial glimpse was obtained by mortals in a momentary gleam, tales were speedily formed, relating the adventures of some who had succeeded in entering these treasure-mountains."

This sudden flash is the smiting of the cloud-rock by the arrow of Ahmed, the resistless hammer of Thor, the spear of Odin, the trident of Poseidon, or the rod of Hermes. The forked streak of light is the archetype of the divining-rod in its oldest form, — that in which it

---

* Mr. Tylor offers a different, and possibly a better, explanation of the Symplegades as the gates of Night through which the solar ship, having passed successfully once, may henceforth pass forever. See the details of the evidence in his Primitive Culture, I. 315.

† The Sanskrit *parvata*, a bulging or inflated body, means both "cloud" and "mountain." "In the Edda, too, the rocks, said to have been fashioned out of Ymir's bones, are supposed to be intended for clouds. In Old Norse *Klakkr* means both cloud and rock ; nay, the English word *cloud* itself has been identified with the Anglo-Saxon *clûd*, rock. See Justi, Orient und Occident, Vol. II. p. 62." Max Müller, Rig-Veda, Vol. I. p. 44.

not only indicates the hidden treasures, but, like the staff
of the Ilsenstein shepherd, bursts open the enchanted
crypt and reveals them to the astonished wayfarer. Hence
the one thing essential to the divining-rod, from whatever
tree it be chosen, is that it shall be forked.

It is not difficult to comprehend the reasons which led
the ancients to speak of the lightning as a worm, serpent,
trident, arrow, or forked wand; but when we inquire
why it was sometimes symbolized as a flower or leaf, or
when we seek to ascertain why certain trees, such as the
ash, hazel, white-thorn, and mistletoe, were supposed to
be in a certain sense embodiments of it, we are entering
upon a subject too complicated to be satisfactorily treated
within the limits of the present paper. It has been said
that the point of resemblance between a cow and a
comet, that both have tails, was quite enough for the
primitive word-maker : it was certainly enough for the
primitive myth-teller.* Sometimes the pinnate shape
of a leaf, the forking of a branch, the tri-cleft corolla, or
even the red colour of a flower, seems to have been
sufficient to determine the association of ideas. The
Hindu commentators of the Veda certainly lay great
stress on the fact that the palasa, one of their lightning-
trees, is trident-leaved. The mistletoe branch is forked,
like a wish-bone,† and so is the stem which bears the

---

* In accordance with the mediæval "doctrine of signatures," it was
maintained "that the hard, stony seeds of the Gromwell must be good
for gravel, and the knotty tubers of scrophularia for scrofulous glands ;
while the scaly pappus of scaliosa showed it to be a specific in leprous
diseases, the spotted leaves of pulmonaria that it was a sovereign remedy
for tuberculous lungs, and the growth of saxifrage in the fissures of
rocks that it would disintegrate stone in the bladder." Prior, Popular
Names of British Plants, Introd., p. xiv. See also Chapiel, La Doctrine
des Signatures. Paris, 1866.

† Indeed, the wish-bone, or forked clavicle of a fowl, itself belongs
to the same family of talismans as the divining-rod.

forget-me-not or wild scorpion grass. So too the leaves
of the Hindu *ficus religiosa* resemble long spear-heads.*
But in many cases it is impossible for us to determine
with confidence the reasons which may have guided
primitive men in their choice of talismanic plants. In
the case of some of these stories, it would no doubt be
wasting ingenuity to attempt to assign a mythical origin
for each point of detail. The ointment of the dervise,
for instance, in the Arabian tale, has probably no special
mythical significance, but was rather suggested by the
exigencies of the story, in an age when the old mythologies were so far disintegrated and mingled together that
any one talisman would serve as well as another the
purposes of the narrator. But the lightning-plants of
Indo-European folk-lore cannot be thus summarily disposed of ; for however difficult it may be for us to perceive any connection between them and the celestial
phenomena which they represent, the myths concerning
them are so numerous and explicit as to render it certain
that some such connection was imagined by the myth-
makers. The superstition concerning the hand of glory
is not so hard to interpret. In the mythology of the
Finns, the storm-cloud is a black man with a bright
copper hand; and in Hindustan, Indra Savitâr, the deity
who slays the demon of the cloud, is golden-handed.
The selection of the hand of a man who has been hanged
is probably due to the superstition which regarded the
storm-god Odin as peculiarly the lord of the gallows.

* The ash, on the other hand, has been from time immemorial used
for spears in many parts of the Aryan domain. The word *œsc* meant,
in Anglo-Saxon, indifferently "ash-tree," or "spear" ; and the same is,
or has been, true of the French *fresne* and the Greek μελία. The root
of *œsc* appears in the Sanskrit *as*, "to throw" or "lance," whence *âsa*,
"a bow," and *asanâ*, "an arrow." See Pictet, Origines Indo-Euro-
péennes, I. 222.

The man who is raised upon the gallows is placed directly in the track of the wild huntsman, who comes with his hounds to carry off the victim; and hence the notion, which, according to Mr. Kelly, is "very common in Germany and not extinct in England," that every suicide by hanging is followed by a storm.

The paths of comparative mythology are devious, but we have now pursued them long enough, I believe, to have arrived at a tolerably clear understanding of the original nature of the divining-rod. Its power of revealing treasures has been sufficiently explained; and its affinity for water results so obviously from the character of the lightning-myth as to need no further comment. But its power of detecting criminals still remains to be accounted for.

In Greek mythology, the being which detects and punishes crime is the Erinys, the prototype of the Latin Fury, figured by late writers as a horrible monster with serpent locks. But this is a degradation of the original conception. The name *Erinys* did not originally mean *Fury*, and it cannot be explained from Greek sources alone. It appears in Sanskrit as *Sáranyu*, a word which signifies the light of morning creeping over the sky. And thus we are led to the startling conclusion that, as the light of morning reveals the evil deeds done under the cover of night, so the lovely Dawn, or Erinys, came to be regarded under one aspect as the terrible detector and avenger of iniquity. Yet startling as the conclusion is, it is based on established laws of phonetic change, and cannot be gainsaid.

But what has the avenging daybreak to do with the lightning and the divining-rod? To the modern mind the association is not an obvious one: in antiquity it was otherwise. Myths of the daybreak and myths of the

3 *

lightning often resemble each other so closely that, except by a delicate philological analysis, it is difficult to
distinguish the one from the other. The reason is obvious. In each case the phenomenon to be explained is
the struggle between the day-god and one of the demons
of darkness. There is essentially no distinction to the
mind of the primitive man between the Panis, who steal
Indra's bright cows and keep them in a dark cavern all
night, and the throttling snake Ahi or Echidna, who imprisons the waters in the stronghold of the thunder-cloud
and covers the earth with a short-lived darkness. And
so the poisoned arrows of Bellerophon, which slay the
storm-dragon, differ in no essential respect from the
shafts with which Odysseus slaughters the night-demons
who have for ten long hours beset his mansion. Thus
the divining-rod, representing as it does the weapon of
the god of day, comes legitimately enough by its function of detecting and avenging crime.

But the lightning not only reveals strange treasures
and gives water to the thirsty land and makes plain what
is doing under cover of darkness; it also sometimes kills,
benumbs, or paralyzes. Thus the head of the Gorgon
Medusa turns into stone those who look upon it. Thus
the ointment of the dervise, in the tale of Baba Abdallah,
not only reveals all the treasures of the earth, but instantly thereafter blinds the unhappy man who tests its
powers. And thus the hand of glory, which bursts open
bars and bolts, benumbs also those who happen to be
near it. Indeed, few of the favoured mortals who were
allowed to visit the caverns opened by sesame or the
luck-flower, escaped without disaster. The monkish tale
of "The Clerk and the Image," in which the primeval
mythical features are curiously distorted, well illustrates
this point.

In the city of Rome there formerly stood an image with its right hand extended and on its forefinger the words "strike here." Many wise men puzzled in vain over the meaning of the inscription; but at last a certain priest observed that whenever the sun shone on the figure, the shadow of the finger was discernible on the ground at a little distance from the statue. Having marked the spot, he waited until midnight, and then began to dig. At last his spade struck upon something hard. It was a trap-door, below which a flight of marble steps descended into a spacious hall, where many men were sitting in solemn silence amid piles of gold and diamonds and long rows of enamelled vases. Beyond this he found another room, a *gynæcium* filled with beautiful women reclining on richly embroidered sofas; yet here, too, all was profound silence. A superb banqueting-hall next met his astonished gaze; then a silent kitchen; then granaries loaded with forage; then a stable crowded with motionless horses. The whole place was brilliantly lighted by a carbuncle which was suspended in one corner of the reception-room; and opposite stood an archer, with his bow and arrow raised, in the act of taking aim at the jewel. As the priest passed back through this hall, he saw a diamond-hilted knife lying on a marble table; and wishing to carry away something wherewith to accredit his story, he reached out his hand to take it; but no sooner had he touched it than all was dark. The archer had shot with his arrow, the bright jewel was shivered into a thousand pieces, the staircase had fled, and the priest found himself buried alive.*

---

* Compare Spenser's story of Sir Guyon, in the "Faëry Queen," where, however, the knight fares better than this poor priest. Usually these lightning-caverns were like Ixion's treasure-house, into which none might look and live. This conception is the foundation of part of the

Usually, however, though the lightning is wont to strike dead, with its basilisk glance, those who rashly enter its mysterious caverns, it is regarded rather as a benefactor than as a destroyer. The feelings with which the myth-making age contemplated the thunder-shower as it revived the earth paralyzed by a long drought, are shown in the myth of Oidipous. The Sphinx, whose name signifies " the one who binds," is the demon who sits on the cloud-rock and imprisons the rain, muttering dark sayings which none but the all-knowing sun may understand. The flash of solar light which causes the monster to fling herself down from the cliff with a fearful roar, restores the land to prosperity. But besides this, the association of the thunder-storm with the approach of summer has produced many myths in which the lightning is symbolized as the life-renewing wand of the victorious sun-god. Hence the use of the divining-rod in the cure of disease; and hence the large family of schamir-myths in which the dead are restored to life by leaves or herbs. In Grimm's tale of the Three Snake Leaves, " a prince is buried alive (like Sindbad) with his dead wife, and seeing a snake approaching her body, he cuts it in three pieces. Presently another snake, crawling from the corner, saw the other lying dead, and going away soon returned with three green leaves in its mouth; then laying the parts of the body together so as to join, it put one leaf on each wound, and the dead snake was alive again. The prince, applying the leaves to his wife's body, restores her also to life." * In the Greek story, told by Ælian and Apollodoros, Polyidos is shut up with the corpse of Glaukos, which he is ordered to restore to

story of Blue-Beard and of the Arabian tale of the third one-eyed Calender.

* Cox, Mythology of the Aryan Nations, Vol. I. p. 161.

life. He kills a dragon which is approaching the body,
but is presently astonished at seeing another dragon come
with a blade of grass and place it upon its dead companion, which instantly rises from the ground. Polyidos
takes the same blade of grass, and with it resuscitates
Glaukos. The same incident occurs in the Hindu story
of Panch Phul Ranee, and in Fouqué's "Sir Elidoc,"
which is founded on a Breton legend.

We need not wonder, then, at the extraordinary thera-
peutic properties which are in all Aryan folk-lore ascribed to the various lightning-plants. In Sweden sani-
tary amulets are made of mistletoe-twigs, and the plant
is supposed to be a specific against epilepsy and an anti-
dote for poisons. In Cornwall children are passed through
holes in ash-trees in order to cure them of hernia. Ash
rods are used in some parts of England for the cure of
diseased sheep, cows, and horses ; and in particular they
are supposed to neutralize the venom of serpents. The
notion that snakes are afraid of an ash-tree is not extinct
even in the United States. The other day I was told,
not by an old granny, but by a man fairly educated and
endowed with a very unusual amount of good common-
sense, that a rattlesnake will sooner go through fire than
creep over ash leaves or into the shadow of an ash-tree.
Exactly the same statement is made by Pliny, who adds
that if you draw a circle with an ash rod around the spot
of ground on which a snake is lying, the animal must die
of starvation, being as effectually imprisoned as Ugolino
in the dungeon at Pisa. In Cornwall it is believed that
a blow from an ash stick will instantly kill any serpent.
The ash shares this virtue with the hazel and fern. A
Swedish peasant will tell you that snakes may be deprived of their venom by a touch with a hazel wand ;
and when an ancient Greek had occasion to make his

bed in the woods, he selected fern leaves if possible, in
the belief that the smell of them would drive away poisonous animals.*

But the beneficent character of the lightning appears
still more clearly in another class of myths. To the primitive man the shaft of light coming down from heaven was
typical of the original descent of fire for the benefit and
improvement of the human race. The Sioux Indians account for the origin of fire by a myth of unmistakable kinship; they say that "their first ancestor obtained his fire
from the sparks which a friendly panther struck from the
rocks as he scampered up a stony hill." † This panther
is obviously the counterpart of the Aryan bird which
drops schamir. But the Aryan imagination hit upon a
far more remarkable conception. The ancient Hindus
obtained fire by a process similar to that employed by
Count Rumford in his experiments on the generation of
heat by friction. They first wound a couple of cords
around a pointed stick in such a way that the unwinding
of the one would wind up the other, and then, placing
the point of the stick against a circular disk of wood,
twirled it rapidly by alternate pulls on the two strings.
This instrument is called a *chark*, and is still used in
South Africa, ‡ in Australia, in Sumatra, and among the
Veddahs of Ceylon. The Russians found it in Kamt-
chatka; and it was formerly employed in America, from
Labrador to the Straits of Magellan. § The Hindus

* Kelly, Indo-European Folk-Lore, pp. 147, 183, 186, 193.
† Brinton, Myths of the New World, p. 151.
‡ Callaway, Zulu Nursery Tales, I. 173, Note 12.
§ Tylor, Early History of Mankind, p. 238 ; Primitive Culture, Vol.
II. p. 254 ; Darwin, Naturalist's Voyage, p. 409.
    "Jacky's next proceeding was to get some dry sticks and wood, and
prepare a fire, which, to George's astonishment, he lighted thus. He
got a block of wood, in the middle of which he made a hole ; then he

churned milk by a similar process;* and in order to explain the thunder-storm, a Sanskrit poem tells how "once upon a time the Devas, or gods, and their opponents, the Asuras, made a truce, and joined together in churning the ocean to procure amrita, the drink of immortality. They took Mount Mandara for a churning-stick, and, wrapping the great serpent Sesha round it for a rope, they made the mountain spin round to and fro, the Devas pulling at the serpent's tail, and the Asuras at its head."† In this myth the churning-stick, with its flying serpent-cords, is the lightning, and the amrita, or drink of immortality, is simply the rain-water, which in Aryan folk-lore possesses the same healing virtues as the lightning. "In Sclavonic myths it is the water of life which restores the dead earth, a water brought by a bird from the depths of a gloomy cave."‡ It is the celestial soma or mead which Indra loves to drink; it is the ambrosial nectar of the Olympian gods; it is the charmed water which in the Arabian Nights restores to human shape the victims of wicked sorcerers; and it is the elixir of life which mediæval philosophers tried to discover, and in quest of which Ponce de Leon traversed the wilds of Florida.§

cut and pointed a long stick, and inserting the point into the block, worked it round between his palms for some time and with increasing rapidity. Presently there came a smell of burning wood, and soon after it burst into a flame at the point of contact. Jacky cut slices of shark and roasted them." — Reade, Never too Late to Mend, chap. xxxviii.

* The production of fire by the drill is often called *churning,* e. g. "He took the *uvati* [chark], and sat down and churned it, and kindled a fire." Callaway, Zulu Nursery Tales, I. 174.

† Kelly, Indo-European Folk-Lore, p. 39. Burnouf, Bhâgavata Purâna, VIII. 6, 32.

‡ Baring-Gould, Curious Myths, p. 149.

§ It is also the regenerating water of baptism, and the "holy water" of the Roman Catholic.

The most interesting point in this Hindu myth is the name of the peaked mountain Mandara, or Manthara, which the gods and devils took for their churning-stick. The word means "a churning-stick," and it appears also, with a prefixed preposition, in the name of the fire-drill, *pramantha.* Now Kuhn has proved that this name, *pramantha*, is etymologically identical with *Prometheus*, the name of the beneficent Titan, who stole fire from heaven and bestowed it upon mankind as the richest of boons. This sublime personage was originally nothing but the celestial drill which churns fire out of the clouds ; but the Greeks had so entirely forgotten his origin that they interpreted his name as meaning "the one who thinks beforehand," and accredited him with a brother, Epimetheus, or "the one who thinks too late." The Greeks had adopted another name, *trypanon*, for their fire-drill, and thus the primitive character of Prometheus became obscured.

I have said above that it was regarded as absolutely essential that the divining-rod should be forked. To this rule, however, there was one exception, and if any further evidence be needed to convince the most sceptical that the divining-rod is nothing but a symbol of the lightning, that exception will furnish such evidence. For this exceptional kind of divining-rod was made of a pointed stick rotating in a block of wood, and it was the presence of hidden water or treasure which was supposed to excite the rotatory motion.

In the myths relating to Prometheus, the lightning-god appears as the originator of civilization, sometimes as the creator of the human race, and always as its friend,* suf-

---

* In the Vedas the rain-god Soma, originally the personification of the sacrificial ambrosia, is the deity who imparts to men life, knowledge, and happiness. See Bréal, Hercule et Cacus, p. 85. Tylor, Primitive Culture, Vol. II. p. 277.

fering in its behalf the most fearful tortures at the hands of the jealous Zeus. In one story he creates man by making a clay image and infusing into it a spark of the fire which he had brought from heaven ; in another story he is himself the first man. In the Peloponnesian myth Phoroneus, who is Prometheus under another name, is the first man, and his mother was an ash-tree. In Norse mythology, also, the gods were said to have made the first man out of the ash-tree Yggdrasil. The association of the heavenly fire with the life-giving forces of nature is very common in the myths of both hemispheres, and in view of the facts already cited it need not surprise us. Hence the Hindu Agni and the Norse Thor were patrons of marriage, and in Norway, the most lucky day on which to be married is still supposed to be Thursday, which in old times was the day of the fire-god.* Hence the light-ning-plants have divers virtues in matters pertaining to marriage. The Romans made their wedding torches of whitethorn ; hazel-nuts are still used all over Europe in divinations relating to the future lover or sweetheart ;† and under a mistletoe bough it is allowable for a gentle-man to kiss a lady. A vast number of kindred supersti-tions are described by Mr. Kelly, to whom I am indebted for many of these examples. ‡

* We may, perhaps, see here the reason for making the Greek fire-god Hephaistos the husband of Aphrodite.

† "Our country maidens are well aware that *triple* leaves plucked at hazard from the common *ash* are worn in the breast, for the purpose of causing prophetic dreams respecting a dilatory lover. The leaves of the yellow trefoil are supposed to possess similar virtues." — Harland and Wilkinson, Lancashire Folk-Lore, p. 20.

‡ "In Peru, a mighty and far-worshipped deity was Catequil, the thunder-god, ... he who in thunder-flash and clap hurls from his sling the small, round, smooth thunder-stones, treasured in the villages as fire-fetishes and charms to kindle the flames of love." — Tylor, op. cit. Vol. II. p. 239.

Thus we reach at last the completed conception of the
divining-rod, or as it is called in this sense the wish-rod,
with its kindred talismans, from Aladdin's lamp and the
purse of Bedreddin Hassan, to the Sangreal, the philosopher's stone, and the goblets of Oberon and Tristram.
These symbols of the reproductive energies of nature,
which give to the possessor every good and perfect gift,
illustrate the uncurbed belief in the power of wish which
the ancient man shared with modern children. In the
Norse story of Frodi's quern, the myth assumes a whim-
sical shape. The prose Edda tells of a primeval age of
gold, when everybody had whatever he wanted. This
was because the giant Frodi had a mill which ground out
peace and plenty and abundance of gold withal, so that
it lay about the roads like pebbles. Through the inex-
cusable avarice of Frodi, this wonderful implement was
lost to the world. For he kept his maid-servants working at the mill until they got out of patience, and began
to make it grind out hatred and war. Then came a
mighty sea-rover by night and slew Frodi and carried
away the maids and the quern. When he got well out
to sea, he told them to grind out salt, and so they did
with a vengeance. They ground the ship full of salt and
sank it, and so the quern was lost forever, but the sea
remains salt unto this day.

Mr. Kelly rightly identifies Frodi with the sun-god Fro
or Freyr, and observes that the magic mill is only another form of the fire-churn, or chark. According to
another version the quern is still grinding away and
keeping the sea salt, and over the place where it lies
there is a prodigious whirlpool or maelstrom which sucks
down ships.

In its completed shape, the lightning-wand is the *ca-
duccus*, or rod of Hermes. I observed, in the preceding

paper, that in the Greek conception of Hermes there have been fused together the attributes of two deities who were originally distinct. The Hermes of the Homeric Hymn is a wind-god; but the later Hermes Agoraios, the patron of gymnasia, the mutilation of whose statues caused such terrible excitement in Athens during the Peloponnesian War, is a very different personage. He is a fire-god, invested with many solar attributes, and represents the quickening forces of nature. In this capacity the invention of fire was ascribed to him as well as to Prometheus; he was said to be the friend of mankind, and was surnamed Ploutodotes, or "the giver of wealth."

The Norse wind-god Odin has in like manner acquired several of the attributes of Freyr and Thor.* His lightning-spear, which is borrowed from Thor, appears by a comical metamorphosis as a wish-rod which will administer a sound thrashing to the enemies of its possessor. Having cut a hazel stick, you have only to lay down an old coat, name your intended victim, wish he was there, and whack away: he will howl with pain at every blow. This wonderful cudgel appears in Dasent's tale of " The Lad who went to the North Wind," with which we may conclude this discussion. The story is told, with little variation, in Hindustan, Germany, and Scandinavia.

The North Wind, representing the mischievous Hermes, once blew away a poor woman's meal. So her boy went to the North Wind and demanded his rights for the meal his mother had lost. " I have n't got your meal," said the Wind, " but here 's a tablecloth which will cover itself with an excellent dinner whenever you tell it to."

* In Polynesia, "the great deity Maui adds a new complication to his enigmatic solar-celestial character by appearing as a wind-god." — Tylor, op. cit. Vol. II. p. 242.

So the lad took the cloth and started for home. At night-fall he stopped at an inn, spread his cloth on the table, and ordered it to cover itself with good things, and so it did. But the landlord, who thought it would be money in his pocket to have such a cloth, stole it after the boy had gone to bed, and substituted another just like it in appearance. Next day the boy went home in great glee to show off for his mother's astonishment what the North Wind had given him, but all the dinner he got that day was what the old woman cooked for him. In his despair he went back to the North Wind and called him a liar, and again demanded his rights for the meal he had lost. "I have n't got your meal," said the Wind, "but here 's a ram which will drop money out of its fleece whenever you tell it to." So the lad travelled home, stopping over night at the same inn, and when he got home he found himself with a ram which did n't drop coins out of its fleece. A third time he visited the North Wind, and obtained a bag with a stick in it which, at the word of command, would jump out of the bag and lay on until told to stop. Guessing how matters stood as to his cloth and ram, he turned in at the same tavern, and going to a bench lay down as if to sleep. The landlord thought that a stick carried about in a bag must be worth some-thing, and so he stole quietly up to the bag, meaning to get the stick out and change it. But just as he got within whacking distance, the boy gave the word, and out jumped the stick and beat the thief until he prom-ised to give back the ram and the tablecloth. And so the boy got his rights for the meal which the North Wind had blown away.

October, 1870.

III.

WEREWOLVES AND SWAN-MAIDENS.

IT is related by Ovid that Lykaon, king of Arkadia, once invited Zeus to dinner, and served up for him a dish of human flesh, in order to test the god's omniscience. But the trick miserably failed, and the impious monarch received the punishment which his crime had merited. He was transformed into a wolf, that he might henceforth feed upon the viands with which he had dared to pollute the table of the king of Olympos. From that time forth, according to Pliny, a noble Arkadian was each year, on the festival of Zeus Lykaios, led to the margin of a certain lake. Hanging his clothes upon a tree, he then plunged into the water and became a wolf. For the space of nine years he roamed about the adjacent woods, and then, if he had not tasted human flesh during all this time, he was allowed to swim back to the place where his clothes were hanging, put them on, and return to his natural form. It is further related of a certain Demainetos, that, having once been present at a human sacrifice to Zeus Lykaios, he ate of the flesh, and was transformed into a wolf for a term of ten years.[*]

These and other similar mythical germs were developed by the mediæval imagination into the horrible superstition of werewolves.

A *werewolf*, or *loup-garou*,[†] was a person who had the

[*] Compare Plato, Republic, VIII. 15.

[†] *Were-wolf = man-wolf*, *wehr* meaning "man." *Garou* is a Gallic corruption of *wehrwolf*, so that *loup-garou* is a tautological expression.

power of transforming himself into a wolf, being endowed, while in the lupine state, with the intelligence
of a man, the ferocity of a wolf, and the irresistible
strength of a demon.   The ancients believed in the existence of such persons; but in the Middle Ages the metamorphosis was supposed to be a phenomenon of daily
occurrence, and even at the present day, in secluded portions of Europe, the superstition is still cherished by
peasants.   The belief, moreover, is supported by a vast
amount of evidence, which can neither be argued nor
pooh-poohed into insignificance.   It is the business of
the comparative mythologist to trace the pedigree of the
ideas from which such a conception may have sprung;
while to the critical historian belongs the task of ascertaining and classifying the actual facts which this particular conception was used to interpret.

The mediæval belief in werewolves is especially adapted
to illustrate the complicated manner in which divers
mythical conceptions and misunderstood natural occurrences will combine to generate a long-enduring superstition.   Mr. Cox, indeed, would have us believe that the
whole notion arose from an unintentional play upon
words; but the careful survey of the field, which has
been taken by Hertz and Baring-Gould, leads to the conclusion that many other circumstances have been at work.
The delusion, though doubtless purely mythical in its
origin, nevertheless presents in its developed state a curious mixture of mythical and historical elements.

With regard to the Arkadian legend, taken by itself,
Mr. Cox is probably right.   The story seems to belong
to that large class of myths which have been devised in
order to explain the meaning of equivocal words whose
true significance has been forgotten.   The epithet *Lykaios,*
as applied to Zeus, had originally no reference to wolves:

it means "the bright one," and gave rise to lycanthropic legends only because of the similarity in sound between the names for "wolf" and "brightness." Aryan mythology furnishes numerous other instances of this confusion. The solar deity, Phoibos Lykegenes, was originally the "offspring of light"; but popular etymology made a kind of werewolf of him by interpreting his name as the "wolf-born." The name of the hero Autolykos means simply the "self-luminous"; but it was more frequently interpreted as meaning "a very wolf," in allusion to the supposed character of its possessor. Bazra, the name of the citadel of Carthage, was the Punic word for "fortress"; but the Greeks confounded it with *byrsa*, "a hide," and hence the story of the ox-hides cut into strips by Dido in order to measure the area of the place to be fortified. The old theory that the Irish were Phœnicians had a similar origin. The name *Fena*, used to designate the old Scoti or Irish, is the plural of *Fion*, "fair," seen in the name of the hero Fion Gall, or "Fingal"; but the monkish chroniclers identified *Fena* with *Phoinix*, whence arose the myth; and by a like misunderstanding of the epithet *Miledh*, or "warrior," applied to Fion by the Gaelic bards, there was generated a mythical hero, *Milesius*, and the soubriquet "Milesian," colloquially employed in speaking of the Irish.* So the Franks explained the name of the town Daras, in Mesopotamia, by the story that the Emperor Justinian once addressed the chief magistrate with the exclamation, *daras*, "thou shalt give" : †
the Greek chronicler, Malalas, who spells the name *Doras*, informs us with equal complacency that it was the place where Alexander overcame Codomannus with δόρυ, "the spear." A certain passage in the Alps is called Scaletta,

---

* Meyer, in Bunsen's Philosophy of Universal History, Vol. I. p. 151.
† Aimoin, De Gestis Francorum, II. 5.

from its resemblance to a staircase; but according to a
local tradition it owes its name to the bleaching *skelctons*
of a company of Moors who were destroyed there in the
eighth century, while attempting to penetrate into Northern Italy. The name of Antwerp denotes the town built
at a "wharf"; but it sounds very much like the Flemish
handt werpen, " hand-throwing": " hence arose the legend
of the giant who cut off the hands of those who passed
his castle without paying him black-mail, and threw them
into the Scheldt."*   In the myth of Bishop Hatto, related
in a previous paper, the Mäuse-thurm is a corruption of
maut-thurm; it means " customs-tower," and has nothing
to do with mice or rats. Doubtless this etymology was
the cause of the floating myth getting fastened to this
particular place; that it did not give rise to the myth
itself is shown by the existence of the same tale in other
places. Somewhere in England there is a place called
Chateau Vert; the peasantry have corrupted it into Shot-
over, and say that it has borne that name ever since
Little John *shot over* a high hill in the neighbourhood.†
Latium means " the flat land"; but, according to Virgil,
it is the place where Saturn once hid (*latuisset*) from the
wrath of his usurping son Jupiter. ‡

---

* Taylor, Words and Places, p. 393.

† Very similar to this is the etymological confusion upon which is
based the myth of the " confusion of tongues" in the eleventh chapter
of Genesis. The name "Babel" is really *Bab-Il,* or "the gate of God";
but the Hebrew writer erroneously derives the word from the root בָּלַל
balal, " to confuse "; and hence arises the mythical explanation, —
that *Babel* was a place where human speech became confused. See Raw-
linson, in Smith's Dictionary of the Bible, Vol. I. p. 149 ; Renan, Histoire des Langues Sémitiques, Vol. I. p. 32 ; Donaldson, New Cratylus,
p. 74, note ; Colenso on the Pentateuch, Vol. IV. p. 268.

‡ Virg. Æn. VIII. 322. With *Latium* compare πλατύς, Skr. *prath*
(to spread out), Eng. *flat.* Ferrar, Comparative Grammar of Greek,
Latin, and Sanskrit, Vol. I. p. 31.

It was in this way that the constellation of the Great Bear received its name. The Greek word *arktos*, answering to the Sanskrit *riksha*, meant originally any bright object, and was applied to the bear — for what reason it would not be easy to state — and to that constellation which was most conspicuous in the latitude of the early home of the Aryans. When the Greeks had long forgotten why these stars were called *arktoi*, they symbolized them as a Great Bear fixed in the sky. So that, as Max Müller observes, "the name of the Arctic regions rests on a misunderstanding of a name framed thousands of years ago in Central Asia, and the surprise with which many a thoughtful observer has looked at these seven bright stars, wondering why they were ever called the Bear, is removed by a reference to the early annals of human speech." Among the Algonquins the sun-god Michabo was represented as a hare, his name being compounded of *michi*, "great," and *wabos*, "a hare"; yet *wabos* also meant "white," so that the god was doubtless originally called simply "the Great White One." The same naïve process has made bears of the Arkadians, whose name, like that of the Lykians, merely signified that they were "children of light"; and the metamorphosis of Kallisto, mother of Arkas, into a bear, and of Lykaon into a wolf, rests apparently upon no other foundation than an erroneous etymology. Originally Lykaon was neither man nor wolf; he was but another form of Phoibos Lykegenes, the light-born sun, and, as Mr. Cox has shown, his legend is but a variation of that of Tantalos, who in time of drought offers to Zeus the flesh of his own offspring, the withered fruits, and is punished for his impiety.

It seems to me, however, that this explanation, though valid as far as it goes, is inadequate to explain all the features of the werewolf superstition, or to account for its presence in all Aryan countries and among many peoples who are not of Aryan origin. There can be no doubt that the myth-makers transformed Lykaon into a wolf because of his unlucky name ; because what really meant "bright man" seemed to them to mean "wolf-man"; but it has by no means been proved that a similar equivocation occurred in the case of all the primitive Aryan were-wolves, nor has it been shown to be probable that among each people the being with the uncanny name got thus accidentally confounded with the particular beast most dreaded by that people. Etymology alone does not explain the fact that while Gaul has been the favourite haunt of the man-wolf, Scandinavia has been preferred by the man-bear, and Hindustan by the man-tiger. To account for such a widespread phenomenon we must seek a more general cause.

Nothing is more strikingly characteristic of primitive thinking than the close community of nature which it assumes between man and brute. The doctrine of metempsychosis, which is found in some shape or other all over the world, implies a fundamental identity between the two ; the Hindu is taught to respect the flocks browsing in the meadow, and will on no account lift his hand against a cow, for who knows but it may be his own grandmother ? The recent researches of Mr. M'Lennan and. Mr. Herbert Spencer have served to connect this feeling with the primeval worship of ancestors and with the savage customs of totemism.*

The worship of ancestors seems to have been every-

---

* M'Lennan, "The Worship of Animals and Plants," Fortnightly Review, N. S. Vol. VI. pp. 407--427, 562--582, Vol. VII. pp. 194--216 ; Spencer, "The Origin of Animal Worship," Id. Vol. VII. pp. 535--550, reprinted in his Recent Discussions in Science, etc., pp. 31--56.

where the oldest systematized form of fetichistic religion. The reverence paid to the chieftain of the tribe while living was continued and exaggerated after his death. The uncivilized man is everywhere incapable of grasping the idea of death as it is apprehended by civilized people. He cannot understand that a man should pass away so as to be no longer capable of communicating with his fellows. The image of his dead chief or comrade remains in his mind, and the savage's philosophic realism far surpasses that of the most extravagant mediæval schoolmen ; to him the persistence of the idea implies the persistence of the reality. The dead man, accordingly, is not really dead ; he has thrown off his body like a husk, yet still retains his old appearance, and often shows himself to his old friends, especially after nightfall. He is no doubt possessed of more extensive powers than before his transformation,* and may very likely have a share in regulating the weather, granting or withholding rain. Therefore, argues the uncivilized mind, he is to be cajoled and propitiated more sedulously now than before his strange transformation.

This kind of worship still maintains a languid existence as the state religion of China, and it still exists as a

---

* Thus is explained the singular conduct of the Hindu, who slays himself before his enemy's door, in order to acquire greater power of injuring him. "A certain Brahman, on whose lands a Kshatriya raja had built a house, ripped himself up in revenge, and became a demon of the kind called Brahmadasyu, who has been ever since the terror of the whole country, and is the most common village-deity in Kharakpur. Toward the close of the last century there were two Brahmans, out of whose house a man had wrongfully, as they thought, taken forty rupees ; whereupon one of the Brahmans proceeded to cut off his own mother's head, with the professed view, entertained by both mother and son, that her spirit, excited by the beating of a large drum during forty days, might haunt. torment, and pursue to death the taker of their money and those concerned with him." Tylor, Primitive Culture, Vol. II. p. 103.

portion of Brahmanism; but in the Vedic religion it is
to be seen in all its vigour and in all its naïve simplicity.
According to the ancient Aryan, the *Pitris*, or " Fathers "
(Lat. *patres*), live in the sky along with Yama, the great
original Pitri of mankind. This first man came down
from heaven in the lightning, and back to heaven both
himself and all his offspring must have gone. There
they distribute light unto men below, and they shine
themselves as stars; and hence the Christianized German peasant, fifty centuries later, tells his children that
the stars are angels' eyes, and the English cottager im-
presses it on the youthful mind that it is wicked to
point at the stars, though why he cannot tell. But
the Pitris are not stars only, nor do they content themselves with idly looking down on the affairs of men, after
the fashion of the *laissez-faire* divinities of Lucretius.
They are, on the contrary, very busy with the weather;
they send rain, thunder, and lightning; and they especially delight in rushing over the housetops in a great
gale of wind, led on by their chief, the mysterious huntsman, Hermes or Odin.

It has been elsewhere shown that the howling dog, or
wish-hound of Hermes, whose appearance under the windows of a sick person is such an alarming portent, is
merely the tempest personified. Throughout all Aryan
mythology the souls of the dead are supposed to ride on
the night-wind, with their howling dogs, gathering into
their throng the souls of those just dying as they pass by
their houses.* Sometimes the whole complex conception
is wrapped up in the notion of a single dog, the messenger of the god of shades, who comes to summon the de-

* Hence, in many parts of Europe, it is still customary to open the
windows when a person dies, in order that the soul may not be hindered
in joining the mystic cavalcade.

parting soul. Sometimes, instead of a dog, we have a great ravening wolf who comes to devour its victim and extinguish the sunlight of life, as that old wolf of the tribe of Fenrir devoured little Red Riding-Hood with her robe of scarlet twilight.* Thus we arrive at a true werewolf myth. The storm-wind, or howling Rakshasa of Hindu folk-lore, is " a great misshapen giant with red beard and red hair, with pointed protruding teeth, ready to lacerate and devour human flesh ; his body is covered with coarse, bristling hair, his huge mouth is open, he looks from side to side as he walks, lusting after the flesh and blood of men, to satisfy his raging hunger and quench his consuming thirst. Towards nightfall his strength increases manifold ; he can change his shape at will ; he haunts the woods, and roams howling through the jungle." †

Now if the storm-wind is a host of Pitris, or one great Pitri who appears as a fearful giant, and is also a pack of wolves or wish-hounds, or a single savage dog or wolf, the inference is obvious to the mythopœic mind that men

* The story of little Red Riding-Hood is "mutilated in the English version, but known more perfectly by old wives in Germany, who can tell that the lovely little maid in her shining red satin cloak was swallowed with her grandmother by the wolf, till they both came out safe and sound when the hunter cut open the sleeping beast." Tylor, Primitive Culture, I. 307, where also see the kindred Russian story of Vasilissa the Beautiful. Compare the case of Tom Thumb, who "was swallowed by the cow and came out unhurt " ; the story of Saktideva swallowed by the fish and cut out again, in Somadeva Bhatta, II. 118–184; and the story of Jonah swallowed by the whale, in the Old Testament. All these are different versions of the same myth, and refer to the alternate swallowing up and casting forth of Day by Night, which is commonly personified as a wolf, and now and then as a great fish. Compare Grimm's story of the Wolf and Seven Kids, Tylor, loc. cit., and see Early History of Mankind, p. 337 ; Hardy, Manual of Budhism, p. 501.

† Baring-Gould, Book of Werewolves, p. 178 ; Muir, Sanskrit Texts, II. 435.

may become wolves, at least after death. And to the uncivilized thinker this inference is strengthened, as Mr. Spencer has shown, by evidence registered on his own tribal totem or heraldic emblem. The bears and lions and leopards of heraldry are the degenerate descendants of the totem of savagery which designated the tribe by a beast-symbol. To the untutored mind there is everything in a name; and the descendant of Brown Bear or Yellow Tiger or Silver Hyæna cannot be pronounced unfaithful to his own style of philosophizing, if he regards his ancestors, who career about his hut in the darkness of night, as belonging to whatever order of beasts his totem associations may suggest.

Thus we not only see a ray of light thrown on the subject of metempsychosis; but we get a glimpse of the curious process by which the intensely realistic mind of antiquity arrived at the notion that men could be transformed into beasts. For the belief that the soul can temporarily quit the body during lifetime has been universally entertained; and from the conception of wolf-like ghosts it was but a short step to the conception of corporeal werewolves. In the Middle Ages the phenomena of trance and catalepsy were cited in proof of the theory that the soul can leave the body and afterwards return to it. Hence it was very difficult for a person accused of witchcraft to prove an *alibi;* for to any amount of evidence showing that the body was innocently reposing at home and in bed, the rejoinder was obvious that the soul may nevertheless have been in attendance at the witches' Sabbath or busied in maiming a neighbour's cattle. According to one mediæval notion, the soul of the werewolf quit its human body, which remained in a trance until its return.*

* In those days even an after-dinner nap seems to have been thought uncanny. See Dasent, Burnt Njal, I. xxi.

The mythological basis of the werewolf superstition is now, I believe, sufficiently indicated. The belief, however, did not reach its complete development, or acquire its most horrible features, until the pagan habits of thought which had originated it were modified by contact with Christian theology. To the ancient there was nothing necessarily diabolical in the transformation of a man into a beast. But Christianity, which retained such a host of pagan conceptions under such strange disguises, which degraded the " All-father " Odin into the ogre of the castle to which Jack climbed on his bean-stalk, and which blended the beneficent lightning-god Thor and the mischievous Hermes and the faun-like Pan into the grotesque Teutonic Devil, did not fail to impart a new and fearful character to the belief in werewolves. Lycanthropy became regarded as a species of witchcraft ; the werewolf was supposed to have obtained his peculiar powers through the favour or connivance of the Devil ; and hundreds of persons were burned alive or broken on the wheel for having availed themselves of the privilege of beast-metamorphosis. The superstition, thus widely extended and greatly intensified, was confirmed by many singular phenomena which cannot be omitted from any thorough discussion of the nature and causes of lycanthropy.

The first of these phenomena is the Berserker insanity, characteristic of Scandinavia, but not unknown in other countries. In times when killing one's enemies often formed a part of the necessary business of life, persons were frequently found who killed for the mere love of the thing ; with whom slaughter was an end desirable in itself, not merely a means to a desirable end. What the miser is in an age which worships mammon, such was the Berserker in an age when the current idea of heaven was that of a place where people could hack each other to pieces through all eternity, and when the man who refused a challenge was punished with confiscation of his estates. With these Northmen, in the ninth century, the chief business and amusement in life was to set sail for some pleasant country, like Spain or France, and make all the coasts and navigable rivers hideous with rapine and massacre. When at home, in the intervals between their freebooting expeditions, they were liable to become possessed by a strange homicidal madness, during which they would array themselves in the skins of wolves or bears, and sally forth by night to crack the backbones, smash the skulls, and sometimes to drink with fiendish glee the blood of unwary travellers or loiterers. These fits of madness were usually followed by periods of utter exhaustion and nervous depression.*

Such, according to the unanimous testimony of historians, was the celebrated " Berserker rage," not peculiar to the Northland, although there most conspicuously manifested. Taking now a step in advance, we find that in comparatively civilized countries there have been many cases of monstrous homicidal insanity. The two most celebrated cases, among those collected by Mr. Baring-Gould, are those of the Maréchal de Retz, in 1440, and of Elizabeth, a Hungarian countess, in the seventeenth century. The Countess Elizabeth enticed young girls into her palace on divers pretexts, and then coolly murdered them, for the purpose of bathing in their blood. The spectacle of human suffering became at last such

---

* See Dasent, Burnt Njal, Vol. I. p. xxii. ; Grettis Saga, by Magnússon and Morris, chap. xix. ; Viga Glum's Saga, by Sir Edmund Head, p. 13, note, where the Berserkers are said to have maddened themselves with drugs. Dasent compares them with the Malays, who work themselves into a frenzy by means of arrack, or hasheesh, and run amuck.

a delight to her, that she would apply with her own hands the most excruciating tortures, relishing the shrieks of her victims as the epicure relishes each sip of his old Château Margaux. In this way she is said to have murdered six hundred and fifty persons before her evil career was brought to an end; though, when one recollects the famous men in buckram and the notorious trio of crows, one is inclined to strike off a cipher, and regard sixty-five as a sufficiently imposing and far less improbable number. But the case of the Maréchal de Retz is still more frightful. A marshal of France, a scholarly man, a patriot, and a man of holy life, he became suddenly possessed by an uncontrollable desire to murder children. During seven years he continued to inveigle little boys and girls into his castle, at the rate of about *two each week*, (?) and then put them to death in various ways, that he might witness their agonies and bathe in their blood; experiencing after each occasion the most dreadful remorse, but led on by an irresistible craving to repeat the crime. When this unparalleled iniquity was finally brought to light, the castle was found to contain bins full of children's bones. The horrible details of the trial are to be found in the histories of France by Michelet and Martin.

Going a step further, we find cases in which the propensity to murder has been accompanied by cannibalism. In 1598 a tailor of Châlons was sentenced by the parliament of Paris to be burned alive for lycanthropy. " This wretched man had decoyed children into his shop, or attacked them in the gloaming when they strayed in the woods, had torn them with his teeth and killed them, after which he seems calmly to have dressed their flesh as ordinary meat, and to have eaten it with a great relish. The number of little innocents whom he destroyed is unknown. A whole caskful of bones was discovered in his house." * About 1850 a beggar in the village of Polomyia, in Galicia, was proved to have killed and eaten fourteen children. A house had one day caught fire and burnt to the ground, roasting one of the inmates, who was unable to escape. The beggar passed by soon after, and, as he was suffering from excessive hunger, could not resist the temptation of making a meal off the charred body. From that moment he was tormented by a craving for human flesh. He met a little orphan girl, about nine years old, and giving her a pinchbeck ring told her to seek for others like it under a tree in the neighbouring wood. She was slain, carried to the beggar's hovel, and eaten. In the course of three years thirteen other children mysteriously disappeared, but no one knew whom to suspect. At last an innkeeper missed a pair of ducks, and having no good opinion of this beggar's honesty, went unexpectedly to his cabin, burst suddenly in at the door, and to his horror found him in the act of hiding under his cloak a severed head; a bowl of fresh blood stood under the oven, and pieces of a thigh were cooking over the fire.†

This occurred only about twenty years ago, and the criminal, though ruled by an insane appetite, is not known to have been subject to any mental delusion. But there have been a great many similar cases, in which the homicidal or cannibal craving has been accompanied by genuine hallucination. Forms of insanity in which the afflicted persons imagine themselves to be brute animals are not perhaps very common, but they are not unknown. I once knew a poor demented old man who believed himself to be a horse, and would stand by the hour together before a manger, nibbling hay, or deluding

---

* Baring-Gould, Werewolves, p. 81.
† Baring-Gould, op. cit. chap. xiv.

himself with the pretence of so doing. Many of the cannibals whose cases are related by Mr. Baring-Gould, in his chapter of horrors, actually believed themselves to have been transformed into wolves or other wild animals. Jean Grenier was a boy of thirteen, partially idiotic, and of strongly marked canine physiognomy; his jaws were large and projected forward, and his canine teeth were unnaturally long, so as to protrude beyond the lower lip. He believed himself to be a werewolf. One evening, meeting half a dozen young girls, he scared them out of their wits by telling them that as soon as the sun had set he would turn into a wolf and eat them for supper. A few days later, one little girl, having gone out at nightfall to look after the sheep, was attacked by some creature which in her terror she mistook for a wolf, but which afterwards proved to be none other than Jean Grenier. She beat him off with her sheep-staff, and fled home. As several children had mysteriously disappeared from the neighbourhood, Grenier was at once suspected. Being brought before the parliament of Bordeaux, he stated that two years ago he had met the Devil one night in the woods and had signed a compact with him and received from him a wolf-skin. Since then he had roamed about as a wolf after dark, resuming his human shape by daylight. He had killed and eaten several children whom he had found alone in the fields, and on one occasion he had entered a house while the family were out and taken the baby from its cradle. A careful investigation proved the truth of these statements, so far as the cannibalism was concerned. There is no doubt that the missing children were eaten by Jean Grenier, and there is no doubt that in his own mind the half-witted boy was firmly convinced that he was a wolf. Here the lycanthropy was complete.

In the year 1598, " in a wild and unfrequented spot near Caude, some countrymen came one day upon the corpse of a boy of fifteen, horribly mutilated and bespattered with blood. As the men approached, two wolves, which had been rending the body, bounded away into the thicket. The men gave chase immediately, following their bloody tracks till they lost them ; when, suddenly crouching among the bushes, his teeth chattering with fear, they found a man half naked, with long hair and beard, and with his hands dyed in blood. His nails were long as claws, and were clotted with fresh gore and shreds of human flesh." *

This man, Jacques Roulet, was a poor, half-witted creature under the dominion of a cannibal appetite. He was employed in tearing to pieces the corpse of the boy when these countrymen came up. Whether there were any wolves in the case, except what the excited imaginations of the men may have conjured up, I will not presume to determine ; but it is certain that Roulet supposed himself to be a wolf, and killed and ate several persons under the influence of the delusion. He was sentenced to death, but the parliament of Paris reversed the sentence, and charitably shut him up in a madhouse.

The annals of the Middle Ages furnish many cases similar to these of Grenier and Roulet. Their share in maintaining the werewolf superstition is undeniable ; but modern science finds in them nothing that cannot be readily explained. That stupendous process of breeding, which we call civilization, has been for long ages strengthening those kindly social feelings by the possession of which we are chiefly distinguished from the brutes, leaving our primitive bestial impulses to die for want of exercise, or checking in every possible way their further

* Baring-Gould, op. cit. p. 82.

expansion by legislative enactments. But this process, which is transforming us from savages into civilized men, is a very slow one ; and now and then there occur cases of what physiologists call atavism, or reversion to an ancestral type of character. Now and then persons are born, in civilized countries, whose intellectual powers are on a level with those of the most degraded Australian savage, and these we call idiots. And now and then persons are born possessed of the bestial appetites and cravings of primitive man, his fiendish cruelty and his liking for human flesh. Modern physiology knows how to classify and explain these abnormal cases, but to the unscientific mediæval mind they were explicable only on the hypothesis of a diabolical metamorphosis. And there is nothing strange in the fact that, in an age when the prevailing habits of thought rendered the transformation of men into beasts an easily admissible notion, these monsters of cruelty and depraved appetite should have been regarded as capable of taking on bestial forms. Nor is it strange that the hallucination under which these unfortunate wretches laboured should have taken such a shape as to account to their feeble intelligence for the existence of the appetites which they were conscious of not sharing with their neighbours and contemporaries. If a myth is a piece of unscientific philosophizing, it must sometimes be applied to the explanation of obscure psychological as well as of physical phenomena. Where the modern calmly taps his forehead and says, " Arrested development," the terrified ancient made the sign of the cross and cried, " Werewolf."

We shall be assisted in this explanation by turning aside for a moment to examine the wild superstitions about " changelings," which contributed, along with so many others, to make the lives of our ancestors anxious and miserable. These superstitions were for the most part attempts to explain the phenomena of insanity, epilepsy, and other obscure nervous diseases. A man who has hitherto enjoyed perfect health, and whose actions have been consistent and rational, suddenly loses all self-control and seems actuated by a will foreign to himself. Modern science possesses the key to this phenomenon; but in former times it was explicable only on the hypothesis that a demon had entered the body of the lunatic, or else that the fairies had stolen the real man and substituted for him a diabolical phantom exactly like him in stature and features. Hence the numerous legends of changelings, some of which are very curious. In Irish folk-lore we find the story of one Rickard, surnamed the Rake, from his worthless character. A good-natured, idle fellow, he spent all his evenings in dancing, — an accomplishment in which no one in the village could rival him. One night, in the midst of a lively reel, he fell down in a fit. "He's struck with a fairy-dart," exclaimed all the friends, and they carried him home and nursed him; but his face grew so thin and his manner so morose that by and by all began to suspect that the true Rickard was gone and a changeling put in his place. Rickard, with all his accomplishments, was no musician; and so, in order to put the matter to a crucial test, a bag-pipe was left in the room by the side of his bed. The trick succeeded. One hot summer's day, when all were supposed to be in the field making hay, some members of the family secreted in a clothes-press saw the bedroom door open a little way, and a lean, foxy face, with a pair of deep-sunken eyes, peer anxiously about the premises. Having satisfied itself that the coast was clear, the face withdrew, the door was closed, and presently such ravishing strains of music were heard as never proceeded from a bagpipe before or since that day. Soon was heard the rustle of innumerable fairies, come to dance to the changeling's music. Then the "fairy-man" of the village, who was keeping watch with the family, heated a pair of tongs red-hot, and with deafening shouts all burst at once into the sick-chamber. The music had ceased and the room was empty, but in at the window glared a fiendish face, with such fearful looks of hatred, that for a moment all stood motionless with terror. But when the fairy-man, recovering himself, advanced with the hot tongs to pinch its nose, it vanished with an unearthly yell, and there on the bed was Rickard, safe and sound, and cured of his epilepsy.*

Comparing this legend with numerous others relating to changelings, and stripping off the fantastic garb of fairy-lore with which popular imagination has invested them, it seems impossible to doubt that they have arisen from myths devised for the purpose of explaining the obscure phenomena of mental disease. If this be so, they afford an excellent collateral illustration of the belief in werewolves. The same mental habits which led men to regard the insane or epileptic person as a changeling, and which allowed them to explain catalepsy as the temporary departure of a witch's soul from its body, would enable them to attribute a wolf's nature to the maniac or idiot with cannibal appetites. And when the myth-forming process had got thus far, it would not stop short of assigning to the unfortunate wretch a tangible lupine body ; for all ancient mythology teemed with precedents for such a transformation.

It remains for us to sum up, — to tie into a bunch the keys which have helped us to penetrate into the secret causes of the werewolf superstition. In a previous

* Kennedy, Fictions of the Irish Celts, p. 90.

paper we saw what a host of myths, fairy-tales, and
superstitious observances have sprung from attempts to
interpret one simple natural phenomenon, — the descent
of fire from the clouds.   Here, on the other hand, we see
what a heterogeneous multitude of mythical elements
may combine to build up in course of time a single enormous superstition, and we see how curiously fàct and
fancy have co-operated in keeping the superstition from
falling.   In the first place the worship of dead ancestors
with wolf totems originated the notion of the transformation of men into divine or superhuman wolves ; and this
notion was confirmed by the ambiguous explanation of
the storm-wind as the rushing of a troop of dead men's
souls or as the howling of wolf-like monsters.   Mediæval
Christianity retained these conceptions, merely changing
the superhuman wolves into evil demons ; and finally the
occurrence of cases of Berserker madness and cannibalism, accompanied by lycanthropic hallucinations, being
interpreted as due to such demoniacal metamorphosis,
gave rise to the werewolf superstition of the Middle
Ages.   The etymological proceedings, to which Mr. Cox
would incontinently ascribe the origin of the entire
superstition, seemed to me to have played a very subor-
dinate part in the matter.   To suppose that Jean Grenier
imagined himself to be a wolf, because the Greek word
for wolf sounded like the word for light, and thus gave
rise to the story of a light-deity who became a wolf,
seems to me quite inadmissible.   Yet as far as such verbal equivocations may have prevailed, they doubtless
helped to sustain the delusion.

Thus we need no longer regard our werewolf as an
inexplicable creature of undetermined pedigree.   But any
account of him would be quite imperfect which should
omit all consideration of the methods by which his

change of form was accomplished. By the ancient Romans the werewolf was commonly called a "skin-changer" or "turn-coat" (*versipellis*), and similar epithets were applied to him in the Middle Ages The mediæval theory was that, while the werewolf kept his human form, his hair grew inwards ; when he wished to become a wolf, he simply turned himself inside out. In many trials on record, the prisoners were closely interrogated as to how this inversion might be accomplished ; but I am not aware that any one of them ever gave a satisfactory answer. At the moment of change their memories seem to have become temporarily befogged. Now and then a poor wretch had his arms and legs cut off, or was partially flayed, in order that the .ingrowing hair might be detected.* Another theory was, that the possessed person had merely to put on a wolf's skin, in order to assume instantly the lupine form and character; and in this may perhaps be seen a vague reminiscence of the alleged fact that Berserkers were in the habit of haunting the woods by night, clothed in the hides of wolves or bears.† Such

---

* "En 1541, à Padoue, dit Wier, un homme qui se croyait changé en loup courait la campagne, attaquant et mettant à mort ceux qu'il rencontrait. Après bien des difficultés, on parvint s'emparer de lui. Il dit en confidence à ceux qui l'arrêtèrent : Je suis vraiment un loup, et si ma peau ne paraît pas être celle d'un loup, c'est parce qu'elle est retournée et que les poils sont en dedans. — Pour s'assurer du fait, on coupa le malheureux aux différentes parties du corps, on lui emporta les bras et les jambes." — Taine, De l'Intelligence, Tom. II. p. 203. See the account of Slavonic werewolves in Ralston, Songs of the Russian People, pp. 404 – 418.

† Mr. Cox, whose scepticism on obscure points in history rather surpasses that of Sir G. C. Lewis, dismisses with a sneer the subject of the Berserker madness, observing that "the unanimous testimony of the Norse historians is worth as much and as little as the convictions of Glanvil and Hale on the reality of witchcraft." I have not the special knowledge requisite for pronouncing an opinion on this point, but Mr. Cox's ordinary methods of disposing of such questions are not such as

a wolfskin was kept by the boy Grenier.   Roulet, on the other hand, confessed to using a magic salve or ointment. A fourth method of becoming a werewolf was to obtain a girdle, usually made of human skin.   Several cases are related in Thorpe's "Northern Mythology."   One hot day in harvest-time some reapers lay down to sleep in the shade ; when one of them, who could not sleep, saw the man next him arise quietly and gird him with a strap, whereupon he instantly vanished, and a wolf jumped up from among the sleepers and ran off across the fields. Another man, who possessed such a girdle, once went away from home without remembering to lock it up. His little son climbed up to the cupboard and got it, and as he proceeded to buckle it around his waist, he became instantly transformed into a strange-looking beast.   Just then his father came in, and seizing the girdle restored the child to his natural shape.   The boy said that no sooner had he buckled it on than he was tormented with a raging hunger.

Sometimes the werewolf transformation led to unlucky accidents.   At Caseburg, as a man and his wife were making hay, the woman threw down her pitchfork and went away, telling her husband that if a wild beast should come to him during her absence he must throw his hat at it.   Presently a she-wolf rushed towards him. The man threw his hat at it, but a boy came up from another part of the field and stabbed the animal with his pitchfork, whereupon it vanished, and the woman's dead body lay at his feet.

A parallel legend shows that this woman wished to

to make one feel obliged to accept his bare assertion, unaccompanied by critical arguments. The madness of the bearsarks may, no doubt, be the same thing as the frenzy of Herakles ; but something more than mere dogmatism is needed to prove it.

have the hat thrown at her, in order that she might be henceforth free from her liability to become a werewolf. A man was one night returning with his wife from a merry-making when he felt the change coming on. Giving his wife the reins, he jumped from the wagon, telling her to strike with her apron at any animal which might come to her. In a few moments a wolf ran up to the side of the vehicle, and, as the woman struck out with her apron, it bit off a piece and ran away. Presently the man returned with the piece of apron in his mouth, and consoled his terrified wife with the information that the enchantment had left him forever.

A terrible case at a village in Auvergne has found its way into the annals of witchcraft. " A gentleman while hunting was suddenly attacked by a savage wolf of monstrous size. Impenetrable by his shot, the beast made a spring upon the helpless huntsman, who in the struggle luckily, or unluckily for the unfortunate lady, contrived to cut off one of its fore-paws. This trophy he placed in his pocket, and made the best of his way homewards in safety. On the road he met a friend, to whom he exhibited a bleeding paw, or rather (as it now appeared) a woman's hand, upon which was a wedding-ring. His wife's ring was at once recognized by the other. His suspicions aroused, he immediately went in search of his wife, who was found sitting by the fire in the kitchen, her arm hidden beneath her apron, when the husband, seizing her by the arm, found his terrible suspicions verified. The bleeding stump was there, evidently just fresh from the wound. She was given into custody, and in the event was burned at Riom, in presence of thousands of spectators." *

---

* Williams, Superstitions of Witchcraft, p. 179. See a parallel case of a cat-woman, in Thorpe's Northern Mythology, II. 26. "Certain witches

Sometimes a werewolf was cured merely by recognizing him while in his brute shape. A Swedish legend tells of a cottager who, on entering the forest one day without recollecting to say his *Pater Noster,* got into the power of a Troll, who changed him into a wolf. For many years his wife mourned him as dead. But one Christmas eve the old Troll, disguised as a beggar-woman, came to the house for alms; and being taken in and kindly treated, told the woman that her husband might very likely appear to her in wolf-shape. Going at night to the pantry to lay aside a joint of meat for to-morrow's dinner, she saw a wolf standing with its paws on the window-sill, looking wistfully in at her. "Ah, dearest," said she, "if I knew that thou wert really my husband, I would give thee a bone." Whereupon the wolf-skin fell off, and her husband stood before her in the same old clothes which he had on the day that the Troll got hold of him.

In Denmark it was believed that if a woman were to creep through a colt's placental membrane stretched between four sticks, she would for the rest of her life bring forth children without pain or illness; but all the boys would in such case be werewolves, and all the girls Maras, or nightmares. In this grotesque superstition appears that curious kinship between the werewolf and the wife or maiden of supernatural race, which serves admirably to illustrate the nature of both conceptions, and the elucidation of which shall occupy us throughout the remainder of this paper.

at Thurso for a long time tormented an honest fellow under the usual form of cats, till one night he put them to flight with his broadsword, and cut off the leg of one less nimble than the rest; taking it up, to his amazement he found it to be a woman's leg, and next morning he discovered the old hag its owner with but one leg left." — Tylor, Primitive Culture, I. 283.

It is, perhaps, needless to state that in the personality of the nightmare, or Mara, there was nothing equine. The Mara was a female demon,* who would come at night and torment men or women by crouching on their chests or stomachs and stopping their respiration. The scene is well enough represented in Fuseli's picture, though the frenzied-looking horse which there accompanies the demon has no place in the original superstition. A Netherlandish story illustrates the character of the Mara. Two young men were in love with the same damsel. One of them, being tormented every night by a Mara, sought advice from his rival, and it was a treacherous counsel that he got. " Hold a sharp knife with the point towards your breast, and you 'll never see the Mara again," said this false friend. The lad thanked him, but when he lay down to rest he thought it as well to be on the safe side, and so held the knife handle downward. So when the Mara came, instead of forcing the blade into his breast, she cut herself badly, and fled howling; and let us hope, though the legend here leaves us in the dark, that this poor youth, who is said to have been the comelier of the two, revenged himself on his malicious rival by marrying the young lady.

But the Mara sometimes appeared in less revolting shape, and became the mistress or even the wife of some mortal man to whom she happened to take a fancy. In such cases she would vanish on being recognized. There is a well-told monkish tale of a pious knight who, journeying one day through the forest, found a beautiful lady stripped naked and tied to a tree, her back all covered with deep gashes streaming with blood, from a flogging

---

* " The *mare* in *nightmare* means spirit, elf, or nymph ; compare Anglo-Saxon *wudumære* (wood-mare) = echo." — Tylor, Primitive Culture, Vol. II. p. 173.

which some bandits had given her. Of course he took
her home to his castle and married her, and for a while
they lived very happily together, and the fame of the
lady's beauty was so great that kings and emperors held
tournaments in honor of her. But this pious knight
used to go to mass every Sunday, and greatly was he
scandalized when he found that his wife would never
stay to assist in the *Credo*, but would always get up and
walk out of church just as the choir struck up. All
her husband's coaxing was of no use; threats and en-
treaties were alike powerless even to elicit an explanation of this strange conduct. At last the good man determined to use force; and so one Sunday, as the lady
got up to go out, according to custom, he seized her by
the arm and sternly commanded her to remain. Her
whole frame was suddenly convulsed, and her dark eyes
gleamed with weird, unearthly brilliancy. The services
paused for a moment, and all eyes were turned toward
the knight and his lady. "In God's name, tell me what
thou art," shouted the knight; and instantly, says the
chronicler, "the bodily form of the lady melted away,
and was seen no more; whilst, with a cry of anguish and
of terror, an evil spirit of monstrous form rose from the
ground, clave the chapel roof asunder, and disappeared in
the air."

In a Danish legend, the Mara betrays her affinity to
the Nixies, or Swan-maidens. A peasant discovered that
his sweetheart was in the habit of coming to him by
night as a Mara. He kept strict watch until he discovered her creeping into the room through a small
knot-hole in the door. Next day he made a peg, and
after she had come to him, drove in the peg so that she
was unable to escape. They were married and lived together many years; but one night it happened that the

man, joking with his wife about the way in which he had
secured her, drew the peg from the knot-hole, that she
might see how she had entered his room. As she peeped
through, she became suddenly quite small, passed out,
and was never seen again.

The well-known pathological phenomena of nightmare
are sufficient to account for the mediæval theory of a
fiend who sits upon one's bosom and hinders respiration;
but as we compare these various legends relating to the
Mara, we see that a more recondite explanation is needed
to account for all her peculiarities. Indigestion may
interfere with our breathing, but it does not make beautiful women crawl through keyholes, nor does it bring
wives from the spirit-world. The Mara belongs to an
ancient family, and in passing from the regions of monkish superstition to those of pure mythology we find that,
like her kinsman the werewolf, she had once seen better
days. Christianity made a demon of the Mara, and adopted
the theory that Satan employed these seductive creatures
as agents for ruining human souls. Such is the character
of the knight's wife, in the monkish legend just cited. But
in the Danish tale the Mara appears as one of that large
family of supernatural wives who are permitted to live
with mortal men under certain conditions, but who are
compelled to flee away when these conditions are broken
as is always sure to be the case. The eldest and one of
the loveliest of this family is the Hindu nymph Urvasi,
whose love adventures with Purûravas are narrated in the
Puranas, and form the subject of the well-known and
exquisite Sanskrit drama by Kalidasa. Urvasi is allowed
to live with Purûravas so long as she does not see him
undressed. But one night her kinsmen, the Gandharvas,
or cloud-demons, vexed at her long absence from heaven,
resolved to get her away from her mortal companion.

They stole a pet lamb which had been tied at the foot of her couch, whereat she bitterly upbraided her husband. In rage and mortification, Purûravas sprang up without throwing on his tunic, and grasping his sword sought the robber. Then the wicked Gandharvas sent a flash of lightning, and Urvasi, seeing her naked husband, instantly vanished.

The different versions of .this legend, which have been elaborately analyzed by comparative mythologists, leave no doubt that Urvasi is one of the dawn-nymphs or bright fleecy clouds of early morning, which vanish as the splendour of the sun is unveiled. We saw, in the preceding paper, that the ancient Aryans regarded the sky as a sea or great lake, and that the clouds were explained variously as Phaiakian ships with bird-like beaks sailing over this lake, or as bright birds of divers shapes and hues. The light fleecy cirrhi were regarded as mermaids, or as swans, or as maidens .with swan's plumage. In Sanskrit they are called *Apsaras*, or "those who move in the water," and the Elves and Maras of Teutonic mythology have the same significance. Urvasi appears in one legend as a bird ; and a South German prescription for getting rid of the Mara asserts that if she be wrapped up in the bedclothes and firmly held, a white dove will forthwith fly from the room, leaving the bedclothes empty.*

In the story of Melusina the cloud-maiden appears as a kind of mermaid, but in other respects the legend resembles that of Urvasi. Raymond, Count de la Forêt, of Poitou, having by an accident killed his patron and benefactor during a hunting excursion, fled in terror and

---

* See Kuhn, Herabkunft des Feuers, p. 91 ; Weber, Indische Studien, I. 197 ; Wolf, Beiträge zur deutschen Mythologie, II. 233 – 281 ; Müller, Chips, II. 114 – 128.

despair into the deep recesses of the forest. All the
afternoon and evening he wandered through the thick
dark woods, until at midnight he came upon a strange
scene. All at once "the boughs of the trees became less
interlaced, and the trunks fewer; next moment his
horse, crashing through the shrubs, brought him out on
a pleasant glade, white with rime, and illumined by the
new moon; in the midst bubbled up a limpid fountain,
and flowed away over a pebbly-floor with a soothing mur-
mur. Near the fountain-head sat three maidens in glim-
mering white dresses, with long waving golden hair, and
faces of inexpressible beauty." * One of them advanced
to meet Raymond, and according to all mythological
precedent, they were betrothed before daybreak. In due
time the fountain-nymph † became Countess de la Forêt,
but her husband was given to understand that all her
Saturdays would be passed in strictest seclusion, upon
which he must never dare to intrude, under penalty of
losing her forever. For many years all went well, save
that the fair Melusina's children were, without exception, misshapen or disfigured. But after a while this
strange weekly seclusion got bruited about all over the
neighbourhood, and people shook their heads and looked
grave about it. So many gossiping tales came to the
Count's ears, that he began to grow anxious and suspicious, and at last he determined to know the worst. He
went one Saturday to Melusina's private apartments, and
going through one empty room after another, at last came
to a locked door which opened into a bath; looking
through a keyhole, there he saw the Countess transformed
from the waist downwards into a fish, disporting herself

---

* Baring-Gould, Curious Myths, II. 207.

† The word *nymph* itself means "cloud-maiden," as is illustrated by
the kinship between the Greek νύμφη and the Latin *nubes*.

like a mermaid in the water. Of course he could not keep the secret, but when some time afterwards they quarrelled, must needs address her as "a vile serpent, contaminator of his honourable race." So she disappeared through the window, but ever afterward hovered about her husband's castle of Lusignan, like a Banshee, whenever one of its lords was about to die.

The well-known story of Undine is similar to that of Melusina, save that the naiad's desire to obtain a human soul is a conception foreign to the spirit of the myth, and marks the degradation which Christianity had inflicted upon the denizens of fairy-land. In one of Dasent's tales the water-maiden is replaced by a kind of werewolf. A white bear marries a young girl, but assumes the human shape at night. She is never to look upon him in his human shape, but how could a young bride be expected to obey such an injunction as that? She lights a candle while he is sleeping, and discovers the handsomest prince in the world; unluckily she drops tallow on his shirt, and that tells the story. But she is more fortunate than poor Raymond, for after a tiresome journey to the "land east of the sun and west of the moon," and an arduous washing-match with a parcel of ugly Trolls, she washes out the spots, and ends her husband's enchantment.*

In the majority of these legends, however, the Apsaras, or cloud-maiden, has a shirt of swan's feathers which plays the same part as the wolfskin cape or girdle of the werewolf. If you could get hold of a werewolf's sack and burn it, a permanent cure was effected. No danger of a relapse, unless the Devil furnished him with a new wolfskin. So the swan-maiden kept her human form, as

---

* This is substantially identical with the stories of Beauty and the Beast, Eros and Psyche, Gandharba Sena, etc.

long as she was deprived of her tunic of feathers. Indo-European folk-lore teems with stories of swan-maidens forcibly wooed and won by mortals who had stolen their clothes. A man travelling along the road passes by a lake where several lovely girls are bathing; their dresses, made of feathers curiously and daintily woven, lie on the shore. He approaches the place cautiously and steals one of these dresses.* When the girls have finished their bathing, they all come and get their dresses and swim away as swans; but the one whose dress is stolen must needs stay on shore and marry the thief. It is needless to add that they live happily together for many years, or that finally the good man accidentally leaves the cupboard door unlocked, whereupon his wife gets back her swan-shirt and flies away from him, never to return. But it is not always a shirt of feathers. In one German story, a nobleman hunting deer finds a maiden bathing in a clear pool in the forest. He runs stealthily up to her and seizes her necklace, at which she loses the power to flee. They are married, and she bears seven sons at once, all of whom have gold chains about their necks, and are able to transform themselves into swans whenever they like. A Flemish legend tells of three Nixies, or water-sprites, who came out of the Meuse one autumn evening, and helped the villagers celebrate the end of the vintage. Such graceful dancers had never been seen in Flanders, and they could sing as well as they could dance. As the night was warm, one of them took off her gloves and gave them to her partner to hold for her. When the clock struck twelve the other two

---

* The feather-dress reappears in the Arabian story of Hassan of El-Basrah, who by stealing it secures possession of the Jinniya. See Lane's Arabian Nights, Vol. III. p. 380. Ralston, Songs of the Russian People, p. 179.

started off in hot haste, and then there was a hue and
cry for gloves. The lad would keep them as love-tokens,
and so the poor Nixie had to go home without them;
but she must have died on the way, for next morning the waters of the Meuse were blood-red, and those
damsels never returned.

In the Faro Islands it is believed that seals cast off
their skins every ninth night, assume human forms, and
sing and dance like men and women until daybreak,
when they resume their skins and their seal natures.
Of course a man once found and hid one of these sealskins, and so got a mermaid for a wife; and of course she
recovered the skin and escaped.* On the coasts of Ireland it is supposed to be quite an ordinary thing for
young sea-fairies to get human husbands in this way;
the brazen things even come to shore on purpose, and
leave their red caps lying around for young men to pick
up; but it behooves the husband to keep a strict watch
over the red cap, if he would not see his children left
motherless.

This mermaid's cap has contributed its quota to the
superstitions of witchcraft. An Irish story tells how Red
James was aroused from sleep one night by noises in the
kitchen. Going down to the door, he saw a lot of old
women drinking punch around the fireplace, and laughing and joking with his housekeeper. When the punch-
bowl was empty, they all put on red caps, and singing

> " By yarrow and rue,
>   And my red cap too,
>   Hie me over to England,"

they flew up chimney. So Jimmy burst into the room,
and seized the housekeeper's cap, and went along with

* Thorpe, Northern Mythology, III. 173; Kennedy, Fictions of the
Irish Celts, p. 123.

them. They flew across the sea to a castle in England, passed through the keyholes from room to room and into the cellar, where they had a famous carouse. Unluckily Jimmy, being unused to such good cheer, got drunk, and forgot to put on his cap when the others did. So next morning the lord's butler found him dead-drunk on the cellar floor, surrounded by empty casks. He was sentenced to be hung without any trial worth speaking of; but as he was carted to the gallows an old woman cried out, "Ach, Jimmy alanna! Would you be afther dyin' in a strange land without your red birredh?" The lord made no objections, and so the red cap was brought and put on him. Accordingly when Jimmy had got to the gallows and was making his last speech for the edification of the spectators, he unexpectedly and somewhat irrelevantly exclaimed, "By yarrow and rue," etc., and was off like a rocket, shooting through the blue air *en route* for old Ireland.*

In another Irish legend an enchanted ass comes into the kitchen of a great house every night, and washes the dishes and scours the tins, so that the servants lead an easy life of it. After a while in their exuberant gratitude they offer him any present for which he may feel inclined to ask. He desires only " an ould coat, to keep the chill off of him these could nights "; but as soon as he gets into the coat he resumes his human form and bids them good by, and thenceforth they may wash their own dishes and scour their own tins, for all him.

But we are diverging from the subject of swan-maidens, and are in danger of losing ourselves in that labyrinth of popular fancies which is more intricate than any that Daidalos ever planned. The significance of all these sealskins and feather-dresses and mermaid caps and were-

---

* Kennedy, Fictions of the Irish Celts, p. 168.

wolf-girdles may best be sought in the etymology of words
like the German *leichnam*, in which the body is described
as a garment of flesh for the soul.* In the naïve philosophy of primitive thinkers, the soul, in passing from
one visible shape to another, had only to put on the outward integument of the creature in which it wished to
incarnate itself. With respect to the mode of metamorphosis, there is little difference between the werewolf and
the swan-maiden; and the similarity is no less striking
between the genesis of the two conceptions. The original werewolf is the night-wind, regarded now as a man-
like deity and now as a howling lupine fiend; and the
original swan-maiden is the light fleecy cloud, regarded
either as a woman-like goddess or as a bird swimming in
the sky sea. The one conception has been productive of
little else but horrors; the other has given rise to a great
variety of fanciful creations, from the treacherous mermaid and the fiendish nightmare to the gentle Undine,
the charming Nausikaa, and the stately Muse of classic
antiquity.

We have seen that the original werewolf, howling in
the wintry blast, is a kind of psychopomp, or leader of
departed souls; he is the wild ancestor of the death-dog,
whose voice under the window of a sick-chamber is even
now a sound of ill-omen. The swan-maiden has also
been supposed to summon the dying to her home in the
Phaiakian land. The Valkyries, with their shirts of swan-
plumage, who hovered over Scandinavian battle-fields to
receive the souls of falling heroes, were identical with
the Hindu Apsaras; and the Houris of the Mussulman
belong to the same family. Even for the angels, —
women with large wings, who are seen in popular pictures
bearing mortals on high towards heaven, — we can hardly

* Baring-Gould, Book of Werewolves, p. 163.

claim a different kinship. Melusina, when she leaves the castle of Lusignan, becomes a Banshee; and it has been a common superstition among sailors, that the appearance of a mermaid, with her comb and looking-glass, foretokens shipwreck, with the loss of all on board.

October, 1870.

IV.

LIGHT AND DARKNESS.

WHEN Maitland blasphemously asserted that God was but " a Bogie of the nursery," he unwittingly made a remark as suggestive in point of philology as it was crude and repulsive in its atheism. When examined with the lenses of linguistic science, the " Bogie " or " Bug-a-boo " or " Bugbear " of nursery lore turns out to be identical, not only with the fairy " Puck," whom Shakespeare has immortalized, but also with the Slavonic " Bog " and the " Baga " of the Cuneiform Inscriptions, both of which are names for the Supreme Being. If we proceed further, and inquire after the ancestral form of these epithets, — so strangely incongruous in their significations, — we shall find it in the Old Aryan " Bhaga," which reappears unchanged in the Sanskrit of the Vedas, and has left a memento of itself in the surname of the Phrygian Zeus " Bagaios." It seems originally to have denoted either the unclouded sun or the sky of noonday illumined by the solar rays. In Sâyana's commentary on the Rig-Veda, Bhaga is enumerated among the seven (or eight) sons of Aditi, the boundless Orient; and he is elsewhere described as the lord of life, the giver of bread, and the bringer of happiness.*

Thus the same name which, to the Vedic poet, to the Persian of the time of Xerxes, and to the modern Rus-

* Muir's Sanskrit Texts, Vol. IV. p. 12 ; Müller, Rig-Veda Sanhita, Vol. I. pp. 230 – 251 ; Fick, Woerterbuch der Indogermanischen Grundsprache, p. 124, s. v. Bhaga.

sian, suggests the supreme majesty of deity, is in English associated with an ugly and ludicrous fiend, closely akin to that grotesque Northern Devil of whom Southey was unable to think without laughing. Such is the irony of fate toward a deposed deity. The German name for idol — *Abgott*, that is, "ex-god," or "dethroned god" — sums up in a single etymology the history of the havoc wrought by monotheism among the ancient symbols of deity. In the hospitable Pantheon of the Greeks and Romans a niche was always in readiness for every new divinity who could produce respectable credentials; but the triumph of monotheism converted the stately mansion into a Pandemonium peopled with fiends. To the monotheist an "ex-god" was simply a devilish deceiver of mankind whom the true God had succeeded in vanquishing; and thus the word *demon,* which to the ancient meant a divine or semi-divine being, came to be applied to fiends exclusively. Thus the Teutonic races, who preserved the name of their highest divinity, Odin, — originally, Guodan, — by which to designate the God of the Christian,* were unable to regard the Bog of ancient tradition as anything but an "ex-god," or vanquished demon.

The most striking illustration of this process is to be found in the word *devil* itself. To a reader unfamiliar with the endless tricks which language delights in playing, it may seem shocking to be told that the Gypsies use the word *devil* as the name of God.† This, however,

---

* In the North American Review, October, 1869, p. 354, I have collected a number of facts which seem to me to prove beyond question that the name *God* is derived from *Guodan,* the original form of *Odin,* the supreme deity of our Pagan forefathers. The case is exactly parallel to that of the French *Dieu,* which is descended from the *Deus* of the pagan Roman.

† See Pott, Die Zigeuner, II. 311 ; Kuhn, Beiträge, I. 147. Yet in the worship of *dewel* by the Gypsies is to be found the element of

is not because these people have made the archfiend an object of worship, but because the Gypsy language, descending directly from the Sanskrit, has retained in its primitive exalted sense a word which the English language has received only in its debased and perverted sense. The Teutonic words *devil, teufel, diuval, djöfull, djevful,* may all be traced back to the Zend *dev,*[*] a name in which is implicitly contained the record of the oldest monotheistic revolution known to history. The influence of the so-called Zoroastrian reform upon the long-subsequent development of Christianity will receive further notice in the course of this paper; for the present it is enough to know that it furnished for all Christendom the name by which it designates the author of evil. To the Parsee follower of Zarathustra the name of the Devil has very nearly the same signification as to the Christian; yet, as Grimm has shown, it is nothing else than a corruption of *deva,* the Sanskrit name for God. When Zarathustra overthrew the primeval Aryan nature-worship in Bactria, this name met the same evil fate which in early Christian times overtook the word *demon,* and from a symbol of reverence became henceforth a symbol of detestation.[†] But throughout the rest of the Aryan world it achieved

---

diabolism invariably present in barbaric worship. "Dewel, the great god in heaven (*dewa, deus*), is rather feared than loved by these weather-beaten outcasts, for he harms them on their wanderings with his thunder and lightning, his snow and rain, and his stars interfere with their dark doings. Therefore they curse him foully when misfortune falls on them; and when a child dies, they say that Dewel has eaten it." Tylor, Primitive Culture, Vol. II. p. 248.

[*] See Grimm, Deutsche Mythologie, 939.

[†] The Buddhistic as well as the Zarathustrian reformation degraded the Vedic gods into demons. "In Buddhism we find these ancient devas, Indra and the rest, carried about at shows, as servants of Buddha, as goblins, or fabulous heroes." Max Müller, Chips, I. 25. This is like the Christian change of Odin into an ogre, and of Thor into the Devil.

a nobler career, producing the Greek *theos,* the Lithuanian
d*:*ewas, the Latin *deus,* and hence the modern French
Dieu, all meaning God.

If we trace back this remarkable word to its primitive
source in that once lost but now partially recovered mother-tongue from which all our Aryan languages are descended, we find a root *div* or *dyu,* meaning " to shine."
From the first-mentioned form comes *deva,* with its numerous progeny of good and evil appellatives; from the
latter is derived the name of Dyaus, with its brethren,
Zeus and Jupiter. In Sanskrit *dyu,* as a noun, means
" sky " and " day "; and there are many passages in the
Rig-Veda where the character of the god Dyaus, as the
personification of the sky or the brightness of the ethereal
heavens, is unmistakably apparent. This key unlocks
for us one of the secrets of Greek mythology. So long
as there was for *Zeus* no better etymology than that
which assigned it to the root *zen,* " to live," [*] there was
little hope of understanding the nature of Zeus. But
when we learn that Zeus is identical with Dyaus, the
bright sky, we are enabled to understand Horace's expression, " sub Jove frigido," and the prayer of the Athenians, " Rain, rain, dear Zeus, on the land of the Athenians, and on the fields." [†] Such expressions as these were
retained by the Greeks and Romans long after they had
forgotten that their supreme deity was once the sky. Yet
even the Brahman, from whose mind the physical signifi-

---

[*] Ζεὺς — Δία — Ζῆνα — δι' ὃν ζῆν ἀεὶ πᾶσι τοῖς ζῶσιν ὑπάρχει. Plato,
Kratylos, p. 396, A., with Stallbaum's note. See also Proklos, Comm.
ad Timæum, II. p. 226, Schneider; and compare Pseudo-Aristotle, De
Mundo, p. 401, a, 15, who adopts the etymology δι' ὃν ζῶμεν. See also
Diogenes Laërtius, VII. 147.

[†] Εὐχὴ Ἀθηναίων, ὗσον, ὗσον, ὦ φίλε Ζεῦ, κατὰ τῆς ἀρούρας τῶν Ἀθηναίων καὶ τῶν πεδίων. Marcus Aurelius, v. 7; ὖε δ' ἄρα Ζεὺς συνεχές.
Hom. Iliad, xii. 25; cf. Petronius Arbiter, Sat. xliv.

cance of the god's name never wholly disappeared, could
speak of him as Father Dyaus, the great Pitri, or ancestor of gods and men ; and in this reverential name *Dyaus
pitar* may be seen the exact equivalent of the Roman's
Jupiter, or Jove the Father. The same root can be followed into Old German, where Zio is the god of day ;
and into Anglo-Saxon, where *Tiwsdaeg,* or the day of
Zeus, is the ancestral form of *Tuesday.*

Thus we again reach the same results which were obtained from the examination of the name *Bhaga.* These
various names for the supreme Aryan god, which without
the help afforded by the Vedas could never have been
interpreted, are seen to have been originally applied to
the sun-illumined firmament. Countless other examples,
when similarly analyzed, show that the earliest Aryan
conception of a Divine Power, nourishing man and sus-
taining the universe, was suggested by the light of the
mighty Sun ; who, as modern science has shown, is the
originator of all life and motion upon the globe, and
whom the ancients delighted to believe the source, not
only of "the golden light," * but of everything that is
bright, joy-giving, and pure. Nevertheless, in accepting
this conclusion as well established by linguistic science,
we must be on our guard against an error into which
writers on mythology are very liable to fall. Neither
sky nor sun nor light of day, neither Zeus nor Apollo,
neither Dyaus nor Indra, was ever worshipped by the
ancient Aryan in anything like a monotheistic sense.
To interpret Zeus or Jupiter as originally the supreme
Aryan god, and to regard classic paganism as one of the
degraded remnants of a primeval monotheism, is to sin
against the canons of a sound inductive philosophy.

* "Il Sol, dell aurea luce eterno fonte." Tasso, Gerusalemme, XV.
47 ; cf. Dante, Paradiso, X. 28.

Philology itself teaches us that this could not have been so. Father Dyaus was originally the bright sky and nothing more. Although his name became generalized, in the classic languages, into *deus*, or God, it is quite certain that in early days, before the Aryan separation, it had acquired no such exalted significance. It was only in Greece and Rome — or, we may say, among the still united Italo-Hellenic tribes — that Jupiter-Zeus attained a pre-eminence over all other deities. The people of Iran quite rejected him, the Teutons preferred Thor and Odin, and in India he was superseded, first by Indra, afterwards by Brahma and Vishnu. We need not, therefore, look for a single supreme divinity among the old Aryans; nor may we expect to find any sense, active or dormant, of monotheism in the primitive intelligence of uncivilized men.* The whole fabric of comparative mythology, as at present constituted, and as described above, in the first of these papers, rests upon the postulate that the earliest religion was pure fetichism.

In the unsystematic nature-worship of the old Aryans the gods are presented to us only as vague powers, with their nature and attributes dimly defined, and their relations to each other fluctuating and often contradictory. There is no theogony, no regular subordination of one deity to another. The same pair of divinities appear now as father and daughter, now as brother and sister,

---

* The Aryans were, however, doubtless better off than the tribes of North America. "In no Indian language could the early missionaries find a word to express the idea of God. *Manitou* and *Oki* meant anything endowed with supernatural powers, from a snake-skin or a greasy Indian conjurer up to Manabozho and Jouskeha. The priests were forced to use a circumlocution, — 'the great chief of men,' or 'he who lives in the sky.'" Parkman, Jesuits in North America, p. lxxix. "The Algonquins used no oaths, for their language supplied none; doubtless because their mythology had no beings sufficiently distinct to swear by." Ibid, p. 31.

now as husband and wife; and again they quite lose
their personality, and are represented as mere natural
phenomena. As Müller observes, "The poets of the
Veda indulged freely in theogonic speculations without
being frightened by any contradictions. They knew of
Indra as the greatest of gods, they knew of Agni as the
god of gods, they knew of Varuna as the ruler of all; but
they were by no means startled at the idea that their
Indra had a mother, or that their Agni [Latin *ignis*] was
born like a babe from the friction of two fire-sticks, or
that Varuna and his brother Mitra were nursed in the
lap of Aditi." *   Thus we have seen Bhaga, the daylight, represented as the offspring of Aditi, the boundless
Orient; but he had several brothers, and among them
were Mitra, the sun, Varuna, the overarching firmament,
and Vivasvat, the vivifying sun. Manifestly we have
here but so many different names for what is at bottom
one and the same conception. The common element
which, in Dyaus and Varuna, in Bhaga and Indra, was
made an object of worship, is the brightness, warmth,
and life of day, as contrasted with the darkness, cold, and
seeming death of the night-time. And this common
element was personified in as many different ways as
the unrestrained fancy of the ancient worshipper saw fit
to devise.†

Thus we begin to see why a few simple objects, like
the sun, the sky, the dawn, and the night, should be represented in mythology by such a host of gods, goddesses,
and heroes. For at one time the Sun is represented as
the conqueror of hydras and dragons who hide away from
men the golden treasures of light and warmth, and at
another time he is represented as a weary voyager trav-

---

* Müller, Rig-Veda-Sanhita, I. 230.
† Compare the remarks of Bréal, Hercule et Cacus, p. 13.

ersing the sky-sea amid many perils, with the steadfast purpose of returning to his western home and his twilight bride; hence the different conceptions of Herakles, Bellerophon, and Odysseus. Now he is represented as the son of the Dawn, and again, with equal propriety, as the son of the Night, and the fickle lover of the Dawn; hence we have, on the one hand, stories of a virgin mother who dies in giving birth to a hero, and, on the other hand, stories of a beautiful maiden who is forsaken and perhaps cruelly slain by her treacherous lover. Indeed, the Sun's adventures with so many dawn-maidens have given him quite a bad character, and the legends are numerous in which he appears as the prototype of Don Juan. Yet again his separation from the bride of his youth is described as due to no fault of his own, but to a resistless decree of fate, which hurries him away, as Aineias was compelled to abandon Dido. Or, according to a third and equally plausible notion, he is a hero of ascetic virtues, and the dawn-maiden is a wicked enchantress, daughter of the sensual Aphrodite, who vainly endeavours to seduce him. In the story of Odysseus these various conceptions are blended together. When enticed by artful women,* he yields for a while to the temptation; but by and by his longing to see Penelope takes him homeward, albeit with a record which Penelope might not altogether have liked. Again, though the Sun, "always roaming with a hungry heart,"

---

* It should be borne in mind, however, that one of the women who tempt Odysseus is not a dawn-maiden, but a goddess of darkness; Kalypso answers to Venus-Ursula in the myth of Tannhäuser. Kirke, on the other hand, seems to be a dawn-maiden, like Medeia, whom she resembles. In her the wisdom of the dawn-goddess Athene, the loftiest of Greek divinities, becomes degraded into the art of an enchantress. She reappears, in the Arabian Nights, as the wicked Queen Labe, whose sorcery none of her lovers can baffle, save Beder, king of Persia.

has seen many cities and customs of strange men, he is
nevertheless confined to a single path, — a circumstance
which seems to have occasioned much speculation in the
primeval mind.   Garcilaso de la Vega relates of a certain
Peruvian Inca, who seems to have been an "infidel"
with reference to the orthodox mythology of his day,
that he thought the Sun was not such a mighty god after
all; for if he were, he would wander about the heavens
at random instead of going forever, like a horse in a
treadmill, along the same course.   The American Indians
explained this circumstance by myths which told how
the Sun was once caught and tied with a chain which
would only let him swing a little way to one side or the
other.   The ancient Aryan developed the nobler myth of
the labours of Herakles, performed in obedience to the
bidding of Eurystheus.   Again, the Sun must needs
destroy its parents, the Night and the Dawn; and
accordingly his parents, forewarned by prophecy, expose
him in infancy, or order him to be put to death; but his
tragic destiny never fails to be accomplished to the letter.
And again the Sun, who engages in quarrels not his own,
is sometimes represented as retiring moodily from the
sight of men, like Achilleus and Meleagros : he is short-
lived and ill-fated, born to do much good and to be
repaid with ingratitude ; his life depends on the duration
of a burning brand, and when that is extinguished he
must die.

The myth of the great Theban hero, Oidipous, well
illustrates the multiplicity of conceptions which clustered
about the daily career of the solar orb.   His father, Laios,
had been warned by the Delphic oracle that he was in
danger of death from his own son.   The newly born
Oidipous was therefore exposed on the hillside ; but, like
Romulus and Remus, and all infants similarly situated

in legend, was duly rescued. He was taken to Corinth, where he grew up to manhood. Journeying once to Thebes, he got into a quarrel with an old man whom he met on the road, and slew him, who was none other than his father, Laios. Reaching Thebes, he found the city harassed by the Sphinx, who afflicted the land with drought until she should receive an answer to her riddles. Oidipous destroyed the monster by solving her dark sayings, and as a reward received the kingdom, with his own mother, Iokaste, as his bride. Then the Erinyes hastened the discovery of these dark deeds; Iokaste died in her bridal chamber; and Oidipous, having blinded himself, fled to the grove of the Eumenides, near Athens, where, amid flashing lightning and peals of thunder, he died.

Oidipous is the Sun. Like all the solar heroes, from Herakles and Perseus to Sigurd and William Tell, he performs his marvellous deeds at the behest of others. His father, Laios, is none other than the Vedic Dasyu, the night-demon who is sure to be destroyed by his solar offspring. In the evening, Oidipous is united to the Dawn, the mother who had borne him at daybreak; and here the original story doubtless ended. In the Vedic hymns we find Indra, the Sun, born of Dahana (Daphne), the Dawn, whom he afterwards, in the evening twilight, marries. To the Indian mind the story was here complete; but the Greeks had forgotten and outgrown the primitive signification of the myth. To them Oidipous and Iokaste were human, or at least anthropomorphic beings; and a marriage between them was a fearful crime which called for bitter expiation. Thus the latter part of the story arose in the effort to satisfy a moral feeling. As the name of Laios denotes the dark night, so, like Iole, Oinone, and Iamos, the word *Iokaste* signifies the delicate *violet* tints of the morning and evening clouds.

Oidipous was exposed, like Paris upon Ida (a Vedic word meaning " the earth "), because the sunlight in the morning lies upon the hillside.* He is borne on to the destruction of his father and the incestuous marriage with his mother by an irresistible Moira, or Fate; the sun cannot but slay the darkness and hasten to the couch of the violet twilight.† The Sphinx is the storm-demon who sits on the cloud-rock and imprisons the rain; she is the same as Medusa, Ahi, or Echidna, and Chimaira, and is akin to the throttling snakes of darkness which the jealous Here sent to destroy Herakles in his cradle. The idea was not derived from Egypt, but the Greeks, on finding Egyptian figures resembling their conception of the Sphinx, called them by the same name. The omniscient Sun comprehends the sense of her dark mutterings, and destroys her, as Indra slays Vritra, bringing down rain upon the parched earth. The Erinyes, who bring to light the crimes of Oidipous, have been explained, in a previous paper, as the personification of daylight, which reveals the evil deeds done under the cover of night. The grove of the Erinyes, like the garden of the Hyperboreans, represents " the fairy network of clouds, which are the first to receive and the last to lose the light of the sun in the morning and in the evening; hence, although Oidipous dies in a thunder-storm, yet the Eumenides are kind to him, and his last hour is one of

---

* The Persian Cyrus is an historical personage; but the story of his perils in infancy belongs to solar mythology as much as the stories of the magic sleep of Charlemagne and Barbarossa. His grandfather, Astyages, is purely a mythical creation, his name being identical with that of the night-demon, Azidahâka, who appears in the Shah-Nameh as the biting serpent Zohâk. See Cox, Mythology of the Aryan Nations, II. 358.

† In mediæval legend this resistless Moira is transformed into the curse which prevents the Wandering Jew from resting until the day of judgment.

deep peace and tranquillity." * To the last remains with him his daughter Antigone, "she who is born opposite," the pale light which springs up opposite to the setting sun.

These examples show that a story-root may be as prolific of heterogeneous offspring as a word-root. Just as we find the root *spak*, "to look," begetting words so various as *sceptic, bishop, speculate, conspicuous, species,* and *spice,* we must expect to find a simple representation of the diurnal course of the sun, like those lyrically given in the Veda, branching off into stories as diversified as those of Oidipous, Herakles, Odysseus, and Siegfried. In fact, the types upon which stories are constructed are wonderfully few. Some clever playwright — I believe it was Scribe — has said that there are only seven possible dramatic situations; that is, all the plays in the world may be classed with some one. of seven archetypal dramas.† If this be true, the astonishing complexity of mythology taken in the concrete, as compared with its extreme simplicity when analyzed, need not surprise us.

The extreme limits of divergence between stories descended from a common root are probably reached in the myths of light and darkness with which the present discussion is mainly concerned. The subject will be best elucidated by taking a single one of these myths and following its various fortunes through different regions of the Aryan world. The myth of Hercules and

* Cox, Manual of Mythology, p. 134.

† In his interesting appendix to Henderson's Folk Lore of the Northern Counties of England, Mr. Baring-Gould has made an ingenious and praiseworthy attempt to reduce the entire existing mass of household legends to about fifty story-roots ; and his list, though both redundant and defective, is nevertheless, as an empirical classification, very instructive.

Cacus has been treated by M. Bréal in an essay which is one of the most valuable contributions ever made to the study of comparative mythology; and while following his footsteps our task will be an easy one.

The battle between Hercules and Cacus, although one of the oldest of the traditions common to the whole Indo-European race, appears in Italy as a purely local legend, and is narrated as such by Virgil, in the eighth book of the Æneid; by Livy, at the beginning of his history; and by Propertius and Ovid. Hercules, journeying through Italy after his victory over Geryon, stops to rest by the bank of the Tiber. While he is taking his repose, the three-headed monster Cacus, a son of Vulcan and a formidable brigand, comes and steals his cattle, and drags them tail-foremost to a secret cavern in the rocks. But the lowing of the cows arouses Hercules, and he runs toward the cavern where the robber, already frightened, has taken refuge. Armed with a huge flinty rock, he breaks open the entrance of the cavern, and confronts the demon within, who vomits forth flames at him and roars like the thunder in the storm-cloud. After a short combat, his hideous body falls at the feet of the invincible hero, who erects on the spot an altar to Jupiter Inventor, in commemoration of the recovery of his cattle. Ancient Rome teemed with reminiscences of this event, which Livy regarded as first in the long series of the exploits of his countrymen. The place where Hercules pastured his oxen was known long after as the *Forum Boarium;* near it the *Porta Trigemina* preserved the recollection of the monster's triple head; and in the time of Diodorus Siculus sight-seers were shown the cavern of Cacus on the slope of the Aventine. Every tenth day the earlier generations of Romans celebrated the victory with solemn sacrifices at the *Ara Maxima;* and on days of triumph the fortunate general deposited there a tithe of his booty, to be distributed among the citizens.

In this famous myth, however, the god Hercules did not originally figure. The Latin Hercules was an essentially peaceful and domestic deity, watching over households and enclosures, and nearly akin to Terminus and the Penates. He does not appear to have been a solar divinity at all. But the purely accidental resemblance of his name to that of the Greek deity Herakles,* and the manifest identity of the Cacus-myth with the story of the victory of Herakles over Geryon, led to the substitution of Hercules for the original hero of the legend, who was none other than Jupiter, called by his Sabine name Sancus. Now Johannes Lydus informs us that, in Sabine, *Sancus* signified "the sky," a meaning which we have already seen to belong to the name *Jupiter*. The same substitution of the Greek hero for the Roman divinity led to the alteration of the name of the demon overcome by his thunderbolts. The corrupted title *Cacus* was supposed to be identical with the Greek word *kakos*, meaning "evil," and the corruption was suggested by the epithet of Herakles, *Alexikakos*, or "the averter of ill." Originally, however, the name was *Cæcius*, "he who

---

* There is nothing in common between the names *Hercules* and *Herakles*. The latter is a compound, formed like *Themistokles*; the former is a simple derivative from the root of *hercere*, "to enclose." If *Herakles* had any equivalent in Latin, it would necessarily begin with S, and not with H, as *septa* corresponds to ἕπτα, *sequor* to ἕπομαι, etc. It should be noted, however, that Mommsen, in the fourth edition of his History, abandons this view, and observes : "Auch der griechische Herakles ist früh als Herclus, Hercoles, Hercules in Italien einheimisch und dort in eigenthümlicher Weise aufgefasst worden, wie es scheint zunächst als Gott des gewagten Gewinns und der ausserordentlichen Vermögensvermehrung." Römische Geschichte, I. 181. One would gladly learn Mommsen's reasons for recurring to this apparently less defensible opinion. ·

blinds or darkens," and it corresponds literally to the
name of the Greek demon *Kaikias,* whom an old proverb,
preserved by Aulus Gellius, describes as a stealer of the
clouds.*

Thus the significance of the myth becomes apparent.
The three-headed Cacus is seen to be a near kinsman of
Geryon's three-headed dog Orthros, and of the three-
headed Kerberos, the hell-hound who guards the dark
regions below the horizon. He is the original werewolf
or Rakshasa, the fiend of the storm who steals the bright
cattle of Helios, and hides them in the black cavernous
rock, from which they are afterwards rescued by the
schamir or lightning-stone of the solar hero. The physical character of the myth is apparent even in the
description of Virgil, which reads wonderfully like a
Vedic hymn in celebration of the exploits of Indra. But
when we turn to the Veda itself, we find the correctness
of the interpretation demonstrated again and again, with
inexhaustible prodigality of evidence. Here we encounter again the three-headed *Orthros* under the identical
title of *Vritra,* "he who shrouds or envelops," called
also *Çushna,* "he who parches," *Pani,* "the robber," and
Ahi, "the strangler." In many hymns of the Rig-Veda
the story is told over and over, like a musical theme
arranged with variations. Indra, the god of light, is a
herdsman who tends a herd of bright golden or violet-
coloured cattle. Vritra, a snake-like monster with three
heads, steals them and hides them in a cavern, but Indra
slays him as Jupiter slew Cæcius, and the cows are
recovered. The language of the myth is so significant,
that the Hindu commentators of the Veda have themselves given explanations of it similar to those proposed

---

* For the relations between Sancus and Herakles, see Preller,
Römische Mythologie, p. 635 ; Vollmer, Mythologie, p. 970.

by modern philologists. To them the legend never became devoid of sense, as the myth of Geryon appeared to Greek scholars like Apollodoros.*

These celestial cattle, with their resplendent coats of purple and gold, are the clouds lit up by the solar rays ; but the demon who steals them is not always the fiend of the storm, acting in that capacity. They are stolen every night by Vritra the concealer, and Cæcius the darkener, and Indra is obliged to spend hours in looking for them, sending Sarama, the inconstant twilight, to negotiate for their recovery. Between the storm-myth and the myth of night and morning the resemblance is sometimes so close as to confuse the interpretation of the two. Many legends which Max Müller explains as myths of the victory of day over night are explained by Dr. Kuhn as storm-myths ; and the disagreement between two such powerful champions would be a standing reproach to what is rather prematurely called the *science* of comparative mythology, were it not easy to show that the difference is merely apparent and non-essential. It is the old story of the shield with two sides ; and a comparison of the ideas fundamental to these myths will show that there is no valid ground for disagreement in the interpretation of them. The myths of schamir and the divining-rod, analyzed in a previous paper, explain the rending of the thunder-cloud and the procuring of water without especial reference to any struggle between opposing divinities. But in the myth of Hercules and Cacus, the fundamental idea is the victory of the solar god over the robber who steals the light. Now whether the robber carries off the light in the evening when Indra has gone to sleep, or boldly rears his black form against the sky during the daytime, causing darkness to spread

* Burnouf, Bhâgavata-Purâna, III. p. lxxxvi ; Bréal, op. cit. p. 98.

over the earth, would make little difference to the framers
of the myth. To a chicken a solar eclipse is the same
thing as nightfall, and he goes to roost accordingly.
Why, then, should the primitive thinker have made a
distinction between the darkening of the sky caused by
black clouds and that caused by the rotation of the
earth? He had no more conception of the scientific
explanation of these phenomena than the chicken has
of the scientific explanation of an eclipse. For him it
was enough to know that the solar radiance was stolen,
in the one case as in the other, and to suspect that the
same demon was to blame for both robberies.

The Veda itself sustains this view. It is certain that
the victory of Indra over Vritra is essentially the same
as his victory over the Panis. Vritra, the storm-fiend, is
himself called one of the Panis; yet the latter are uni-
formly represented as night-demons. They steal Indra's
golden cattle and drive them by circuitous paths to a
dark hiding-place near the eastern horizon. Indra sends
the dawn-nymph, Sarama, to search for them, but as she
comes within sight of the dark stable, the Panis try to
coax her to stay with them: "Let us make thee our
sister, do not go away again; we will give thee part of
the cows, O darling." * According to the text of this
hymn, she scorns their solicitations, but elsewhere the
fickle dawn-nymph is said to coquet with the powers
of darkness. She does not care for their cows, but will
take a drink of milk, if they will be so good as to get it
for her. Then she goes back and tells Indra that she
cannot find the cows. He kicks her with his foot, and
she runs back to the Panis, followed by the god, who
smites them all with his unerring arrows and recovers
the stolen light. From such a simple beginning as this

* Max Müller, Science of Language, II. 484.

has been deduced the Greek myth of the faithlessness of Helen.*

These night-demons, the Panis, though not apparently regarded with any strong feeling of moral condemnation, are nevertheless hated and dreaded as the authors of calamity. They not only steal the daylight, but they parch the earth and wither the fruits, and they slay vegetation during the winter months. As *Cæcius*, the "darkener," became ultimately changed into *Cacus*, the "evil one," so the name of *Vritra*, the "concealer," the most famous of the Panis, was gradually generalized until it came to mean "enemy," like the English word *fiend*, and began to be applied indiscriminately to any kind of evil spirit. In one place he is called Adeva, the "enemy of the gods," an epithet exactly equivalent to the Persian *dev*.

In the Zendavesta the myth of Hercules and Cacus has given rise to a vast system of theology. The fiendish Panis are concentrated in Ahriman or Anro-mainyas, whose name signifies the "spirit of darkness," and who carries on a perpetual warfare against Ormuzd or Ahura-mazda, who is described by his ordinary surname, Spento-mainyas, as the "spirit of light." The ancient polytheism here gives place to a refined dualism, not very different from what in many Christian sects has passed current as monotheism. Ahriman is the archfiend, who struggles with Ormuzd, not for the possession of a herd of perisha-ble cattle, but for the dominion of the universe. Ormuzd creates the world pure and beautiful, but Ahriman comes

* As Max Müller observes, "apart from all mythological considera-tions, *Saramâ* in Sanskrit is the same word as *Helena* in Greek." Op. cit. p. 490. The names correspond phonetically letter for letter, as *Surya* corresponds to *Helios*, *Sâramêyas* to *Hermeias*, and *Aharyu* to *Achilleus*. Müller has plausibly suggested that *Paris* similarly answers to the *Panis*.

after him and creates everything that is evil in it. He not only keeps the earth covered with darkness during half of the day, and withholds the rain and destroys the crops, but he is the author of all evil thoughts and the instigator of all wicked actions. Like his progenitor Vritra and his offspring Satan, he is represented under the form of a serpent; and the destruction which ultimately awaits these demons is also in reserve for him. Eventually there is to be a day of reckoning, when Ahriman will be bound in chains and rendered powerless, or when, according to another account, he will be converted to righteousness, as Burns hoped and Origen believed would be the case with Satan.

This dualism of the ancient Persians has exerted a powerful influence upon the development of Christian theology. The very idea of an archfiend Satan, which Christianity received from Judaism, seems either to have been suggested by the Persian Ahriman, or at least to have derived its principal characteristics from that source. There is no evidence that the Jews, previous to the Babylonish captivity, possessed the conception of a Devil as the author of all evil. In the earlier books of the Old Testament Jehovah is represented as dispensing with his own hand the good and the evil, like the Zeus of the Iliad.* The story of the serpent in Eden — an Aryan story in every particular, which has crept into the Pentateuch — is not once alluded to in the Old Testament; and the notion of Satan as the author of evil appears only in the later books, composed after the Jews had come into close contact with Persian ideas.† In the

---

* "I create evil," Isaiah xlv. 7 ; "Shall there be evil in the city, and the Lord hath not done it?" Amos iii. 6; cf. Iliad, xxiv. 527, and contrast 2 Samuel xxiv. 1 with 1 Chronicles xxi. 1.

† Nor is there any ground for believing that the serpent in the Eden-

Book of Job, as Réville observes, Satan is "still a member of the celestial court, being one of the sons of the Elohim, but having as his special office the continual accusation of men, and having become so suspicious by his practice as public accuser, that he believes in the virtue of no one, and always presupposes interested motives for the purest manifestations of human piety." In this way the character of this angel became injured, and he became more and more an object of dread and dislike to men, until the later Jews ascribed to him all the attributes of Ahriman, and in this singularly altered shape he passed into Christian theology. Between the Satan of the Book of Job and the mediæval Devil the metamorphosis is as great as that which degraded the stern Erinys, who brings evil deeds to light, into the demon-like Fury who torments wrong-doers in Tartarus; and, making allowance for difference of circumstances, the process of degradation has been very nearly the same in the two cases.

The mediæval conception of the Devil is a grotesque compound of elements derived from all the systems of pagan mythology which Christianity superseded. He is primarily a rebellious angel, expelled from heaven along with his followers, like the giants who attempted to scale Olympos, and like the impious Efreets of Arabian legend who revolted against the beneficent rule of Solomon. As the serpent prince of the outer darkness, he retains the old characteristics of Vritra, Ahi, Typhon, and Echidna.

myth is intended for Satan. The identification is entirely the work of modern dogmatic theology, and is due, naturally enough, to the habit, so common alike among theologians and laymen, of reasoning about the Bible as if it were a single book, and not a collection of writings of different ages and of very different degrees of historic authenticity. In a future work, entitled "Aryana Vaëdjo," I hope to examine, at considerable length, this interesting myth of the garden of Eden.

As the black dog which appears behind the stove in Dr.
Faust's study, he is the classic hell-hound Kerberos, the
Vedic Çarvara. From the sylvan deity Pan he gets his
goat-like body, his horns and cloven hoofs. Like the
wind-god Orpheus, to whose music the trees bent their
heads to listen, he is an unrivalled player on the bagpipes.
Like those other wind-gods the psychopomp Hermes and
the wild huntsman Odin, he is the prince of the powers
of the air: his flight through the midnight sky, attended
by his troop of witches mounted on their brooms, which
sometimes break the boughs and sweep the leaves from
the trees, is the same as the furious chase of the Erlking
Odin or the Burckar Vittikâb. He is Dionysos, who
causes red wine to flow from the dry wood, alike on the
deck of the Tyrrhenian pirate-ship and in Auerbach's
cellar at Leipzig. He is Wayland, the smith, a skilful
worker in metals and a wonderful architect, like the classic
fire-god Hephaistos or Vulcan; and, like Hephaistos, he
is lame from the effects of his fall from heaven. From
the lightning-god Thor he obtains his red beard, his
pitchfork, and his power over thunderbolts; and, like
that ancient deity, he is in the habit of beating his wife
behind the door when the rain falls during sunshine.
Finally, he takes a hint from Poseidon and from the
swan-maidens, and appears as a water-imp or Nixy
(whence probably his name of Old Nick), and as the
Davy (*deva*) whose " locker " is situated at the bottom
of the sea.*

According to the Scotch divines of the seventeenth
century, the Devil is a learned scholar and profound
thinker. Having profited by six thousand years of in-

---

* For further particulars see Cox, Mythology of the Aryan Nations,
Vol. II. pp. 358, 366 ; to which I am indebted for several of the details
here given. Compare Welcker, Griechische Götterlehre, I. 661, *seq.*

tense study and meditation, he has all science, philosophy, and theology at his tongue's end; and, as his skill
has increased with age, he is far more than a match for
mortals in cunning.* Such, however, is not the view
taken by mediæval mythology, which usually represents
his stupidity as equalling his malignity. The victory of
Hercules over Cacus is repeated in a hundred mediæval
legends in which the Devil is overreached and made a
laughing-stock. The germ of this notion may be found
in the blinding of Polyphemos by Odysseus, which is itself a victory of the sun-hero over the night-demon, and
which curiously reappears in a Middle-Age story narrated
by Mr. Cox. "The Devil asks a man who is moulding
buttons what he may be doing; and when the man answers that he is moulding eyes, asks him further whether
he can give him a pair of new eyes. He is told to come
again another day; and when he makes his appearance
accordingly, the man tells him that the operation cannot
be performed rightly unless he is first tightly bound with
his back fastened to a bench. While he is thus pinioned
he asks the man's name. The reply is Issi ('himself').
When the lead is melted, the Devil opens his eyes wide
to receive the deadly stream. As soon as he is blinded,
he starts up in agony, bearing away the bench to which
he had been bound; and when some workpeople in the
fields ask him who had thus treated him, his answer is,
'Issi teggi' ('Self did it'). With a laugh they bid him
lie on the bed which he has made: 'selbst gethan, selbst
habe.' The Devil died of his new eyes, and was never
seen again."

---

* Many amusing passages from Scotch theologians are cited in Buckle's
History of Civilization, Vol. II. p. 368. The same belief is implied in
the quaint monkish tale of "Celestinus and the Miller's Horse." See
Tales from the Gesta Romanorum, p. 134.

In his attempts to obtain human souls the Devil is frequently foiled by the superior cunning of mortals. Once, he agreed to build a house for a peasant in exchange for the peasant's soul ; but if the house were not finished before cockcrow, the contract was to be null and void. Just as the Devil was putting on the last tile the man imitated a cockcrow and waked up all the roosters in the neighbourhood, so that the fiend had his labour for his pains. A merchant of Louvain once sold himself to the Devil, who heaped upon him all manner of riches for seven years, and then came to get him. The merchant "took the Devil in a friendly manner by the hand and, as it was just evening, said, ' Wife, bring a light quickly for the gentleman.' ' That is not at all necessary,' said the Devil ; ' I am merely come to fetch you.' ' Yes, yes, that I know very well,' said the merchant, ' only just grant me the time till this little candle-end is burnt out, as I have a few letters to sign and to put on my coat.' ' Very well,' said the Devil, ' but only till the candle is burnt out.' ' Good,' said the merchant, and going into the next room, ordered the maid-servant to place a large cask full of water close to a very deep pit that was dug in the garden. The men-servants also carried, each of them, a cask to the spot ; and when all was done, they were ordered each to take a shovel, and stand round the pit. The merchant then returned to the Devil, who seeing that not more than about an inch of candle remained, said, laughing, ' Now get yourself ready, it will soon be burnt out.' ' That I see, and am content ; but I shall hold you to your word, and stay till it *is* burnt.' ' Of course,' answered the Devil ; ' I stick to my word.' ' It is dark in the next room,' continued the merchant, ' but I must find the great book with clasps, so let me just take the light for one moment.' ' Certainly,' said the

Devil, ' But I 'll go with you.' He did so, and the merchant's trepidation was now on the increase. When in
the next room he said on a sudden, ' Ah, now I know,
the key is in the garden door.' And with these words he
ran out with the light into the garden, and before the
Devil could overtake him, threw it into the pit, and the
men and the maids poured water upon it, and then filled
up the hole with earth. Now came the Devil into the
garden and asked, ' Well, did you get the key ? and how
is it with the candle ? where is it ? ' ' The candle ? ' said
the merchant. ' Yes, the candle.' ' Ha, ha, ha ! it is not
yet burnt out,' answered the merchant, laughing, ' and
will not be burnt out for the next fifty years ; it lies
there a hundred fathoms deep in the earth.' When the
Devil heard this he screamed awfully, and went off with
a most intolerable stench." *

One day a fowler, who was a terrible bungler and
could n't hit a bird at a dozen paces, sold his soul to the
Devil in order to become a Freischütz. The fiend was to
come for him in seven years, but must be always able to
name the animal at which he was shooting, otherwise the
compact was to be nullified. After that day the fowler
never missed his aim, and never did a fowler command
such wages. When the seven years were out the fowler
told all these things to his wife, and the twain hit upon
an expedient for cheating the Devil. The woman
stripped herself, daubed her whole body with molasses,
and rolled herself up in a feather-bed, cut open for this
purpose. Then she hopped and skipped about the field
where her husband stood parleying with Old Nick.
"There 's a shot for you, fire away," said the Devil. " Of
course I 'll fire, but do you first tell me what kind of a
bird it is ; else our agreement is cancelled, Old Boy."

* Thorpe, Northern Mythology, Vol. II. p. 258.

There was no help for it; the Devil had to own himself nonplussed, and off he fled, with a whiff of brimstone which nearly suffocated the Freischütz and his good woman.*

In the legend of Gambrinus, the fiend is still more ingloriously defeated. Gambrinus was a fiddler, who, being jilted by his sweetheart, went out into the woods to hang himself. As he was sitting on the bough, with the cord about his neck, preparatory to taking the fatal plunge, suddenly a tall man in a green coat appeared before him, and offered his services. He might become as wealthy as he liked, and make his sweetheart burst with vexation at her own folly, but in thirty years he must give up his soul to Beelzebub. The bargain was struck, for Gambrinus thought thirty years a long time to enjoy one's self in, and perhaps the Devil might get him in any event; as well be hung for a sheep as for a lamb. Aided by Satan, he invented chiming-bells and lager-beer, for both of which achievements his name is held in grateful remembrance by the Teuton. No sooner had the Holy Roman Emperor quaffed a gallon or two of the new beverage than he made Gambrinus Duke of Brabant and Count of Flanders, and then it was the fiddler's turn to laugh at the discomfiture of his old sweetheart. Gambrinus kept clear of women, says the legend, and so lived in peace. For thirty years he sat beneath his belfry with the chimes, meditatively drinking beer with his nobles and burghers around him. Then Beelzebub sent Jocko, one of his imps, with orders to

* Thorpe, Northern Mythology, Vol. II. p. 259. In the Norse story of " Not a Pin to choose between them," the old woman is in doubt as to her own identity, on waking up after the butcher has dipped her in a tar-barrel and rolled her on a heap of feathers ; and when Tray barks at her, her perplexity is as great as the Devil's when fooled by the Freischütz. See Dasent, Norse Tales, p. 199.

bring back Gambrinus before midnight. But Jocko was, like Swiveller's Marchioness, ignorant of the taste of beer, never having drunk of it even in a sip, and the Flemish *schoppen* were too much for him. He fell into a drunken sleep, and did not wake up until noon next day, at which he was so mortified that he had not the face to go back to hell at all. So Gambrinus lived on tranquilly for a century or two, and drank so much beer that he turned into a beer-barrel.*

The character of gullibility attributed to the Devil in these legends is probably derived from the Trolls, or "night-folk," of Northern mythology. In most respects the Trolls resemble the Teutonic elves and fairies, and the Jinn or Efreets of the Arabian Nights ; but their pedigree is less honourable. The fairies, or "White Ladies," were not originally spirits of darkness, but were nearly akin to the swan-maidens, dawn-nymphs, and dryads, and though their wrath was to be dreaded, they were not malignant by nature. Christianity, having no place for such beings, degraded them into something like imps ; the most charitable theory being that they were angels who had remained neutral during Satan's rebellion, in punishment for which Michael expelled them from heaven, but has left their ultimate fate unannounced until the day of judgment. The Jinn appear to have been similarly degraded on the rise of Mohammedanism. But the Trolls were always imps of darkness. They are descended from the Jötuns, or Frost-Giants of Northern paganism, and they correspond to the Panis, or night-demons of the Veda. In many Norse tales they are said to burst when they see the risen sun.† They eat human flesh, are ignorant of the simplest arts, and live in the

---

* See Deulin, Contes d'un Buveur de Bière, pp. 3 – 29.

† Dasent, Popular Tales from the Norse, No. III. and No. XLII.

deepest recesses of the forest or in caverns on the hillside, where the sunlight never penetrates. Some of these
characteristics may very likely have been suggested by
reminiscences of the primeval Lapps, from whom the
Aryan invaders wrested the dominion of Europe.* In
some legends the Trolls are represented as an ancient
race of beings now superseded by the human race.
"'What sort of an earth-worm is this?' said one Giant
to another, when they met a man as they walked.
'These are the earth-worms that will one day eat us up,
brother,' answered the other; and soon both Giants left
that part of Germany." "'See what pretty playthings,
mother!' cries the Giant's daughter, as she unties her
apron, and shows her a plough, and horses, and a peasant.
'Back with them this instant,' cries the mother in wrath,
'and put them down as carefully as you can, for these
playthings can do our race great harm, and when these
come we must budge.'" Very naturally the primitive
Teuton, possessing already the conception of night-demons, would apply it to these men of the woods whom even
to this day his uneducated descendants believe to be sorcerers, able to turn men into wolves. But whatever contributions historical fact may have added to his character,
the Troll is originally a creation of mythology, like Polyphemos, whom he resembles in his uncouth person, his
cannibal appetite, and his lack of wit. His ready gullibility is shown in the story of "Boots who ate a Match
with the Troll." Boots, the brother of Cinderella, and
the counterpart alike of Jack the Giant-killer, and of
Odysseus, is the youngest of three brothers who go into
a forest to cut wood. The Troll appears and threatens to
kill any one who dares to meddle with his timber. The

---

* See Dasent's Introduction, p. cxxxix; Campbell, Tales of the West
Highlands, Vol. IV. p. 344; and Williams, Indian Epic Poetry, p. 10.

elder brothers flee, but Boots puts on a bold face. He pulled a cheese out of his scrip and squeezed it till the whey began to spurt out. "Hold your tongue, you dirty Troll," said he, "or I'll squeeze you as I squeeze this stone." So the Troll grew timid and begged to be spared,* and Boots let him off on condition that he would hew all day with him. They worked till nightfall, and the Troll's giant strength accomplished wonders. Then Boots went home with the Troll, having arranged that he should get the water while his host made the fire. When they reached the hut there were two enormous iron pails, so heavy that none but a Troll could lift them, but Boots was not to be frightened. "Bah!" said he. "Do you suppose I am going to get water in those paltry hand-basins? Hold on till I go and get the spring itself!" "O dear!" said the Troll, "I'd rather not; do you make the fire, and I'll get the water." Then when the soup was made, Boots challenged his new friend to an eating-match; and tying his scrip in front of him, proceeded to pour soup into it by the ladleful. By and by the giant threw down his spoon in despair, and owned himself conquered. "No, no! don't give it up yet," said Boots, "just cut a hole in your stomach like this, and you can eat forever." And suiting the action to the words, he ripped open his scrip. So the silly Troll cut himself open and died, and Boots carried off all his gold and silver.

Once there was a Troll whose name was Wind-and-

---

* "A Leopard was returning home from hunting on one occasion, when he lighted on the kraal of a Ram. Now the Leopard had never seen a Ram before, and accordingly, approaching submissively, he said, 'Good day, friend! what may your name be?' The other, in his gruff voice, and striking his breast with his forefoot, said, 'I am a Ram; who are you?' 'A Leopard,' answered the other, more dead than alive; and then, taking leave of the Ram, he ran home as fast as he could." Bleek, Hottentot Fables, p. '24.

Weather, and Saint Olaf hired him to build a church.
If the church were completed within a certain specified
time, the Troll was to get possession of Saint Olaf. The
saint then planned such a stupendous edifice that he
thought the giant would be forever building it; but the
work went on briskly, and at the appointed day nothing
remained but to finish the point of the spire. In his
consternation Olaf rushed about until he passed by the
Troll's den, when he heard the giantess telling her children that their father, Wind-and-Weather, was finishing
his church, and would be home to-morrow with Saint
Olaf. So the saint ran back to the church and bawled
out, "Hold on, Wind-and-Weather, your spire is crook-
ed!" Then the giant tumbled down from the roof and
broke into a thousand pieces. As in the cases of the
Mara and the werewolf, the enchantment was at an end
as soon as the enchanter was called by name.

These Trolls, like the Arabian Efreets, had an ugly
habit of carrying off beautiful princesses. This is strictly
in keeping with their character as night-demons, or Panis.
In the stories of Punchkin and the Heartless Giant, the
night-demon carries off the dawn-maiden after having
turned into stone her solar brethren. But Boots, or Indra, in search of his kinsfolk, by and by arrives at the
Troll's castle, and then the dawn-nymph, true to her
fickle character, cajoles the Giant and enables Boots to
destroy him. In the famous myth which serves as the
basis for the Völsunga Saga and the Nibelungenlied, the
dragon Fafnir steals the Valkyrie Brynhild and keeps
her shut up in a castle on the Glistening Heath, until
some champion shall be found powerful enough to rescue
her. The castle is as hard to enter as that of the Sleeping Beauty; but Sigurd, the Northern Achilleus, riding
on his deathless horse, and wielding his resistless sword

Gram, forces his way in, slays Fafnir, and recovers the Valkyrie.

In the preceding paper the Valkyries were shown to belong to the class of cloud-maidens ; and between the tale of Sigurd and that of Hercules and Cacus there is no difference, save that the bright sunlit clouds which are represented in the one as cows are in the other represented as maidens. In the myth of the Argonauts they reappear as the Golden Fleece, carried to the far east by Phrixos and Helle, who are themselves Niblungs, or " Children of the Mist " (Nephele), and there guarded by a dragon. In all these myths a treasure is stolen by a fiend of darkness, and recovered by a hero of light, who slays the demon. And — remembering what Scribe said about the fewness of dramatic types — I believe we are warranted in asserting that all the stories of lovely women held in bondage by monsters, and rescued by heroes who perform wonderful tasks, such as Don Quixote burned to achieve, are derived ultimately from solar myths, like the myth of Sigurd and Brynhild. I do not mean to say that the story-tellers who beguiled their time in stringing together the incidents which make up these legends were conscious of their solar character. They did not go to work, with malice prepense, to weave allegories and apologues. The Greeks who first told the story of Perseus and Andromeda, the Arabians who devised the tale of Codadad and his brethren, the Flemings who listened over their beer-mugs to the adventures of Culotte-Verte, were not thinking of sun-gods or dawn-maidens, or night-demons ; and no theory of mythology can be sound which implies such an extravagance. Most of these stories have lived on the lips of the common people ; and illiterate persons are not in the habit of allegorizing in the style of mediæval monks or rabbinical

commentators. But what has been amply demonstrated
is, that the sun and the clouds, the light and the darkness, were once supposed to be actuated by wills analogous to the human will; that they were personified and
worshipped or propitiated by sacrifice; and that their
doings were described in language which applied so well
to the deeds of human or quasi-human beings that in
course of time its primitive purport faded from recollection. No competent scholar now doubts that the myths
of the Veda and the Edda originated in this way, for
philology itself shows that the names employed in them
are the names of the great phenomena of nature. And
when once a few striking stories had thus arisen, — when
once it had been told how Indra smote the Panis, and
how Sigurd rescued Brynhild, and how Odysseus blinded
the Kyklops, — then certain mythic or dramatic types
had been called into existence; and to these types, preserved in the popular imagination, future stories would
inevitably conform. We need, therefore, have no hesita-
tion in admitting a common origin for the vanquished
Panis and the outwitted Troll or Devil; we may securely
compare the legends of St. George and Jack the Giant-
killer with the myth of Indra slaying Vritra; we may
see in the invincible Sigurd the prototype of many a
doughty knight-errant of romance; and we may learn
anew the lesson, taught with fresh emphasis by modern
scholarship, that in the deepest sense there is nothing
new under the sun.

I am the more explicit on this point, because it seems
to me that the unguarded language of many students of
mythology is liable to give rise to misapprehensions, and
to discredit both the method which they employ and the
results which they have obtained. If we were to give
full weight to the statements which are sometimes made,

we should perforce believe that primitive men had nothing to do but to ponder about the sun and the clouds, and
to worry themselves over the disappearance of daylight.
But there is nothing in the scientific interpretation of
myths which obliges us to go any such length. I do not
suppose that any ancient Aryan, possessed of good di-
gestive powers and endowed with sound common-sense,
ever lay awake half the night wondering whether the
sun would come back again.* The child and the savage
believe of necessity that the future will resemble the
past, and it is only philosophy which raises doubts on
the subject.† The predominance of solar legends in
most systems of mythology is not due to the lack of
" that Titanic assurance with which we say, the sun *must*
rise " ;‡ nor again to the fact that the phenomena of day
and night are the most striking phenomena in nature.
Eclipses and earthquakes and floods are phenomena of
the most terrible and astounding kind, and they have
all generated myths; yet their contributions to folk-lore
are scanty compared with those furnished by the strife
between the day-god and his enemies. The sun-myths
have been so prolific because the dramatic types to which
they have given rise are of surpassing human interest.
The dragon who swallows the sun is no doubt a fearful
personage ; but the hero who toils for others, who slays
hydra-headed monsters, and dries the tears of fair-haired

* I agree, most heartily, with Mr. Mahaffy's remarks, Prolegomena
to Ancient History, p. 69.

† Sir George Grey once told some Australian natives about the countries within the arctic circle where during part of the year the sun never
sets. "Their astonishment now knew no bounds. ' Ah ! that must be
another sun, not the same as the one we see here,' said an old man ; and
in spite of all my arguments to the contrary, the others adopted this
opinion." Grey's Journals, I. 293, cited in Tylor, Early History of
Mankind, p. 301.

‡ Max Müller, Chips, II. 96.

damsels, and achieves success in spite of incredible obsta-
cles, is a being with whom we can all sympathize, and of
whom we never weary of hearing.

With many of these legends which present the myth
of light and darkness in its most attractive form, the
reader is already acquainted, and it is needless to retail
stories which have been told over and over again in books
which every one is presumed to have read. I will content myself with a weird Irish legend, narrated by Mr.
Patrick Kennedy,* in which we here and there catch
glimpses of the primitive mythical symbols, as fragments
of gold are seen gleaming through the crystal of quartz.

Long before the Danes ever came to Ireland, there died
at Muskerry a Sculloge, or country farmer, who by dint
of hard work and close economy had amassed enormous
wealth. His only son did not resemble him. When the
young Sculloge looked about the house, the day after his
father's death, and saw the big chests full of gold and
silver, and the cupboards shining with piles of sovereigns,
and the old stockings stuffed with large and small coin,
he said to himself, "Bedad, how shall I ever be able to
spend the likes o' that!" And so he drank, and gam-
bled, and wasted his time in hunting and horse-racing,
until after a while he found the chests empty and the
cupboards poverty-stricken, and the stockings lean and
penniless. Then he mortgaged his farm-house and gam-
bled away all the money he got for it, and then he be-
thought him that a few hundred pounds might be raised
on his mill. But when he went to look at it, he found
"the dam broken, and scarcely a thimbleful of water in
the mill-race, and the wheel rotten, and the thatch of the
house all gone, and the upper millstone lying flat on the
lower one, and a coat of dust and mould over every-

* Fictions of the Irish Celts, pp. 255 – 270.

thing." So he made up his mind to borrow a horse and take one more hunt to-morrow and then reform his habits.

As he was returning late in the evening from this farewell hunt, passing through a lonely glen he came upon an old man playing backgammon, betting on his left hand against his right, and crying and cursing because the right *would* win. " Come and bet with me," said he to Sculloge. "Faith, I have but a sixpence in the world," was the reply ; " but, if you like, I 'll wager that on the right." " Done," said the old man, who was a Druid ; "if you win I 'll give you a hundred guineas." So the game was played, and the old man, whose right hand was always the winner, paid over the guineas and told Sculloge to go to the Devil with them.

Instead of following this bit of advice, however, the young farmer went home and began to pay his debts, and next week he went to the glen and won another game, and made the Druid rebuild his mill. So Sculloge became prosperous again, and by and by he tried his luck a third time, and won a game played for a beautiful wife. The Druid sent her to his house the next morning before he was out of bed, and his servants came knocking at the door and crying, " Wake up ! wake up ! Master Sculloge, there 's a young lady here to see you." " Bedad, it 's the vanithee * herself," said Sculloge ; and getting up in a hurry, he spent three quarters of an hour in dressing himself. At last he went down stairs, and there on the sofa was the prettiest lady ever seen in Ireland ! Naturally, Sculloge's heart beat fast and his voice trembled, as he begged the lady's pardon for this Druidic style of wooing, and besought her not to feel obliged to stay with him unless she really liked him. But the young lady,

---

* A corruption of Gaelic *bhan a teaigh*, " lady of the house."

who was a king's daughter from a far country, was won-
drously charmed with the handsome farmer, and so well
did they get along that the priest was sent for without
further delay, and they were married before sundown.
Sabina was the vanithee's name; and she warned her
husband to have no more dealings with Lassa Buaicht,
the old man of the glen. So for a while all went happily,
and the Druidic bride was as good as she was beautiful.
But by and by Sculloge began to think he was not earn-
ing money fast enough. He could not bear to see his
wife's white hands soiled with work, and thought it
would be a fine thing if he could only afford to keep a
few more servants, and drive about with Sabina in an
elegant carriage, and see her clothed in silk and adorned
with jewels.

" I will play one more game and set the stakes high,"
said Sculloge to himself one evening, as he sat pondering
over these things; and so, without consulting Sabina, he
stole away to the glen, and played a game for ten thousand guineas. But the evil Druid was now ready to
pounce on his prey, and he did not play as of old. Sculloge broke into a cold sweat with agony and terror as he
saw the left hand win! Then the face of Lassa Buaicht
grew dark and stern, and he laid on Sculloge the curse
which is laid upon the solar hero in misfortune, that he
should never sleep twice under the same roof, or ascend
the couch of the dawn-nymph, his wife, until he should
have procured and brought to him the sword of light.
When Sculloge reached home, more dead than alive, he
saw that his wife knew all. Bitterly they wept together,
but she told him that with courage all might be set right.
She gave him a Druidic horse, which bore him swiftly
over land and sea, like the enchanted steed of the Arabian
Nights, until he reached the castle of his wife's father,

who, as Sculloge now learned, was a good Druid, the brother of the evil Lassa Buaicht. This good Druid told him that the sword of light was kept by a third brother, the powerful magician, Fiach O'Duda, who dwelt in an enchanted castle, which many brave heroes had tried to enter, but the dark sorcerer had slain them all. Three high walls surrounded the castle, and many had scaled the first of these, but none had ever returned alive. But Sculloge was not to be daunted, and, taking from his father-in-law a black steed, he set out for the fortress of Fiach O'Duda. Over the first high wall nimbly leaped the magic horse, and Sculloge called aloud on the Druid to come out and surrender his sword. Then came out a tall, dark man, with coal-black eyes and hair and melancholy visage, and made a furious sweep at Sculloge with the flaming blade. But the Druidic beast sprang back over the wall in the twinkling of an eye and rescued his rider, leaving, however, his tail behind in the court-yard. Then Sculloge returned in triumph to his father-in-law's palace, and the night was spent in feasting and revelry.

Next day Sculloge rode out on a white horse, and when he got to Fiach's castle, he saw the first wall lying in rubbish. He leaped the second, and the same scene occurred as the day before, save that the horse escaped unharmed.

The third day Sculloge went out on foot, with a harp like that of Orpheus in his hand, and as he swept its strings the grass bent to listen and the trees bowed their heads. The castle walls all lay in ruins, and Sculloge made his way unhindered to the upper room, where Fiach lay in Druidic slumber, lulled by the harp. He seized the sword of light, which was hung by the chimney sheathed in a dark scabbard, and making the best of his way back to the good king's palace, mounted his wife's steed, and scoured over land and sea until he found himself in the gloomy glen where Lassa Buaicht was still crying and cursing and betting on his left hand against his right.

"Here, treacherous fiend, take your sword of light!" shouted Sculloge in tones of thunder; and as he drew it from its sheath the whole valley was lighted up as with the morning sun, and next moment the head of the wretched Druid was lying at his feet, and his sweet wife, who had come to meet him, was laughing and crying in his arms.

November, 1870.

V.

MYTHS OF THE BARBARIC WORLD.

THE theory of mythology set forth in the four preceding papers, and illustrated by the examination of numerous myths relating to the lightning, the storm-wind, the clouds, and the sunlight, was originally framed with reference solely to the mythic and legendary lore of the Aryan world. The phonetic identity of the names of many Western gods and heroes with the names of those Vedic divinities which are obviously the personifications of natural phenomena, suggested the theory which philosophical considerations had already foreshadowed in the works of Hume and Comte, and which the exhaustive analysis of Greek, Hindu, Keltic, and Teutonic legends has amply confirmed. Let us now, before proceeding to the consideration of barbaric folk-lore, briefly recapitulate the results obtained by modern scholarship working strictly within the limits of the Aryan domain.

In the first place, it has been proved once for all that the languages spoken by the Hindus, Persians, Greeks, Romans, Kelts, Slaves, and Teutons are all descended from a single ancestral language, the Old Aryan, in the same sense that French, Italian, and Spanish are descended from the Latin. And from this undisputed fact it is an inevitable inference that these various races contain, along with other elements, a race-element in common, due to their Aryan pedigree. That the Indo-European races are wholly Aryan is very improbable, for in every case the countries overrun by them were occupied

by inferior races, whose blood must have mingled in vary-
ing degrees with that of their conquerors; but that every
Indo-European people is in great part descended from a
common Aryan stock is not open to question.

In the second place, along with a common fund of
moral and religious ideas and of legal and ceremonial observances, we find these kindred peoples possessed of a
common fund of myths, superstitions, proverbs, popular
poetry, and household legends. The Hindu mother
amuses her child with fairy-tales which often correspond,
even in minor incidents, with stories in Scottish or
Scandinavian nurseries; and she tells them in words
which are phonetically akin to words in Swedish and
Gaelic. No doubt many of these stories might have
been devised in a dozen different places independently
of each other; and no doubt many of them have been
transmitted laterally from one people to another; but a
careful examination shows that such cannot have been
the case with the great majority of legends and beliefs.
The agreement between two such stories, for instance, as
those of Faithful John and Rama and Luxman is so close
as to make it incredible that they should have been independently fabricated, while the points of difference are
so important as to make it extremely improbable that the
one was ever copied from the other. Besides which, the
essential identity of such myths as those of Sigurd and
Theseus, or of Helena and Saramâ, carries us back histor-
ically to a time when the scattered Indo-European tribes
had not yet begun to hold commercial and intellectual
intercourse with each other, and consequently could not
have interchanged their epic materials or their household
stories. We are therefore driven to the conclusion —
which, startling as it may seem, is after all the most
natural and plausible one that can be stated — that the

Aryan nations, which have inherited from a common ancestral stock their languages and their customs, have inherited also from the same common original their fireside legends. They have preserved Cinderella and Punchkin just as they have preserved the words for *father* and *mother*, *ten* and *twenty*; and the former case, though more imposing to the imagination, is scientifically no less intelligible than the latter.

Thirdly, it has been shown that these venerable tales may be grouped in a few pretty well defined classes; and that the archetypal myth of each class — the primitive story in conformity to which countless subsequent tales have been generated — was originally a mere description of physical phenomena, couched in the poetic diction of an age when everything was personified, because all natural phenomena were supposed to be due to the direct workings of a volition like that of which men were conscious within themselves. Thus we are led to the striking conclusion that mythology has had a common root, both with science and with religious philosophy. The myth of Indra conquering Vritra was one of the theorems of primitive Aryan science; it was a provisional explanation of the thunder-storm, satisfactory enough until extended observation and reflection supplied a better one. It also contained the germs of a theology; for the life-giving solar light furnished an important part of the primeval conception of deity. And finally, it became the fruitful parent of countless myths, whether embodied in the stately epics of Homer and the bards of the Nibelungenlied, or in the humbler legends of St. George and William Tell and the ubiquitous Boots.

Such is the theory which was suggested half a century ago by the researches of Jacob Grimm, and which, so far as concerns the mythology of the Aryan race, is now

victorious along the whole line. It remains for us to
test the universality of the general principles upon which
it is founded, by a brief analysis of sundry legends and
superstitions of the barbaric world. Since the fetichistic
habit of explaining the outward phenomena of nature
after the analogy of the inward phenomena of conscious
intelligence is not a habit peculiar to our Aryan ancestors, but is, as psychology shows, the inevitable result of
the conditions under which uncivilized thinking proceeds, we may expect to find the barbaric mind personi-
fying the powers of nature and making myths about their
operations the whole world over. And we need not be
surprised if we find in the resulting mythologic structures
a strong resemblance to the familiar creations of the
Aryan intelligence. In point of fact, we shall often be
called upon to note such resemblance ; and it accordingly
behooves us at the outset to inquire how far a similarity
between mythical tales shall be taken as evidence of a
common traditional origin, and how far it may be interpreted as due merely to the similar workings of the untrained intelligence in all ages and countries.

Analogies drawn from the comparison of languages
will here be of service to us, if used discreetly ; otherwise they are likely to bewilder far more than to en-
lighten us. A theorem which Max Müller has laid down
for our guidance in this kind of investigation furnishes
us with an excellent example of the tricks which a
superficial analogy may play even with the trained
scholar, when temporarily off his guard. Actuated by a
praiseworthy desire to raise the study of myths to something like the high level of scientific accuracy already
attained by the study of words, Max Müller endeavours
to introduce one of the most useful canons of philology
into a department of inquiry where its introduction

could only work the most hopeless confusion. One of
the earliest lessons to be learned by the scientific student of linguistics is the uselessness of comparing together directly the words contained in derivative languages. For example, you might set the English *twelve*
side by side with the Latin *duodecim*, and then stare at
the two words to all eternity without any hope of reaching a conclusion, good or bad, about either of them :
least of all would you suspect that they are descended
from the same radical. But if you take each word by
itself and trace it back to its primitive shape, explaining
every change of every letter as you go, you will at last
reach the old Aryan *dvadakan*, which is the parent of
both these strangely metamorphosed words.* Nor will it
do, on the other hand, to trust to verbal similarity without a historical inquiry into the origin of such similarity.
Even in the same language two words of quite different
origin may get their corners rubbed off till they look as
like one another as two pebbles. The French words *souris*,
a "mouse," and *souris*, a "smile," are spelled exactly
alike; but the one comes from Latin *sorex* and the other
from Latin *subridere*.

Now Max Müller tells us that this principle, which is
indispensable in the study of words, is equally indispensable in the study of myths.† That is, you must not
rashly pronounce the Norse story of the Heartless Giant
identical with the Hindu story of Punchkin, although the
two correspond in every essential incident. In both
legends a magician turns several members of the same
family into stone; the youngest member of the family
comes to the rescue, and on the way saves the lives of

* For the analysis of *twelve*, see my essay on "The Genesis of Language," North American Review, October, 1869, p. 320.

† Chips from a German Workshop, Vol. II. p. 246.

sundry grateful beasts ; arrived at the magician's castle,
he finds a captive princess ready to accept his love and
to play the part of Delilah to the enchanter. In both
stories the enchanter's life depends on the integrity of
something which is elaborately hidden in a far-distant
island, but which the fortunate youth, instructed by the
artful princess and assisted by his menagerie of grateful
beasts, succeeds in obtaining. In both stories the youth
uses his advantage to free all his friends from their enchantment, and then proceeds to destroy the villain who
wrought all this wickedness. Yet, in spite of this agreement, Max Müller, if I understand him aright, would not
have us infer the identity of the two stories until we have
taken each one separately and ascertained its primitive
mythical significance. Otherwise, for aught we can tell,
the resemblance may be purely accidental, like that of
the French words for " mouse " and " smile."

A little reflection, however, will relieve us from this
perplexity, and assure us that the alleged analogy between the comparison of words and the comparison of
stories is utterly superficial. The transformations of
words — which are often astounding enough — depend
upon a few well-established physiological principles of
utterance ; and since philology has learned to rely upon
these principles, it has become nearly as sure in its
methods and results as one of the so-called " exact
sciences." Folly enough is doubtless committed within
its precincts by writers who venture there without the
laborious preparation which this science, more than almost any other, demands. But the proceedings of the
trained philologist are no more arbitrary than those of
the trained astronomer. And though the former may
seem to be straining at a gnat and swallowing a camel
when he coolly tells you that *violin* and *fiddle* are the

same word, while English *care* and Latin *cura* have
nothing to do with each other, he is nevertheless no
more indulging in guess-work than the astronomer who
confesses his ignorance as to the habitability of Venus
while asserting his knowledge of the existence of hydro-
gen in the atmosphere of Sirius. To cite one example
out of a hundred, every philologist knows that *s* may
become *r*, and that the broad *a*-sound may dwindle into
the closer *o*-sound; but when you adduce some plausible
etymology based on the assumption that *r* has changed
into *s*, or *o* into *a*, apart from the demonstrable influence
of some adjacent letter, the philologist will shake his
head.

Now in the study of stories there are no such simple
rules all cut and dried for us to go by. There is no uniform psychological principle which determines that the
three-headed snake in one story shall become a three-
headed man in the next. There is no Grimm's Law in
mythology which decides that a Hindu magician shall
always correspond to a Norwegian Troll or a Keltic
Druid. The laws of association of ideas are not so
simple in application as the laws of utterance. In short,
the study of myths, though it can be made sufficiently
scientific in its methods and results, does not constitute
a science by itself, like philology. It stands on a footing
similar to that occupied by physical geography, or what
the Germans call " earth-knowledge." No one denies that
all the changes going on over the earth's surface conform
to physical laws; but then no one pretends that there is
any single proximate principle which governs all the
phenomena of rain-fall, of soil-crumbling, of magnetic
variation, and of the distribution of plants and animals.
All these things are explained by principles obtained from
the various sciences of physics, chemistry, geology, and

physiology. And in just the same way the development
and distribution of stories is explained by the help of
divers resources contributed by philology, psychology,
and history. There is therefore no real analogy between
the cases cited by Max Müller. Two unrelated words
may be ground into exactly the same shape, just as a
pebble from the North Sea may be undistinguishable
from another pebble on the beach of the Adriatic; but
two stories like those of Punchkin and the Heartless
Giant are no more likely to arise independently of each
other than two coral reefs on opposite sides of the globe
are likely to develop into exactly similar islands.

Shall we then say boldly, that close similarity between
legends is proof of kinship, and go our way without further misgivings? Unfortunately we cannot dispose of
the matter in quite so summary a fashion; for it remains
to decide what kind and degree of similarity shall be considered satisfactory evidence of kinship. And it is just
here that doctors may disagree. Here is the point at
which our " science " betrays its weakness as compared
with the sister study of philology. Before we can decide with confidence in any case, a great mass of evidence must be brought into court. So long as we remained on Aryan ground, all went smoothly enough,
because all the external evidence was in our favour. We
knew at the outset, that the Aryans inherit a common
language and a common civilization, and therefore we
found no difficulty in accepting the conclusion that they
have inherited, among other things, a common stock of
legends. In the barbaric world it is quite otherwise.
Philology does not pronounce in favour of a common
origin for all barbaric culture, such as it is. The notion
of a single primitive language, standing in the same relation to all existing dialects as the relation of old Aryan

to Latin and English, or that of old Semitic to Hebrew and Arabic, was a notion suited only to the infancy of linguistic science. As the case now stands, it is certain that all the languages actually existing cannot be referred to a common ancestor, and it is altogether probable that there never was any such common ancestor. I am not now referring to the question of the unity of the human race. That question lies entirely outside the sphere of philology. The science of language has nothing to do with skulls or complexions, and no comparison of words can tell us whether the black men are brethren of the white men, or whether yellow and red men have a common pedigree : these questions belong to comparative physiology. But the science of language can and does tell us that a certain amount of civilization is requisite for the production of a language sufficiently durable and wide-spread to give birth to numerous mutually resembling offspring. Barbaric languages are neither widespread nor durable. Among savages each little group of families has its own dialect, and coins its own expressions at pleasure ; and in the course of two or three generations a dialect gets so strangely altered as virtually to lose its identity. Even numerals and personal pronouns, which the Aryan has preserved for fifty centuries, get lost every few years in Polynesia. Since the time of Captain Cook the Tahitian language has thrown away five out of its ten simple numerals, and replaced them by brand-new ones ; and on the Amazon you may acquire a fluent command of some Indian dialect, and then, coming back after twenty years, find yourself worse off than Rip Van Winkle, and your learning all antiquated and useless. How absurd, therefore, to suppose that primeval savages originated a language which has held its own like the old Aryan, and become the prolific mother of the

three or four thousand dialects now in existence! Before
a durable language can arise, there must be an aggrega-
tion of numerous tribes into a people, so that there may
be need of communication on a large scale, and so that
tradition may be strengthened. Wherever mankind have
associated in nations, permanent languages have arisen,
and their derivative dialects bear the conspicuous marks
of kinship; but where mankind have remained in their
primitive savage isolation, their languages have remained
sporadic and transitory, incapable of organic development, and showing no traces of a kinship which never
existed.

The bearing of these considerations upon the origin
and diffusion of barbaric myths is obvious. The development of a common stock of legends is, of course, impossible, save where there is a common language; and
thus philology pronounces against the kinship of barbaric myths with each other and with similar myths of
the Aryan and Semitic worlds. Similar stories told in
Greece and Norway are likely to have a common pedigree, because the persons who have preserved them in
recollection speak a common language and have inherited
the same civilization. But similar stories told in Labrador and South Africa are not likely to be genealogi-
cally related, because it is altogether probable that the
Esquimaux and the Zulu had acquired their present race
characteristics before either of them possessed a language
or a culture sufficient for the production of myths. According to the nature and extent of the similarity, it
must be decided whether such stories have been carried
about from one part of the world to another, or have
been independently originated in many different places.

Here the methods of philology suggest a rule which
will often be found useful. In comparing the vocabula-

ries of different languages, those words which directly
imitate natural sounds — such as *whiz, crash, crackle* —
are not admitted as evidence of kinship between the
languages in which they occur. Resemblances between
such words are obviously no proof of a common ancestry;
and they are often met with in languages which have
demonstrably had no connection with each other. So in
mythology, where we find two stories of which the primitive character is perfectly transparent, we need have no
difficulty in supposing them to have originated independently. The myth of Jack and his Beanstalk is
found all over the world; but the idea of a country
above the sky, to which persons might gain access by
climbing, is one which could hardly fail to occur to every
barbarian. Among the American tribes, as well as
among the Aryans, the rainbow and the Milky-Way
have contributed the idea of a Bridge of the Dead, over
which souls must pass on the way to the other world.
In South Africa, as well as in Germany, the habits of the
fox and of his brother the jackal have given rise to fables
in which brute force is overcome by cunning. In many
parts of the world we find curiously similar stories devised to account for the stumpy tails of the bear and
hyæna, the hairless tail of the rat, and the blindness of
the mole. And in all countries may be found the beliefs that men may be changed into beasts, or plants, or
stones; that the sun is in some way tethered or constrained to follow a certain course; that the storm-cloud
is a ravenous dragon; and that there are talismans which
will reveal hidden treasures. All these conceptions are
so obvious to the uncivilized intelligence, that stories
founded upon them need not be supposed to have a common origin, unless there turns out to be a striking similarity among their minor details. On the other hand,

the numerous myths of an all-destroying deluge have doubtless arisen partly from reminiscences of actually occurring local inundations, and partly from the fact that the Scriptural account of a deluge has been carried all over the world by Catholic and Protestant missionaries.[*]

By way of illustrating these principles, let us now cite a few of the American myths so carefully collected by Dr. Brinton in his admirable treatise. We shall not find in the mythology of the New World the wealth of wit and imagination which has so long delighted us in the stories of Herakles, Perseus, Hermes, Sigurd, and Indra. The mythic lore of the American Indians is comparatively scanty and prosaic, as befits the product of a lower grade of culture and a more meagre intellect. Not only are the personages less characteristically pourtrayed, but there is a continual tendency to extravagance, the sure index of an inferior imagination. Nevertheless, after making due allowances for differences in the artistic method of treatment, there is between the mythologies of the Old and the New Worlds a fundamental resemblance. We come upon solar myths and myths of the storm curiously blended with culture-myths, as in the cases of Hermes, Prometheus, and Kadmos. The American parallels to these are to be found in the stories of Michabo, Viracocha, Ioskeha, and Quetzalcoatl. "As elsewhere the world over, so in America, many tribes had to tell of . . . . an august character, who taught them what they knew, — the tillage of the soil, the properties of plants, the art of picture-writing, the secrets of magic; who founded their institutions and established their religions; who governed them long with glory abroad and

---

[*] For various legends of a deluge, see Baring-Gould, Legends of the Patriarchs and Prophets, pp. 85 – 106.

peace at home; and finally did not die, but, like Frederic Barbarossa, Charlemagne, King Arthur, and all great heroes, vanished mysteriously, and still lives somewhere, ready at the right moment to return to his beloved people and lead them to victory and happiness." * Every one is familiar with the numerous legends of white-skinned, full-bearded heroes, like the mild Quetzalcoatl, who in times long previous to Columbus came from the far East to impart the rudiments of civilization and religion to the red men. By those who first heard these stories they were supposed, with naïve Euhemerism, to refer to pre-Columbian visits of Europeans to this continent, like that of the Northmen in the tenth century. But a scientific study of the subject has dissipated such notions. These legends are far too numerous, they are too similar to each other, they are too manifestly symbolical, to admit of any such interpretation. By comparing them carefully with each other, and with correlative myths of the Old World, their true character soon becomes apparent.

One of the most widely famous of these culture-heroes was Manabozho or Michabo, the Great Hare. With entire unanimity, says Dr. Brinton, the various branches of the Algonquin race, " the Powhatans of Virginia, the Lenni Lenape of the Delaware, the warlike hordes of New England, the Ottawas of the far North, and the Western tribes, perhaps without exception, spoke of ' this chimerical beast,' as one of the old missionaries calls it, as their common ancestor. The *totem*, or clan, which bore his name was looked up to with peculiar respect." Not only was Michabo the ruler and guardian of these numerous tribes, — he was the founder of their religious rites, the inventor of picture-writing, the ruler of the weather, the creator and preserver of earth and

---

* Brinton, Myths of the New World, p. 160.

7 *

heaven. "From a grain of sand brought from the bottom of the primeval ocean he fashioned the habitable land, and set it floating on the waters till it grew to such a size that a strong young wolf, running constantly, died of old age ere he reached its limits." He was also, like Nimrod, a mighty hunter. "One of his footsteps measured eight leagues, the Great Lakes were the beaver-dams he built, and when the cataracts impeded his progress he tore them away with his hands." "Sometimes he was said to dwell in the skies with his brother, the Snow, or, like many great spirits, to have built his wigwam in the far North on some floe of ice in the Arctic Ocean. . . . . But in the oldest accounts of the missionaries he was alleged to reside toward the East; and in the holy formulæ of the *meda* craft, when the winds are invoked to the medicine lodge, the East is summoned in his name, the door opens in that direction, and there, at the edge of the earth where the sun rises, on the shore of the infinite ocean that surrounds the land, he has his house, and sends the luminaries forth on their daily journeys." * From such accounts as this we see that Michabo was no more a wise instructor and legislator than Minos or Kadmos. Like these heroes, he is a personification of the solar life-giving power, which daily comes forth from its home in the east, making the earth to rejoice. The etymology of his name confirms the otherwise clear indications of the legend itself. It is compounded of *michi*, "great," and *wabos*, which means alike "hare" and "white." "Dialectic forms in Algonquin for white are *wabi, wape, wampi,* etc.; for morning, *wapan, wapanch, opah;* for east, *wapa, wanbun,* etc.; for day, *wompan, oppan;* for light, *oppung.*" So that Michabo is the Great White One, the God of the Dawn and the East.

* Brinton, op. cit. p. 163.

And the etymological confusion, by virtue of which he acquired his soubriquet of the Great Hare, affords a curious parallel to what has often happened in Aryan and Semitic mythology, as we saw when discussing the subject of werewolves.

Keeping in mind this solar character of Michabo, let us note how full of meaning are the myths concerning him. In the first cycle of these legends, " he is grandson of the Moon, his father is the West Wind, and his mother, a maiden, dies in giving him birth at the moment of conception. For the Moon is the goddess of night ; the Dawn is her daughter, who brings forth the Morning, and perishes herself in the act; and the West, the spirit of darkness, as the East is of light, precedes, and as it were begets the latter, as the evening does the morning. Straightway, however, continues the legend, the son sought the unnatural father to revenge the death of his mother, and then commenced a long and desperate struggle. It began on the mountains. The West was forced to give ground. Manabozho drove him across rivers and over mountains and lakes, and at last he came to the brink of this world. ' Hold,' cried he, ' my son, you know my power, and that it is impossible to kill me.' What is this but the diurnal combat of light and darkness, carried on from what time ' the jocund morn stands tiptoe on the misty mountain-tops,' across the wide world to the sunset, the struggle that knows no end, for both the opponents are immortal ? " *

Even the Veda nowhere affords a more transparent narrative than this. The Iroquois tradition is very similar. In it appear twin brothers,† born of a virgin mother,

---

* Brinton, op. cit. p. 167.

† Corresponding, in various degrees, to the Asvins, the Dioskouroi, and the brothers True and Untrue of Norse mythology.

daughter of the Moon, who died in giving them life. Their names, Ioskeha and Tawiskara, signify in the Oneida dialect the White One and the Dark One. Under the influence of Christian ideas the contest between the brothers has been made to assume a moral character, like the strife between Ormuzd and Ahriman. But no such intention appears in the original myth, and Dr. Brinton has shown that none of the American tribes had any conception of a Devil. When the quarrel came to blows, the dark brother was signally discomfited; and the victorious Ioskeha, returning to his grandmother, " established his lodge in the far East, on the borders of the Great Ocean, whence the sun comes. In time he became the father of mankind, and special guardian of the Iroquois." He caused the earth to bring forth, he stocked the woods with game, and taught his children the use of fire. " He it was who watched and watered their crops ; ' and, indeed, without his aid,' says the old missionary, quite out of patience with their puerilities, ' they think they could not boil a pot.' " There was more in it than poor Brébeuf thought, as we are forcibly reminded by recent discoveries in physical science. Even civilized men would find it difficult to boil a pot without the aid of solar energy. Call him what we will, — Ioskeha, Michabo, or Phoibos, — the beneficent Sun is the master and sustainer of us all ; and if we were to relapse into heathenism, like Erckmann-Chatrian's innkeeper, we could not do better than to select him as our chief object of worship.

The same principles by which these simple cases are explained furnish also the key to the more complicated mythology of Mexico and Peru. Like the deities just discussed, Viracocha, the supreme god of the Quichuas, rises from the bosom of Lake Titicaca and journeys west-

ward, slaying with his lightnings the creatures who op-
pose him, until he finally disappears in the Western
Ocean. Like Aphrodite, he bears in his name the evidence of his origin, *Viracocha* signifying "foam of the
sea"; and hence the "White One" (*l'aube*), the god of
light rising white on the horizon, like the foam on the
surface of the waves. The Aymaras spoke of their original ancestors as white; and to this day, as Dr. Brinton
informs us, the Peruvians call a white man *Viracocha*.
The myth of Quetzalcoatl is of precisely the same character. All these solar heroes present in most of their qualities and achievements a striking likeness to those of the
Old World. They combine the attributes of Apollo,
Herakles, and Hermes. Like Herakles, they journey
from east to west, smiting the powers of darkness, storm,
and winter with the thunderbolts of Zeus or the unerring
arrows of Phoibos, and sinking in a blaze of glory on
the western verge of the world, where the waves meet
the firmament. Or like Hermes, in a second cycle of
legends, they rise with the soft breezes of a summer morning, driving before them the bright celestial cattle whose
udders are heavy with refreshing rain, fanning the flames
which devour the forests, blustering at the doors of wig-
wams, and escaping with weird laughter through vents
and crevices. The white skins and flowing beards of
these American heroes may be aptly compared to the fair
faces and long golden locks of their Hellenic compeers.
Yellow hair was in all probability as rare in Greece as a
full beard in Peru or Mexico; but in each case the description suits the solar character of the hero. One
important class of incidents, however is apparently quite
absent from the American legends. We frequently see
the Dawn described as a virgin mother who dies in giving birth to the Day; but nowhere do we remember see-

ing her pictured as a lovely or valiant or crafty maiden,
ardently wooed, but speedily forsaken by her solar lover.
Perhaps in no respect is the superior richness and beauty
of the Aryan myths more manifest than in this.   Brynhild, Urvasi, Medeia, Ariadne, Oinone, and countless other
kindred heroines, with their brilliant legends, could not
be spared from the mythology of our ancestors without
leaving it meagre indeed.   These were the materials
which Kalidasa, the Attic dramatists, and the bards of
the Nibelungen found ready, awaiting their artistic treatment.   But the mythology of the New World, with all
its pretty and agreeable *naïveté*, affords hardly enough,
either of variety in situation or of complexity in motive,
for a grand epic or a genuine tragedy.

But little reflection is needed to assure us that the
imagination of the barbarian, who either carries away his
wife by brute force or buys her from her relatives as he
would buy a cow, could never have originated legends in
which maidens are lovingly solicited, or in which their
favour is won by the performance of deeds of valour.
These stories owe their existence to the romantic turn of
mind which has always characterized the Aryan, whose
civilization, even in the times before the dispersion of his
race, was sufficiently advanced to allow of his entertaining such comparatively exalted conceptions of the relations between men and women.   The absence of these
myths from barbaric folk-lore is, therefore, just what
might be expected ; but it is a fact which militates
against any possible hypothesis of the common origin
of Aryan and barbaric mythology.   If there were any
genetic relationship between Sigurd and Ioskeha, between Herakles and Michabo, it would be hard to tell
why Brynhild and Iole should have disappeared entirely
from one whole group of legends, while retained, in some

form or other, throughout the whole of the other group.
On the other hand, the resemblances above noticed between Aryan and American mythology fall very far short
of the resemblances between the stories told in different
parts of the Aryan domain. No barbaric legend, of genuine barbaric growth, has yet been cited which resembles
any Aryan legend as the story of Punchkin resembles the
story of the Heartless Giant. The myths of Michabo and
Viracocha are direct copies, so to speak, of natural phenomena, just as imitative words are direct copies of natural sounds. Neither the Redskin nor the Indo-European
had any choice as to the main features of the career of
his solar divinity. He must be born of the Night, — or
of the Dawn, — must travel westward, must slay harass-
ing demons. Eliminating these points of likeness, the
resemblance between the Aryan and barbaric legends is
at once at an end. Such an identity in point of details
as that between the wooden horse which enters Ilion, and
the horse which bears Sigurd into the place where Brynhild is imprisoned, and the Druidic steed which leaps
with Sculloge over the walls of Fiach's enchanted castle,
is, I believe, nowhere to be found after we leave Indo-
European territory.

Our conclusion, therefore, must be, that while the
legends of the Aryan and the non-Aryan worlds contain
common mythical elements, the legends themselves are
not of common origin. The fact that certain mythical
ideas are possessed alike by different races, shows that in
each case a similar human intelligence has been at work
explaining similar phenomena ; but in order to prove a
family relationship between the culture of these different races, we need something more than this. We need
to prove not only a community of mythical ideas, but
also a community between the stories based upon these

ideas. We must show not only that Michabo is like
Herakles in those striking features which the contemplation of solar phenomena would necessarily suggest to the
imagination of the primitive myth-maker, but also that
the two characters are similarly conceived, and that the
two careers agree in seemingly arbitrary points of detail,
as is the case in the stories of Punchkin and the Heartless Giant. The mere fact that solar heroes, all over the
world, travel in a certain path and slay imps of darkness
is of great value as throwing light upon primeval habits
of thought, but it is of no value as evidence for or against
an alleged community of civilization between different
races. The same is true of the sacredness universally
attached to certain numbers. Dr. Brinton's opinion that
the sanctity of the number *four* in nearly all systems of
mythology is due to a primitive worship of the cardinal
points, becomes very probable when we recollect that the
similar pre-eminence of *seven* is almost demonstrably connected with the adoration of the sun, moon, and five visible planets, which has left its record in the structure and
nomenclature of the Aryan and Semitic week.*

In view of these considerations, the comparison of barbaric myths with each other and with the legends of the
Aryan world becomes doubly interesting, as illustrating
the similarity in the workings of the untrained intelligence the world over. In our first paper we saw how the
moon-spots have been variously explained by Indo-Europeans, as a man with a thorn-bush or as two children
bearing a bucket of water on a pole. In Ceylon it is

---

* See Humboldt's Kosmos, Tom. III. pp. 469 – 476. A fetichistic
regard for the cardinal points has not always been absent from the minds
of persons instructed in a higher theology ; as witness a well-known
passage in Irenæus, and the theories of Bancroft and Whitgift, in accordance with which English churches were at one time built in a line
east and west.

said that as Sakyamuni was one day wandering half
starved in the forest, a pious hare met him, and offered
itself to him to be slain and cooked for dinner; whereupon the holy Buddha set it on high in the moon, that
future generations of men might see it and marvel at its
piety. In the Samoan Islands these dark patches are
supposed to be portions of a woman's figure. A certain
woman was once hammering something with a mallet,
when the moon arose, looking so much like a bread-fruit
that the woman asked it to come down and let her child
eat off a piece of it; but the moon, enraged at the insult,
gobbled up woman, mallet, and child, and there, in the
moon's belly, you may still behold them. According to
the Hottentots, the Moon once sent the Hare to inform
men that as she died away and rose again, so should men
die and again come to life. But the stupid Hare forgot
the purport of the message, and, coming down to the earth,
proclaimed it far and wide that though the Moon was invariably resuscitated whenever she died, mankind, on the
other hand, should die and go to the Devil. When the
silly brute returned to the lunar country and told what
he had done, the Moon was so angry that she took up an
axe and aimed a blow at his head to split it. But the
axe missed and only cut his lip open; and that was the
origin of the "hare-lip." Maddened by the pain and the
insult, the Hare flew at the Moon and almost scratched
her eyes out; and to this day she bears on her face the
marks of the Hare's claws.*

Again, every reader of the classics knows how Selene
cast Endymion into a profound slumber because he refused her love, and how at sundown she used to come

---

* Bleek, Hottentot Fables and Tales, p. 72. Compare the Fiji story
of Ra Vula, the Moon, and Ra Kalavo, the Rat, in Tylor, Primitive
Culture, I. 321.

and stand above him on the Latmian hill, and watch him
as he lay asleep on the marble steps of a temple half
hidden among drooping elm-trees, over which clambered
vines heavy with dark blue grapes. This represents the
rising moon looking down on the setting sun; in Labrador a similar phenomenon has suggested a somewhat different story. Among the Esquimaux the Sun is a maiden
and the Moon is her brother, who is overcome by a wicked passion for her. Once, as this girl was at a dancing-
party in a friend's hut, some one came up and took hold
of her by the shoulders and shook her, which is (according to the legend) the Esquimaux manner of declaring
one's love. She could not tell who it was in the dark,
and so she dipped her hand in some soot and smeared
one of his cheeks with it. When a light was struck in
the hut, she saw, to her dismay, that it was her brother,
and, without waiting to learn any more, she took to her
heels. He started in hot pursuit, and so they ran till
they got to the end of the world, — the jumping-off
place, — when they both jumped into the sky. There
the Moon still chases his sister, the Sun ; and every now
and then he turns his sooty cheek toward the earth, when
he becomes so dark that you cannot see him.*

Another story, which I cite from Mr. Tylor, shows that
Malays, as well as Indo-Europeans, have conceived of the
clouds as swan-maidens. In the island of Celebes it is
said that " seven heavenly nymphs came down from the
sky to bathe, and they were seen by Kasimbaha, who
thought first that they were white doves, but in the bath
he saw that they were women. Then he stole one of the
thin robes that gave the nymphs their power of flying,
and so he caught Utahagi, the one whose robe he had
stolen, and took her for his wife, and she bore him a son.

* Tylor, Early History of Mankind, p. 327.

Now she was called Utahagi from a single white hair she had, which was endowed with magic power, and this hair her husband pulled out. As soon as he had done it, there arose a great storm, and Utahagi went up to heaven. The child cried for its mother, and Kasimbaha was in great grief, and cast about how he should follow Utahagi up into the sky." Here we pass to the myth of Jack and the Beanstalk. " A rat gnawed the thorns off the rattans, and Kasimbaha clambered up by them with his son upon his back, till he came to heaven. There a little bird showed him the house of Utahagi, and after various adventures he took up his abode among the gods."*

In Siberia we find a legend of swan-maidens, which also reminds us of the story of the Heartless Giant. A certain Samojed once went out to catch foxes, and found seven maidens swimming in a lake surrounded by gloomy pine-trees, while their feather dresses lay on the shore. He crept up and stole one of these dresses, and by and by the swan-maiden came to him shivering with cold and promising to become his wife if he would only give her back her garment of feathers. The ungallant fellow, however, did not care for a wife, but a little revenge was not unsuited to his way of thinking. There were seven robbers who used to prowl about the neighbourhood, and who, when they got home, finding their hearts in the way, used to hang them up on some pegs in the tent. One of these robbers had killed the Samojed's mother; and so he promised to return the swan-maiden's dress after she should have procured for him these seven hearts. So she stole the hearts, and the Samojed smashed six of them, and then woke up the seventh robber, and told him to restore his mother to life, on pain of instant death.

* Tylor, op. cit., p. 346.

Then the robber produced a purse containing the old woman's soul, and going to the graveyard shook it over her bones, and she revived at once. Then the Samojed smashed the seventh heart, and the robber died; and so the swan-maiden got back her plumage and flew away rejoicing.*

Swan-maidens are also, according to Mr. Baring-Gould, found among the Minussinian Tartars. But there they appear as foul demons, like the Greek Harpies, who delight in drinking the blood of men slain in battle. There are forty of them, who darken the whole firmament in their flight; but sometimes they all coalesce into one great black storm-fiend, who rages for blood, like a werewolf.

In South Africa we find the werewolf himself.† A certain Hottentot was once travelling with a Bushwoman and her child, when they perceived at a distance a troop of wild horses. The man, being hungry, asked the woman to turn herself into a lioness and catch one of these horses, that they might eat of it; whereupon the woman set down her child, and taking off a sort of petticoat made of human skin became instantly transformed into a lioness, which rushed across the plain, struck down a wild horse and lapped its blood. The man climbed a tree in terror, and conjured his companion to resume her natural shape. Then the lioness came back, and putting on the skirt made of human skin reappeared as a woman, and took up her child, and the two friends resumed their journey after making a meal of the horse's flesh.‡

---

* Baring-Gould, Curious Myths, II. 299–302.

† Speaking of beliefs in the Malay Archipelago, Mr. Wallace says: "It is universally believed in Lombock that some men have the power to turn themselves into crocodiles, which they do for the sake of devouring their enemies, and many strange tales are told of such transformations." Wallace, Malay Archipelago, Vol. I. p. 251.

‡ Bleek, Hottentot Fables and Tales, p. 58.

The werewolf also. appears in North America, duly furnished with his wolf-skin sack; but neither in America nor in Africa is he the genuine European werewolf, inspired by a diabolic frenzy, and ravening for human flesh. The barbaric myths testify to the belief that men can be changed into beasts or have in some cases descended from beast ancestors, but the application of this belief to the explanation of abnormal cannibal cravings seems to have been confined to Europe. The werewolf of the Middle Ages was not merely a transformed man, — he was an insane cannibal, whose monstrous appetite, due to the machinations of the Devil, showed its power over his physical organism by changing the shape of it. The barbaric werewolf is the product of a lower and simpler kind of thinking. There is no diabolism about him; for barbaric races, while believing in the existence of hurtful and malicious fiends, have not a sufficiently vivid sense of moral abnormity to form the conception of diabolism. And the cannibal craving, which to the mediæval European was a phenomenon so strange as to demand a mythological explanation, would not impress the barbarian as either very exceptional or very blameworthy.

In the folk-lore of the Zulus, one of the most quick-witted and intelligent of African races, the cannibal possesses many features in common with the Scandinavian Troll, who also has a liking for human flesh. As we saw in the preceding paper, the Troll has very likely derived some of his characteristics from reminiscences of the barbarous races who preceded the Aryans in Central and Northern Europe. In like manner the long-haired cannibal of Zulu nursery literature, who is always represented as belonging to a distinct race, has been supposed to be explained by the existence of inferior races con-

quered and displaced by the Zulus. Nevertheless, as
Dr. Callaway observes, neither the long-haired mountain
cannibals of Western Africa, nor the Fulahs, nor the
tribes of Eghedal described by Barth, "can be considered
as answering to the description of long-haired as given
in the Zulu legends of cannibals ; neither could they
possibly have formed their historical basis. . . . . It is
perfectly clear that the cannibals of the Zulu legends are
not common men ; they are magnified into giants and
magicians ; they are remarkably swift and enduring ;
fierce and terrible warriors." Very probably they may
have a mythical origin in modes of thought akin to those
which begot the Panis of the Veda and the Northern
Trolls. The parallelism is perhaps the most remarkable
one which can be found in comparing barbaric with
Aryan folk-lore. Like the Panis and Trolls, the cannibals are represented as the foes of the solar hero Uthla-
kányana, who is almost as great a traveller as Odysseus,
and whose presence of mind amid trying circumstances
is not to be surpassed by that of the incomparable Boots.
Uthlakanyana is as precocious as Herakles or Hermes.
He speaks before he is born, and no sooner has he entered the world than he begins to outwit other people
and get possession of their property. He works bitter
ruin for the cannibals, who, with all their strength and
fleetness, are no better endowed with quick wit than the
Trolls, whom Boots invariably victimizes. On one of his
journeys, Uthlakanyana fell in with a cannibal. Their
greetings were cordial enough, and they ate a bit of leopard together, and began to build a house, and killed a
couple of cows, but the cannibal's cow was lean, while
Uthlakanyana's was fat. Then the crafty traveller, fear-
ing that his companion might insist upon having the fat
cow, turned and said, " ' Let the house be thatched now ;

then we can eat our meat. You see the sky, that we shall get wet.' The cannibal said, ' You are right, child of my sister ; you are a man indeed in saying, let us thatch the house, for we shall get wet.' Uthlakanyana said, ' Do you do it then ; I will go inside, and push the thatching-needle for you, in the house.' The cannibal went up. His hair was very, very long. Uthlakanyana went inside and pushed the needle for him. He thatched in the hair of the cannibal, tying it very tightly ; he knotted it into the thatch constantly, taking it by separate locks and fastening it firmly, that it might be tightly fastened to the house." Then the rogue went outside and began to eat of the cow which was roasted. " The cannibal said, ' What are you about, child of my sister ? Let us just finish the house ; afterwards we can do that ; we will do it together.' Uthlakanyana replied, ' Come down then. I cannot go into the house any more. The thatching is finished.' The cannibal assented. When he thought he was going to quit the house, he was unable to quit it. He cried out saying, ' Child of my sister, how have you managed your thatching ? ' Uthlakanyana said, ' See to it yourself. I have thatched well, for I shall not have any dispute. Now I am about to eat in peace ; I no longer dispute with anybody, for I am now alone with my cow.' " So the cannibal cried and raved and appealed in vain to Uthlakanyana's sense of justice, until by and by " the sky came with hailstones and lightning. Uthlakanyana took all the meat into the house ; he stayed in the house and lit a fire. It hailed and rained. The cannibal cried on the top of the house ; he was struck with the hailstones, and died there on the house. It cleared. Uthlakanyana went out and said, ' Uncle, just come down, and come to me. It has become clear. It no longer rains, and there is no more hail, neither is there any more lightning. Why are you silent?' So Uthlakanyana ate his cow alone, until he had finished it. He then went on his way." *

In another Zulu legend, a girl is stolen by cannibals, and shut up in the rock Itshe-likantunjambili, which, like the rock of the Forty Thieves, opens and shuts at the command of those who understand its secret. She gets possession of the secret and escapes, and when the monsters pursue her she throws on the ground a calabash full of sesame, which they stop to eat. At last, getting tired of running, she climbs a tree, and there she finds her brother, who, warned by a dream, has come out to look for her. They ascend the tree together until they come to a beautiful country well stocked with fat oxen. They kill an ox, and while its flesh is roasting they amuse themselves by making a stout thong of its hide. By and by one of the cannibals, smelling the cooking meat, comes to the foot of the tree, and looking up discovers the boy and girl in the sky-country! They invite him up there to share in their feast, and throw him an end of the thong by which to climb up. When the cannibal is dangling midway between earth and heaven, they let go the rope, and down he falls with a terrible crash.†

In this story the enchanted rock opened by a talismanic formula brings us again into contact with Indo-European folk-lore. And that the conception has in both cases been suggested by the same natural phenomenon is rendered probable by another Zulu tale, in which the cannibal's cave is opened by a swallow which flies in the air. Here we have the elements of a genuine lightning-

---

* Callaway, Zulu Nursery Tales, pp. 27–30.

† Callaway, op. cit. pp. 142–152 ; cf. a similar story in which the lion is fooled by the jackal. Bleek, op. cit. p. 7. I omit the sequel of the tale.

myth. We see that among these African barbarians, as well as among our own forefathers, the clouds have been conceived as birds carrying the lightning which can cleave the rocks. In America we find the same notion prevalent. The Dakotahs explain the thunder as "the sound of the cloud-bird flapping his wings," and the Caribs describe the lightning as a poisoned dart which the bird blows through a hollow reed, after the Carib style of shooting.*
On the other hand, the Kamtchatkans know nothing of a cloud-bird, but explain the lightning as something analogous to the flames of a volcano. The Kamtchatkans say that when the mountain goblins have got their stoves well heated up, they throw overboard, with true barbaric shiftlessness, all the brands not needed for immediate use, which makes a volcanic eruption. So when it is summer on earth, it is winter in heaven; and the gods, after heating up their stoves, throw away their spare kindling-wood, which makes the lightning.†

When treating of Indo-European solar myths, we saw the unvarying, unresting course of the sun variously explained as due to the subjection of Herakles to Eurystheus, to the anger of Poseidon at Odysseus, or to the curse laid upon the Wandering Jew. The barbaric mind has worked at the same problem; but the explanations which it has given are more childlike and more grotesque. A Polynesian myth tells how the Sun used to race through the sky so fast that men could not get enough daylight to hunt game for their subsistence. By and by an inventive genius, named Maui, conceived the idea of catching the Sun in a noose and making him go more deliberately. He plaited ropes and made a strong net, and, arming himself with the jawbone of his ancestress, Muri-ranga-whenua, called together all his brethren, and

---

* Brinton, op. cit. p. 104. † Tylor, op. cit. p. 320.

they journeyed to the place where the Sun rises, and
there spread the net. When the Sun came up, he stuck
his head and fore-paws into the net, and while the brothers tightened the ropes so that they cut him and made
him scream for mercy, Maui beat him with the jawbone
until he became so weak that ever since he has only been
able to crawl through the sky. According to another
Polynesian myth, there was once a grumbling Radical,
who never could be satisfied with the way in which
things are managed on this earth. This bold Radical set
out to build a stone house which should last forever; but
the days were so short and the stones so heavy that he
despaired of ever accomplishing his project. One night,
as he lay awake thinking the matter over, it occurred to
him that if he could catch the Sun in a net, he could
have as much daylight as was needful in order to finish
his house. So he borrowed a noose from the god Itu,
and, it being autumn, when the Sun gets sleepy and stupid, he easily caught the luminary. The Sun cried till
his tears made a great freshet which nearly drowned the
island; but it was of no use; there he is tethered to this
day.

Similar stories are met with in North America. A
Dog-Rib Indian once chased a squirrel up a tree until he
reached the sky. There he set a snare for the squirrel
and climbed down again. Next day the Sun was caught
in the snare, and night came on at once. That is to say,
the sun was eclipsed. "Something wrong up there,"
thought the Indian, "I must have caught the Sun"; and
so he sent up ever so many animals to release the captive.
They were all burned to ashes, but at last the mole,
going up and burrowing out through the *ground of the
sky*, (!) succeeded in gnawing asunder the cords of the
snare. Just as it thrust its head out through the opening

made in the sky-ground, it received a flash of light which put its eyes out, and that is why the mole is blind. The Sun got away, but has ever since travelled more deliberately.*

These sun-myths, many more of which are to be found collected in Mr. Tylor's excellent treatise on "The Early History of Mankind," well illustrate both the similarity and the diversity of the results obtained by the primitive mind, in different times and countries, when engaged upon similar problems. No one would think of referring these stories to a common traditional origin with the myths of Herakles and Odysseus; yet both classes of tales were devised to explain the same phenomenon. Both to the Aryan and to the Polynesian the steadfast but deliberate journey of the sun through the firmament was a strange circumstance which called for explanation; but while the meagre intelligence of the barbarian could only attain to the quaint conception of a man throwing a noose over the sun's head, the rich imagination of the Indo-European created the noble picture of Herakles doomed to serve the son of Sthenelos, in accordance with the resistless decree of fate.

Another world-wide myth, which shows how similar are the mental habits of uncivilized men, is the myth of the tortoise. The Hindu notion of a great tortoise that lies beneath the earth and keeps it from falling is familiar to every reader. According to one account, this tortoise, swimming in the primeval ocean, bears the earth on his back; but by and by, when the gods get ready to destroy mankind, the tortoise will grow weary and sink under his load, and then the earth will be overwhelmed by a deluge. Another legend tells us that when the gods and demons took Mount Mandara for a churning-stick

* Tylor, op. cit. pp. 338 – 343.

and churned the ocean to make ambrosia, the god Vishnu took on the form of a tortoise and lay at the bottom of the sea, as a pivot for the whirling mountain to rest upon. But these versions of the myth are not primitive. In the original conception the world is itself a gigantic tortoise swimming in a boundless ocean; the flat surface of the earth is the lower plate which covers the reptile's belly; the rounded shell which covers his back is the sky; and the human race lives and moves and has its being inside of the tortoise. Now, as Mr. Tylor has pointed out, many tribes of Redskins hold substantially the same theory of the universe. They regard the tortoise as the symbol of the world, and address it as the mother of mankind. Once, before the earth was made, the king of heaven quarrelled with his wife, and gave her such a terrible kick that she fell down into the sea. Fortunately a tortoise received her on his back, and proceeded to raise up the earth, upon which the heavenly woman became the mother of mankind. These first men had white faces, and they used to dig in the ground to catch badgers. One day a zealous burrower thrust his knife too far and stabbed the tortoise, which immediately sank into the sea and drowned all the human race save one man.* In Finnish mythology the world is not a tortoise, but it is an egg, of which the white part is the ocean, the yolk is the earth, and the arched shell is the sky. In India this is the mundane egg of Brahma; and it reappears among the Yorubas as a pair of calabashes put together like oyster-shells, one making a dome over the other. In Zulu-land the earth is a huge beast called Usilosimapundu, whose face is a rock, and whose mouth is very large and broad and red: "in some countries which were on his body it was win-

* Tylor, op. cit. p. 336.

ter, and in others it was early harvest." Many broad rivers flow over his back, and he is covered with forests and hills, as is indicated in his name, which means "the rugose or knotty-backed beast." In this group of conceptions may be seen the origin of Sindbad's great fish, which lay still so long that sand and clay gradually accumulated upon its back, and at last it became covered with trees. And lastly, passing from barbaric folk-lore and from the Arabian Nights to the highest level of Indo-European intelligence, do we not find both Plato and Kepler amusing themselves with speculations in which the earth figures as a stupendous animal?

November, 1870.

VI.

JUVENTUS MUNDI.*

TWELVE years ago, when, in concluding his "Studies on Homer and the Homeric Age," Mr. Gladstone applied to himself the warning addressed by Agamemnon to the priest of Apollo, "Let not Nemesis catch me by the swift ships,

ἢ νῦν δηθύνοντ᾽, ἢ ὕστερον αὖθις ἰόντα,"

he would seem to have intended it as a last farewell to classical studies. Yet, whatever his intentions may have been, they have yielded to the sweet desire of revisiting familiar ground, — a desire as strong in the breast of the classical scholar as was the yearning which led Odysseus to reject the proffered gift of immortality, so that he might but once more behold the wreathed smoke curling about the roofs of his native Ithaka. In this new treatise, on the "Youth of the World," Mr. Gladstone discusses the same questions which were treated in his earlier work; and the main conclusions reached in the "Studies on Homer" are here so little modified with reference to the recent progress of archæological inquiries, that the book can hardly be said to have had any other reason for appearing, save the desire of loitering by the ships of the Argives, and of returning thither as often as possible.

* Juventus Mundi. The Gods and Men of the Heroic Age. By the Rt. Hon. William Ewart Gladstone. Boston : Little, Brown, & Co. 1869.

The title selected by Mr. Gladstone for his new work is either a very appropriate one or a strange misnomer, according to the point of view from which it is regarded. Such being the case, we might readily acquiesce in its use, and pass it by without comment, trusting that the author understood himself when he adopted it, were it not that by incidental references, and especially 'by his allusions to the legendary literature of the Jews, Mr. Gladstone shows that he means more by the title than it can fairly be made to express. An author who seeks to determine prehistoric events by references to Kadmos, and Danaos, and Abraham, is at once liable to the suspicion of holding very inadequate views as to the character of the epoch which may properly be termed the "youth of the world." Often in reading Mr. Gladstone we are reminded of Renan's strange suggestion that an exploration of the Hindu Kush territory, whence probably came the primitive Aryans, might throw some new light on the origin of language. Nothing could well be more futile. The primitive Aryan language has already been partly reconstructed for us; its grammatical forms and syntactic devices are becoming familiar to scholars ; one great philologist has even composed a tale in it; yet in studying this long-buried dialect we are not much nearer the first beginnings of human speech than in studying the Greek of Homer, the Sanskrit of the Vedas, or the Umbrian of the Iguvine Inscriptions. The Aryan mother-tongue had passed into the last of the three stages of linguistic growth long before the break-up of the tribal communities in Aryana-vaëdjo, and at that early date presented a less primitive structure than is to be seen in the Chinese or the Mongolian of our own times. So the state of society depicted in the Homeric poems, and well illustrated by Mr. Gladstone, is many degrees

less primitive than that which is revealed to us by the
archæological researches either of Pictet and Windisch-
mann, or of Tylor, Lubbock, and M'Lennan. We shall
gather evidences of this as we proceed. Meanwhile let
us remember that at least eleven thousand years before
the Homeric age men lived in communities, and manu-
factured pottery on the banks of the Nile; and let us
not leave wholly out of sight that more distant period,
perhaps a million years ago, when sparse tribes of savage
men, contemporaneous with the mammoths of Siberia
and the cave-tigers of Britain, struggled against the intense cold of the glacial winters.

Nevertheless, though the Homeric age appears to be a
late one when considered with reference to the whole
career of the human race, there is a point of view from
which it may be justly regarded as the "youth of the
world." However long man may have existed upon the
earth, he becomes thoroughly and distinctly human in
the eyes of the historian only at the epoch at which he
began to create for himself a literature. As far back as
we can trace the progress of the human race continuously
by means of the written word, so far do we feel a true
historical interest in its fortunes, and pursue our studies
with a sympathy which the mere lapse of time is powerless to impair. But the primeval man, whose history
never has been and never will be written, whose career
on the earth, dateless and chartless, can be dimly revealed to us only by palæontology, excites in us a very
different feeling. Though with the keenest interest we
ransack every nook and corner of the earth's surface for
information about him, we are all the while aware that
what we are studying is human zoölogy and not history.
Our Neanderthal man is a specimen, not a character. We
cannot ask him the Homeric question, what is his name,

who were his parents, and how did he get where we found him. His language has died with him, and he can render no account of himself. We can only regard him specifically as *Homo Anthropos*, a creature of bigger brain than his congener *Homo Pithekos*, and of vastly greater promise. But this, we say, is physical science, and not history.

For the historian, therefore, who studies man in his various social relations, the youth of the world is the period at which literature begins. We regard the history of the western world as beginning about the tenth century before the Christian era, because at that date we find literature, in Greece and Palestine, beginning to throw direct light upon the social and intellectual condition of a portion of mankind. That great empires, rich in historical interest and in materials for sociological generalizations, had existed for centuries before that date, in Egypt and Assyria, we do not doubt, since they appear at the dawn of history with all the marks of great antiquity; but the only steady historical light thrown upon them shines from the pages of Greek and Hebrew authors, and these know them only in their latest period. For information concerning their early careers we must look, not to history, but to linguistic archæology, a science which can help us to general results, but cannot enable us to fix dates, save in the crudest manner.

We mention the tenth century before Christ as the earliest period at which we can begin to study human society in general and Greek society in particular, through the medium of literature. But, strictly speaking, the epoch in question is one which cannot be fixed with accuracy. The earliest ascertainable date in Greek history is that of the Olympiad of Koroibos, B. C. 776. There is no doubt that the Homeric poems were written

before this date, and that Homer is therefore strictly
prehistoric. Had this fact been duly realized by those
scholars who have not attempted to deny it, a vast
amount of profitless discussion might have been avoided.
Sooner or later, as Grote says, " the lesson must be learnt,
hard and painful though it be, that no imaginable reach
of critical acumen will of itself enable us to discriminate
fancy from reality, in the absence of a tolerable stock of
evidence." We do not know who Homer was; we do
not know where or when he lived ; and in all probability
we shall never know. The data for settling the question
are not now accessible, and it is not likely that they will
ever be discovered. Even in early antiquity the question
was wrapped in an obscurity as deep as that which
shrouds it to-day. The case between the seven or eight
cities which claimed to be the birthplace of the poet,
and which Welcker has so ably discussed, cannot be
decided. The feebleness of the evidence brought into
court may be judged from the fact that the claims of
Chios and the story of the poet's blindness rest alike
upon a doubtful allusion in the Hymn to Apollo, which
Thukydides (III. 104) accepted as authentic. The majority of modern critics have consoled themselves with the
vague conclusion that, as between the two great divisions
of the early Greek world, Homer at least belonged to
the Asiatic. But Mr. Gladstone has shown good reasons
for doubting this opinion. He has pointed out several
instances in which the poems seem to betray a closer
topographical acquaintance with European than with
Asiatic Greece, and concludes that Athens and Argos
have at least as good a claim to Homer as Chios or
Smyrna.

It is far more desirable that we should form an approx-
imate opinion as to the date of the Homeric poems, than

that we should seek to determine the exact locality in which they originated. Yet the one question is hardly less obscure than the other. Different writers of antiquity assigned eight different epochs to Homer, of which the earliest is separated from the most recent by an interval of four hundred and sixty years,— a period as long as that which separates the Black Prince from the Duke of Wellington, or the age of Perikles from the Christian era. While Theopompos quite preposterously brings him down as late as the twenty-third Olympiad, Krates removes him to the twelfth century B. C. The date ordinarily accepted by modern critics is the one assigned by Herodotos, 880 B. C. Yet Mr. Gladstone shows reasons, which appear to me convincing, for doubting or rejecting this date.

I refer to the much-abused legend of the Children of Herakles, which seems capable of yielding an item of trustworthy testimony, provided it be circumspectly dealt with. I differ from Mr. Gladstone in not regarding the legend as historical in its present shape. In my apprehension, Hyllos and Oxylos, as historical personages, have no value whatever; and I faithfully follow Mr. Grote, in refusing to accept any date earlier than the Olympiad of Koroibos. The tale of the " Return of the Herakleids " is undoubtedly as unworthy of credit as the legend of Hengst and Horsa; yet, like the latter, it doubtless embodies a historical occurrence. One cannot approve, as scholarlike or philosophical, the scepticism of Mr. - Cox, who can see in the whole narrative nothing but a solar myth. There certainly was a time when the Dorian tribes — described in the legend as the allies of the Children of Herakles — conquered Peloponnesos; and that time was certainly subsequent to the composition of the Homeric poems. It is incredible that the Iliad and the

Odyssey should ignore the existence of Dorians in Peloponnesos, if there were Dorians not only dwelling but
ruling there at the time when the poems were written.
The poems are very accurate and rigorously consistent
in their use of ethnical appellatives; and their author,
in speaking of Achaians and Argives, is as evidently
alluding to peoples directly known to him, as is Shakespeare when he mentions Danes and Scotchmen. Now
Homer knows Achaians, Argives, and Pelasgians dwelling in Peloponnesos ; and he knows Dorians also, but
only as a people inhabiting Crete. (Odyss. XIX. 175.)
With Homer, moreover, the Hellenes are not the Greeks
in general, but only a people dwelling in the north, in
Thessaly. When these poems were written, Greece was
not known as Hellas, but as Achaia,— the whole country
taking its name from the Achaians, the dominant race in
Peloponnesos. Now at the beginning of the truly historical period, in the eighth century B. C., all this is
changed. The Greeks as a people are called Hellenes ;
the Dorians rule in Peloponnesos, while their lands are
tilled by Argive Helots ; and the Achaians appear only
as an insignificant people occupying the southern shore
of the Corinthian Gulf. How this change took place we
cannot tell. The explanation of it can never be obtained
from history, though some light may perhaps be thrown
upon it by linguistic archæology. But at all events it
was a great change, and could not have taken place in a
moment. It is fair to suppose that the Helleno-Dorian
conquest must have begun at least a century before the
first Olympiad ; for otherwise the geographical limits
of the various Greek races would not have been so completely established as we find·them to have been at that
date. The Greeks, indeed, supposed it to have begun at
least three centuries earlier, but it is impossible to collect

evidence which will either refute or establish that opinion. For our purposes it is enough to know that the conquest could not have taken place later than 900 B. C. ;
and if this be the case, the *minimum date* for the composition of the Homeric poems must be the tenth century
before Christ; which is, in fact, the date assigned by
Aristotle. Thus far, and no farther, I believe it possible
to go with safety. Whether the poems were composed in
the tenth, eleventh, or twelfth century cannot be determined. We are justified only in placing them far enough
back to allow the Helleno-Dorian conquest to intervene
between their composition and the beginning of recorded
history. The tenth century B. C. is the latest date which
will account for all the phenomena involved in the case,
and with this result we must be satisfied. Even on this
showing, the Iliad and Odyssey appear as the oldest existing specimens of Aryan literature, save perhaps the
hymns of the Rig-Veda and the sacred books of the
Avesta.

The apparent difficulty of preserving such long poems
for three or four centuries without the aid of writing may
seem at first sight to justify the hypothesis of Wolf, that
they are mere collections of ancient ballads, like those
which make up the Mahabharata, preserved in the
memories of a dozen or twenty bards, and first arranged
under the orders of Peisistratos. But on a careful examination this hypothesis is seen to raise more difficulties than it solves. What was there in the position of
Peisistratos, or of Athens itself in the sixth century
B. C., so authoritative as to compel all Greeks to recog-
nize the recension then and there made of their revered
poet? Besides which the celebrated ordinance of Solon
respecting the *rhapsodes* at the Panathenaia obliges us
to infer the existence of written manuscripts of Homer

previous to 550 B. C. As Mr. Grote well observes, the interference of Peisistratos " presupposes a certain fore-known and ancient aggregate, the main lineaments of which were familiar to the Grecian public, although many of the *rhapsodes* in their practice may have de-viated from it both by omission and interpolation. In correcting the Athenian recitations conformably with such understood general type, Peisistratos might hope both to procure respect for Athens and to constitute a fashion for the rest of Greece. But this step of ' collect-ing the torn body of sacred Homer ' is something gener-ically different from the composition of a new Iliad out of pre-existing songs : the former is as easy, suitable, and promising as the latter is violent and gratuitous." *

As for Wolf's objection, that the Iliad and Odyssey are too long to have been preserved by memory, it may be met by a simple denial. It is a strange objection indeed, coming from a man of Wolf's retentive memory. I do not see how the acquisition of the two poems can be regarded as such a very arduous task ; and if literature were as scanty now as in Greek antiquity, there are doubtless many scholars who would long since have had them at their tongues' end. Sir G. C. Lewis, with but little conscious effort, managed to carry in his head a very considerable portion of Greek and Latin classic literature ; and Niebuhr (who once restored from recol-lection a book of accounts which had been accidentally destroyed) was in the habit of referring to book and chapter of an ancient author without consulting his notes. Nay, there is Professor Sophocles, of Harvard University, who, if you suddenly stop and interrogate him in the street, will tell you just how many times any given Greek word occurs in Thukydides, or in Æschylos,

* Hist. Greece, Vol. II. p. 208.

or in Plato, and will obligingly rehearse for you the con-
text.   If all extant copies of the Homeric poems were
to be gathered together and burnt up to-day, like Don
Quixote's library, or like those Arabic manuscripts of
which Cardinal Ximenes made a bonfire in the streets
of Granada, the poems could very likely be reproduced
and orally transmitted for several generations ; and much
easier must it have been for the Greeks to preserve these
books, which their imagination invested with a quasi-
sanctity, and which constituted the greater part of the
literary furniture of their minds.   In Xenophon's time
there were educated gentlemen at Athens who could repeat both Iliad and Odyssey verbatim.   (Xenoph. Sym-
pos., III. 5.)   Besides this, we know that at Chios there
was a company of bards, known as Homerids, whose
business it was to recite these poems from memory; and
from the edicts of Solon and the Sikyonian Kleisthenes
(Herod., V. 67), we may infer that the case was the same
in other parts of Greece.   Passages from the Iliad used
to be sung at the Pythian festivals, to the accompani-
ment of the harp (Athenæus, XIV. 638), and in at least
two of the Ionic islands of the Ægæan there were regular
competitive exhibitions by trained young men, at which
prizes were given to the best reciter.   The difficulty of
preserving the poems, under such circumstances, becomes
very insignificant ; and the Wolfian argument quite van-
ishes when we reflect that it would have been no easier
to preserve a dozen or twenty short poems than two long
ones.   Nay, the coherent, orderly arrangement of the
Iliad and Odyssey would make them even easier to remember than a group of short rhapsodies not consecu-
tively arranged.

When we come to interrogate the poems themselves,
we find in them quite convincing evidence that they

were originally composed for the ear alone, and without reference to manuscript assistance. They abound in catchwords, and in verbal repetitions. The "Catalogue of Ships," as Mr. Gladstone has acutely observed, is arranged in well-defined sections, in such a way that the end of each section suggests the beginning of the next one. It resembles the *versus memoriales* found in old-fashioned grammars. But the most convincing proof of all is to be found in the changes which Greek pronunciation went through between the ages of Homer and Peisistratos. "At the time when these poems were composed, the digamma (or *w*) was an effective consonant, and figured as such in the structure of the verse; at the time when they were committed to writing, it had ceased to be pronounced, and therefore never found a place in any of the manuscripts, — insomuch that the Alexandrian critics, though they knew of its existence in the much later poems of Alkaios and Sappho, never recognized it in Homer. The hiatus, and the various perplexities of metre, occasioned by the loss of the digamma, were corrected by different grammatical stratagems. But the whole history of this lost letter is very curious, and is rendered intelligible only by the supposition that the Iliad and Odyssey belonged for a wide space of time to the memory, the voice, and the ear exclusively."*

Many of these facts are of course fully recognized by the Wolfians; but the inference drawn from them, that the Homeric poems began to exist in a piecemeal condition, is, as we have seen, unnecessary. These poems may indeed be compared, in a certain sense, with the early sacred and epic literature of the Jews, Indians, and Teutons. But if we assign a plurality of composers to the Psalms and Pentateuch, the Mahabharata, the Vedas,

---

* Grote, Hist. Greece, Vol. II. p. 198.

and the Edda, we do so because of internal evidence
furnished by the books themselves, and not because
these books could not have been preserved by oral tradition. Is there, then, in the Homeric poems any such
internal evidence of dual or plural origin as is furnished
by the interlaced Elohistic and Jehovistic documents of
the Pentateuch? A careful investigation will show that
there is not. Any scholar who has given some attention
to the subject can readily distinguish the Elohistic from
the Jehovistic portions of the Pentateuch; and, save in
the case of a few sporadic verses, most Biblical critics
coincide in the separation which they make between the
two. But the attempts which have been made to break
up the Iliad and Odyssey have resulted. in no such harmonious agreement. There are as many systems as there
are critics, and naturally enough. For the Iliad and the
Odyssey are as much alike as two peas, and the resemblance which holds between the two holds also between
the different parts of each poem. From the appearance
of the injured Chryses in the Grecian camp down to the
intervention of Athene on the field of contest at Ithaka,
we find in each book and in each paragraph the same
style, the same peculiarities of expression, the same habits
of thought, the same quite unique manifestations of the
faculty of observation. Now if the style were common-
place, the observation slovenly, or the thought trivial, as
is wont to be the case in ballad-literature, this argument
from similarity might not carry with it much conviction.
But when we reflect that throughout the whole course
of human history no other works, save the best tragedies
of Shakespeare, have ever been written which for combined keenness of observation, elevation of ·thought, and
sublimity of style can compare with the Homeric poems,
we must admit that the argument has very great weight

indeed. Let us take, for example, the sixth and twenty-fourth books of the Iliad. According to the theory of Lachmann, the most eminent champion of the Wolfian hypothesis, these are by different authors. Human speech has perhaps never been brought so near to the limit of its capacity of expressing deep emotion as in the scene between Priam and Achilleus in the twenty-fourth book; while the interview between Hektor and Andromache in the sixth similarly wellnigh exhausts the power of language. Now, the literary critic has a right to ask whether it is probable that two such passages, agreeing perfectly in turn of expression, and alike exhibiting the same unapproachable degree of excellence, could have been produced by two different authors. And the physiologist — with some inward misgivings suggested by Mr. Galton's theory that the Greeks surpassed us in genius even as we surpass the negroes — has a right to ask whether it is in the natural course of things for two such wonderful poets, strangely agreeing in their minutest psychological characteristics, to be produced at the same time. And the difficulty thus raised becomes overwhelming when we reflect that it is the coexistence of not two only, but at least twenty such geniuses which the Wolfian hypothesis requires us to account for. That theory worked very well as long as scholars thoughtlessly assumed that the Iliad and Odyssey were analogous to ballad poetry. But, except in the simplicity of the primitive diction, there is no such analogy. The power and beauty of the Iliad are never so hopelessly lost as when it is rendered into the style of a modern ballad. One might as well attempt to preserve the grandeur of the triumphant close of Milton's Lycidas by turning it into the light Anacreontics of the ode to "Eros stung by a Bee." The peculiarity of the Homeric poetry, which

defies translation, is its union of the simplicity characteristic of an early age with a sustained elevation of style,
which can be explained only as due to individual genius.

The same conclusion is forced upon us when we examine the artistic structure of these poems. With regard
to the Odyssey in particular, Mr. Grote has elaborately
shown that its structure is so thoroughly integral, that no
considerable portion could be subtracted without con-
verting the poem into a more or less admirable fragment.
The Iliad stands in a somewhat different position. There
are unmistakable peculiarities in its structure, which
have led even Mr. Grote, who utterly rejects the Wolfian hypothesis, to regard it as made up of two poems;
although he inclines to the belief that the later poem
was grafted upon the earlier by its own author, by way
of further elucidation and expansion; just as Goethe, in
his old age, added a new part to "Faust." According to
Mr. Grote, the Iliad, as originally conceived, was properly
an *Achilleis;* its design being, as indicated in the opening
lines of the poem, to depict the wrath of Achilleus and
the unutterable woes which it entailed upon the Greeks.
The plot of this primitive Achilleis is entirely contained
in Books I., VIII., and XI. – XXII.; and, in Mr. Grote's
opinion, the remaining books injure the symmetry of this
plot by unnecessarily prolonging the duration of the
Wrath, while the embassy to Achilleus, in the ninth book,
unduly anticipates the conduct of Agamemnon in the
nineteenth, and is therefore, as a piece of bungling work,
to be referred to the hands of an inferior interpolator.
Mr. Grote thinks it probable that these books, with the
exception of the ninth, were subsequently added by the
poet, with a view to enlarging the original Achilleis into
a real Iliad, describing the war of the Greeks against
Troy. With reference to this hypothesis, I gladly admit

that Mr. Grote is, of all men now living, the one best
entitled to a reverential hearing on almost any point
connected with Greek antiquity. Nevertheless it seems
to me that his theory rests solely upon imagined difficulties which have no real existence. I doubt if any scholar,
reading the Iliad ever so much, would ever be struck by
these alleged inconsistencies of structure, unless they
were suggested by some *a priori* theory. And I fear
that the Wolfian theory, in spite of Mr. Grote's emphatic
rejection of it, is responsible for some of these over-refined
criticisms. Even as it stands, the Iliad is not an account
of the war against Troy. It begins in the tenth year of the
siege, and it does not continue to the capture of the city.
It is simply occupied with an episode in the war, — with
the wrath of Achilleus and its consequences, according
to the plan marked out in the opening lines. The supposed additions, therefore, though they may have given
to the poem a somewhat wider scope, have not at any
rate changed its primitive character of an Achilleis. To
my mind they seem even called for by the original
conception of the consequences of the wrath. To
have inserted the battle at the ships, in which Sarpedon
breaks down the wall of the Greeks, immediately after
the occurrences of the first book, would have been too
abrupt altogether. Zeus, after his reluctant promise to
Thetis, must not be expected so suddenly to exhibit such
fell determination. And after the long series of books
describing the valorous deeds of Aias, Diomedes, Agamemnon, Odysseus, and Menelaos, the powerful intervention of Achilleus appears in far grander proportions than
would otherwise be possible. As for the embassy to
Achilleus, in the ninth book, I am unable to see how the
final reconciliation with Agamemnon would be complete
without it. As Mr. Gladstone well observes, what Achil-

leus wants is not restitution, but apology; and Agamemnon offers no apology until the nineteenth book. In
his answer to the ambassadors, Achilleus scornfully rejects the proposals which imply that the mere return of
Briseis will satisfy his righteous resentment, unless it be
accompanied with that public humiliation to which circumstances have not yet compelled the leader of the
Greeks to subject himself. Achilleus is not to be bought
or cajoled. Even the extreme distress of the Greeks in
the thirteenth book does not prevail upon him; nor is
there anything in the poem to show that he ever would
have laid aside his wrath, had not the death of Patroklos
supplied him with a new and wholly unforeseen motive.
It seems to me that his entrance into the battle after the
death of his friend would lose half its poetic effect, were
it not preceded by some such scene as that in the ninth
book, in which he is represented as deaf to all ordinary
inducements. As for the two concluding books, which
Mr. Grote is inclined to regard as a subsequent addition,
not necessitated by the plan of the poem, I am at a loss
to see how the poem can be considered complete without
them. To leave the bodies of Patroklos and Hektor
unburied would be in the highest degree shocking to
Greek religious feelings. Remembering the sentence in-
curred, in far less superstitious times, by the generals at
Arginusai, it is impossible to believe that any conclusion
which left Patroklos's manes unpropitiated, and the mutilated corpse of Hektor unransomed, could have satisfied
either the poet or his hearers. For further particulars I
must refer the reader to the excellent criticisms of Mr.
Gladstone, and also to the article on "Greek History and
Legend" in the second volume of Mr. Mill's "Disserta-
tions and Discussions." A careful study of the arguments
of these writers, and, above all, a thorough and independent

examination of the Iliad itself, will, I believe, convince the student that this great poem is from beginning to end the consistent production of a single author.

The arguments of those who would attribute the Iliad and Odyssey, taken as wholes, to two different authors, rest chiefly upon some apparent discrepancies in the mythology of the two poems; but many of these difficulties have been completely solved by the recent progress of the science of comparative mythology. Thus, for example, the fact that, in the Iliad, Hephaistos is called the husband of Charis, while in the Odyssey he is called the husband of Aphrodite, has been cited even by Mr. Grote as evidence that the two poems are not by the same author. It seems to me that one such discrepancy, in the midst of complete general agreement, would be much better explained as Cervantes explained his own inconsistency with reference to the stealing of Sancho's mule, in the twenty-second chapter of "Don Quixote." But there is no discrepancy. Aphrodite, though originally the moon-goddess, like the German Hörsel, had before Homer's time acquired many of the attributes of the dawn-goddess Athene, while her lunar characteristics had been to a great extent transferred to Artemis and Persephone. In her renovated character, as goddess of the dawn, Aphrodite became identified with Charis, who appears in the Rig-Veda as dawn-goddess. In the post-Homeric mythology, the two were again separated, and Charis, becoming divided in personality, appears as the Charites, or Graces, who were supposed to be constant attendants of Aphrodite. But in the Homeric poems the two are still identical, and either Charis or Aphrodite may be called the wife of the fire-god, without inconsistency.

Thus to sum up, I believe that Mr. Gladstone is quite

right in maintaining that both the Iliad and Odyssey are, from beginning to end, with the exception of a few insignificant interpolations, the work of a single author, whom we have no ground for calling by any other name than that of Homer. I believe, moreover, that this author lived before the beginning of authentic history, and that we can determine neither his age nor his country with precision. We can only decide that he was a Greek who lived at some time previous to the year 900 B.C.

Here, however, I must begin to part company with Mr. Gladstone, and shall henceforth unfortunately have frequent occasion to differ from him on points of fundamental importance. For Mr. Gladstone not only regards the Homeric age as strictly within the limits of authentic history, but he even goes much further than this. He would not only fix the date of Homer positively in the twelfth century B. C., but he regards the Trojan war as a purely historical event, of which Homer is the authentic historian and the probable eye-witness. Nay, he even takes the word of the poet as proof conclusive of the historical character of events happening several generations before the Troika, according to the legendary chronology. He not only regards Agamemnon, Achilleus, and Paris as actual personages, but he ascribes the same reality to characters like Danaos, Kadmos, and Perseus, and talks of the Pelopid and Aiolid dynasties, and the empire of Minos, with as much confidence as if he were dealing with Karlings or Capetians, or with the epoch of the Crusades.

It is disheartening, at the present day, and after so much has been finally settled by writers like Grote, Mommsen, and Sir G. C. Lewis, to come upon such views in the work of a man of scholarship and intelligence. One begins to wonder how many more times it will be neces-

sary to prove that dates and events are of no historical
value, unless attested by nearly contemporary evidence.
Pausanias and Plutarch were able men no doubt, and
Thukydides was a profound historian ; but what these
writers thought of the Herakleid invasion, the age of
Homer, and the war of Troy, can have no great weight
with the critical historian, since even in the time of
Thukydides these events were as completely obscured by
lapse of time as they are now. There is no literary Greek
history before the age of Hekataios and Herodotos, three
centuries subsequent to the first recorded Olympiad. A
portion of this period is satisfactorily covered by inscriptions, but even these fail us before we get within a century of this earliest ascertainable date. Even the career
of the lawgiver Lykourgos, which seems to belong to
the commencement of the eighth century B. C., presents
us, from lack of anything like contemporary records,
with many insoluble problems. The Helleno-Dorian
conquest, as we have seen, must have occurred at some
time or other ; but it evidently did not occur within two
centuries of the earliest known inscription, and it is
therefore folly to imagine that we can determine its date
or ascertain the circumstances which attended it. An-
terior to this event there is but one fact in Greek antiquity directly known to us, — the existence of the
Homeric poems. The belief that there was a Trojan war
rests exclusively upon the contents of those poems : there
is no other independent testimony to it whatever. But
the Homeric poems are of no value as testimony to the
truth of the statements contained in them, unless it can
be proved that their author was either contemporary with
the Troika, or else derived his information from contemporary witnesses. This can never be proved. To assume,
as Mr. Gladstone does, that Homer lived within fifty

years after the Troika, is to make a purely gratuitous
assumption. For aught the wisest historian can tell, the
interval may have been five hundred years, or a thousand.
Indeed the Iliad itself expressly declares that it is dealing with an ancient state of things which no longer exists. It is difficult to see what else can be meant by the
statement that the heroes of the Troika belong to an
order of men no longer seen upon the earth. (Iliad, V. 304.)
Most assuredly Achilleus the son of Thetis, and Sarpedon
the son of Zeus, and Helena the daughter of Zeus, are no
ordinary mortals, such as might have been seen and con-
versed with by the poet's grandfather. They belong to
an inferior order of gods, according to the peculiar an-
thropomorphism of the Greeks, in which deity and humanity are so closely mingled that it is difficult to tell
where the one begins and the other ends. Diomedes,
single-handed, vanquishes not only the gentle Aphrodite,
but even the god of battles himself, the terrible Ares.
Nestor quaffs lightly from a goblet which, we are told,
not two men among the poet's contemporaries could by
their united exertions raise and place upon a table. Aias
and Hektor and Aineias hurl enormous masses of rock as
easily as an ordinary man would throw a pebble. All this
shows that the poet, in his naïve way, conceiving of these
heroes as personages of a remote past, was endeavouring
as far as possible to ascribe to them the attributes of
superior beings. If all that were divine, marvellous, or
superhuman were to be left out of the poems, the supposed historical residue would hardly be worth the trou-
ble of saving. As Mr. Cox well observes, "It is of the
very essence of the narrative that Paris, who has deserted
Oinone, the child of the stream Kebren, and before
whom Here, Athene, and Aphrodite had appeared as
claimants for the golden apple, steals from Sparta the

beautiful sister of the Dioskouroi; that the chiefs are
summoned together for no other purpose than to avenge
her woes and wrongs; that Achilleus, the son of the sea-
nymph Thetis, the wielder of invincible weapons and the
lord of undying horses, goes to fight in a quarrel which
is not his own; that his wrath is roused because he is
robbed of the maiden Briseis, and that henceforth he
takes no part in the strife until his friend Patroklos has
been slain; that then he puts on the new armour which
Thetis brings to him from the anvil of Hephaistos, and
goes forth to win the victory. The details are throughout
of the same nature. Achilleus sees and converses with
Athene; Aphrodite is wounded by Diomedes, and Sleep
and Death bear away the lifeless Sarpedon on their
noiseless wings to the far-off land of light." In view of
all this it is evident that Homer was not describing, like
a salaried historiographer, the state of things which existed
in the time of his father or grandfather. To his mind
the occurrences which he described were those of a remote, a wonderful, a semi-divine past.

This conclusion, which I have thus far supported
merely by reference to the Iliad itself, becomes irresistible as soon as we take into account the results obtained
during the past thirty years by the science of comparative mythology. As long as our view was restricted to
Greece, it was perhaps excusable that Achilleus and
Paris should be taken for exaggerated copies of actual
persons. Since the day when Grimm laid the founda-
tions of the science of mythology, all this has been
changed. It is now held that Achilleus and Paris and
Helena are to be found, not only in the Iliad, but also in
the Rig-Veda, and therefore, as mythical conceptions,
date, not from Homer, but from a period preceding the
dispersion of the Aryan nations. The tale of the Wrath

of Achilleus, far from originating with Homer, far from being recorded by the author of the Iliad as by an eye-witness, must have been known in its essential features in Aryana-vaëdjo; at that remote epoch when the Indian, the Greek, and the Teuton were as yet one and the same. For the story has been retained by the three races alike, in all its principal features; though the Veda has left it in the sky where it originally belonged, while the Iliad and the Nibelungenlied have brought it down to earth, the one locating it in Asia Minor, and the other in Northwestern Europe.*

* For the precise extent to which I would indorse the theory that the Iliad-myth is an account of the victory of light over darkness, let me refer to what I have said above on p. 134. I do not suppose that the struggle between light and darkness was Homer's subject in the Iliad any more than it was Shakespeare's subject in "Hamlet." Homer's subject was the wrath of the Greek hero, as Shakespeare's subject was the vengeance of the Danish prince. Nevertheless, the story of Hamlet, when traced back to its Norse original, is unmistakably the story of the quarrel be-tween summer and winter; and the moody prince is as much a solar hero as Odin himself. See Simrock, Die Quellen des Shakespeare, I. 127–133. Of course Shakespeare knew nothing of this, as Homer knew nothing of the origin of his Achilleus. The two stories, therefore, are not to be taken as sun-myths in their present form. They are the off-spring of other stories which were sun-myths; they are stories which conform to the sun-myth type after the manner above illustrated in the paper on Light and Darkness. [Hence there is nothing unintelligible in the inconsistency — which seems to puzzle Max Müller (Science of Language, 6th ed. Vol. II. p. 516, note 20) — of investing Paris with many of the characteristics of the children of light. Supposing, as we must, that the primitive sense of the Iliad-myth had as entirely disap-peared in the Homeric age, as the primitive sense of the Hamlet-myth had disappeared in the times of Elizabeth, the fit ground for wonder is that such inconsistencies are not more numerous.] The physical theory of myths will be properly presented and comprehended, only when it is understood that we accept the physical derivation of such stories as the Iliad-myth in much the same way that we are bound to accept the phys-ical etymologies of such words as *soul, consider, truth, convince, deliber-ate,* and the like. The late Dr. Gibbs of Yale College, in his "Philo-logical Studies," — a little book which I used to read with delight when

In the Rig-Veda the Panis are the genii of night and winter, corresponding to the Nibelungs, or "Children of the Mist," in the Teutonic legend, and to the children of Nephele (cloud) in the Greek myth of the Golden Fleece. The Panis steal the cattle of the Sun (Indra, Helios, Herakles), and carry them by an unknown route to a dark cave eastward. Sarama, the creeping Dawn, is sent by Indra to find and recover them. The Panis then tamper with Sarama, and try their best to induce her to betray her solar lord. For a while she is prevailed upon to dally with them; yet she ultimately returns to give Indra the information needful in order that he might conquer the Panis, just as Helena, in the slightly altered version, ultimately returns to her western home, carrying with her the treasures (κτήματα, Iliad, II. 285) of which Paris had robbed Menelaos. But, before the bright Indra and his solar heroes can reconquer their treasures they must take captive the offspring of Brisaya, the violet light of morning. Thus Achilleus, answering to the solar champion Aharyu, takes captive the daughter of Brises. But as the sun must always be parted from the morning-light, to return to it again just before setting, so Achilleus loses Briseis, and regains her only just before his final struggle. In similar wise Herakles is parted from Iole ("the violet one"), and Sigurd from Brynhild. In sullen wrath the hero retires from the conflict, and his Myrmidons are no longer seen on the battle-field, as the sun hides behind the dark cloud and his rays no longer appear about him. Yet toward the

---

a boy, — describes such etymologies as "faded metaphors." In similar wise, while refraining from characterizing the Iliad or the tragedy of Hamlet — any more than I would characterize *Le Juif Errant* by Sue, or *La Maison Forestière* by Erckmann-Chatrian — as nature-myths, I would at the same time consider these poems well described as embodying "faded nature-myths."

evening, as Briseis returns, he appears in his might, clothed in the dazzling armour wrought for him by the fire-god Hephaistos, and with his invincible spear slays the great storm-cloud, which during his absence had wellnigh prevailed over the champions of the daylight. But his triumph is short-lived; for having trampled on the clouds that had opposed him, while yet crimsoned with the fierce carnage, the sharp arrow of the night-demon Paris slays him at the Western Gates. We have not space to go into further details. In Mr. Cox's "Mythology of the Aryan Nations," and "Tales of Ancient Greece," the reader will find the entire contents of the Iliad and Odyssey thus minutely illustrated by comparison with the Veda, the Edda, and the Lay of the Nibelungs.

Ancient as the Homeric poems undoubtedly are, they are modern in comparison with the tale of Achilleus and Helena, as here unfolded. The date of the entrance of the Greeks into Europe will perhaps never be determined; but I do not see how any competent scholar can well place it at less than eight hundred or a thousand years before the time of Homer. Between the two epochs the Greek, Latin, Umbrian, and Keltic languages had time to acquire distinct individualities. Far earlier, therefore, than the Homeric "juventus mundi" was that "youth of the world," in which the Aryan forefathers, knowing no abstract terms, and possessing no philosophy but fetichism, deliberately spoke of the Sun, and the Dawn, and the Clouds, as persons or as animals. The Veda, though composed much later than this, — perhaps as late as the Iliad, — nevertheless preserves the record of the mental life of this period. The Vedic poet is still dimly aware that Sarama is the fickle twilight, and the Panis the night-demons who strive

to coax her from her allegiance to the day-god. He
keeps the scene of action in the sky. But the Homeric
Greek had long since forgotten that Helena and Paris
were anything more than semi-divine mortals, the daughter of Zeus and the son of the Zeus-descended Priam.
The Hindu understood that *Dyaus* ("the bright one")
meant the sky, and *Sarama* ("the creeping one") the
dawn, and spoke significantly when he called the latter
the daughter of the former. But the Greek could not
know that *Zeus* was derived from a root *div*, "to shine,"
or that *Helena* belonged to a root *sar*, "to creep." Phonetic change thus helped him to rise from fetichism to
polytheism. His nature-gods became thoroughly anthropomorphic; and he probably no more remembered that
Achilleus originally signified the sun, than we remember
that the word *God*, which we use to denote the most vast
of conceptions, originally meant simply the Storm-wind.
Indeed, when the fetichistic tendency led the Greek
again to personify the powers of nature, he had recourse
to new names formed from his own language. Thus, beside Apollo we have Helios; Selene beside Artemis and
Persephone; Eos beside Athene; Gaia beside Demeter.
As a further consequence of this decomposition and new
development of the old Aryan mythology, we find, as
might be expected, that the Homeric poems are not
always consistent in their use of their mythic materials.
Thus, Paris, the night-demon, is — to Max Müller's perplexity — invested with many of the attributes of the
bright solar heroes. "Like Perseus, Oidipous, Romulus,
and Cyrus, he is doomed to bring ruin on his parents;
like them he is exposed in his infancy on the hillside,
and rescued by a shepherd." All the solar heroes begin
life in this way. Whether, like Apollo, born of the
dark night (Leto), or like Oidipous, of the violet dawn

(Iokaste), they are alike destinèd to bring destruction on their parents, as the night and the dawn are both destroyed by the sun. The exposure of the child in infancy represents the long rays of the morning-sun resting on the hillside. Then Paris forsakes Oinone ("the *wine-coloured* one"), but meets her again at the gloaming when she lays herself by his side amid the crimson flames of the funeral pyre. Sarpedon also, a solar hero, is made to fight on the side of the Niblungs or Trojans, attended by his friend Glaukos ("the brilliant one"). They command the Lykians, or "children of light"; and with them comes also Memnon, son of the Dawn, from the fiery land of the Aithiopes, the favourite haunt of Zeus and the gods of Olympos.

The Iliad-myth must therefore have been current many ages before the Greeks inhabited Greece, long before there was any Ilion to be conquered. Nevertheless, this does not forbid the supposition that the legend, as we have it, may have been formed by the crystallization of mythical conceptions about a nucleus of genuine tradition. In this view I am upheld by a most sagacious and accurate scholar, Mr. E. A. Freeman, who finds in Carlovingian romance an excellent illustration of the problem before us.

The Charlemagne of romance is a mythical personage. He is supposed to have been a Frenchman, at a time when neither the French nation nor the French language can properly be said to have existed; and he is represented as a doughty crusader, although crusading was not thought of until long after the Karolingian era. The legendary deeds of Charlemagne are not conformed to the ordinary rules of geography and chronology. He is a myth, and, what is more, he is a solar myth, — an *avatar*, or at least a representative, of Odin in his solar

capacity. If in his case legend were not controlled and
rectified by history, he would be for us as unreal as
Agamemnon.

History, however, tells us that there was an Emperor
Karl, German in race, name, and language, who was one
of the two or three greatest men of action that the world
has ever seen, and who in the ninth century ruled over all
Western Europe. To the historic Karl corresponds in
many particulars the mythical Charlemagne. The legend
has preserved the fact, which without the information
supplied by history we might perhaps set down as a
fiction, that there was a time when Germany, Gaul, Italy,
and part of Spain formed a single empire. And, as Mr.
Freeman has well observed, the mythical crusades of
Charlemagne are good evidence that there were crusades,
although the real Karl had nothing whatever to do with
one.

Now the case of Agamemnon may be much like that
of Charlemagne, except that we no longer have history
to help us in rectifying the legend. The Iliad preserves
the tradition of a time when a large portion of the islands
and mainland of Greece were at least partially subject
to a common suzerain ; and, as Mr. Freeman has again
shrewdly suggested, the assignment of a place like
Mykenai, instead of Athens or Sparta or Argos, as the
seat of the suzerainty, is strong evidence of the trust-
worthiness of the tradition. It appears to show that the
legend was constrained by some remembered fact, instead
of being guided by general probability. Charlemagne's
seat of government has been transferred in romance from
Aachen to Paris ; had it really been at Paris, says Mr.
Freeman, no one would have thought of transferring it to
Aachen. Moreover, the story of Agamemnon, though
uncontrolled by historic records, is here at least sup-

ported by archæologic remains, which prove Mykenai to have been at some time or other a place of great consequence. Then, as to the Trojan war, we know that the Greeks several times crossed the Ægæan and colonized a large part of the seacoast of Asia Minor. In order to do this it was necessary to oust from their homes many warlike communities of Lydians and Bithynians, and we may be sure that this was not done without prolonged fighting. There may very probably have been now and then a levy *en masse* in prehistoric Greece, as there was in mediæval Europe; and whether the great suzerain at Mykenai ever attended one or not, legend would be sure to send him on such an expedition, as it afterwards sent Charlemagne on a crusade.

It is therefore quite possible that· Agamemnon and Menelaos may represent dimly remembered sovereigns or heroes, with their characters and actions distorted to suit the exigencies of a narrative founded upon a solar myth. The character of the Nibelungenlied here well illustrates that of the Iliad. Siegfried and Brunhild, Hagen and Gunther, seem to be mere personifications of physical phenomena; but Etzel and Dietrich are none other than Attila and Theodoric surrounded with mythical attributes; and even the conception of Brunhild has been supposed to contain elements derived from the traditional recollection of the historical Brunehault. When, therefore, Achilleus is said, like a true sun-god, to have died by a wound from a sharp instrument in the only vulnerable part of his body, we may reply that the legendary Charlemagne conducts himself in many respects like a solar deity. If Odysseus detained by Kalypso represents the sun ensnared and held captive by the pale goddess of night, the legend of Frederic Barbarossa asleep in a Thuringian mountain embodies a portion of a kindred conception. We know that Charlemagne and Frederic have been substituted for Odin; we may suspect that with the mythical impersonations of Achilleus and Odysseus some traditional figures may be blended. We should remember that in early times the solar-myth was a sort of type after which all wonderful stories would be patterned, and that to such a type tradition also would be made to conform.

In suggesting this view, we are not opening the door to Euhemerism. If there is any one conclusion concerning the Homeric poems which the labours of a whole generation of scholars may be said to have satisfactorily established, it is this, that no trustworthy history can be obtained from either the Iliad or the Odyssey merely by sifting out the mythical element. Even if the poems contain the faint reminiscence of an actual event, that event is inextricably wrapped up in mythical phraseology, so that by no cunning of the scholar can it be construed into history. In view of this it is quite useless for Mr. Gladstone to attempt to base historical conclusions upon the fact that Helena is always called "Argive Helen," or to draw ethnological inferences from the circumstances that Menelaos, Achilleus, and the rest of the Greek heroes, have yellow hair, while the Trojans are never so described. The Argos of the myth is not the city of Peloponnesos, though doubtless so construed even in Homer's time. It is "the bright land" where Zeus resides, and the epithet is applied to his wife Here and his daughter Helena, as well as to the dog of Odysseus, who reappears with Sarameyas in the Veda. As for yellow hair, there is no evidence that Greeks have ever commonly possessed it; but no other colour would do for a solar hero, and it accordingly characterizes the entire company of them, wherever found, while for the Trojans, or children of night, it is not required.

A wider acquaintance with the results which have been obtained during the past thirty years by the comparative study of languages and mythologies would have led Mr. Gladstone to reconsider many of his views concerning the Homeric poems, and might perhaps have led him to cut out half or two thirds of his book as hopelessly antiquated. The chapter on the divinities of Olympos would certainly have had to be rewritten, and the ridiculous theory of a primeval revelation abandoned. One can hardly preserve one's gravity when Mr. Gladstone derives Apollo from the Hebrew Messiah, and Athene from the Logos. To accredit Homer with an acquaintance with the doctrine of the Logos, which did not exist until the time of Philo, and did not receive its authorized Christian form until the middle of the second century after Christ, is certainly a strange proceeding. We shall next perhaps be invited to believe that the authors of the Völsunga Saga obtained the conception of Sigurd from the " Thirty-Nine Articles." It is true that these deities, Athene and Apollo, are wiser, purer, and more dignified, on the whole, than any of the other divinities of the Homeric Olympos. They alone, as Mr. Gladstone truly observes, are never deceived or frustrated. For all Hellas, Apollo was the interpreter of futurity, and in the maid Athene we have perhaps the highest conception of deity to which the Greek mind had attained in the early times. In the Veda, Athene is nothing but the dawn; but in the Greek mythology, while the merely sensuous glories of daybreak are assigned to Eos, Athene becomes the impersonation of the illuminating and knowledge-giving light of the sky. As the dawn, she is daughter of Zeus, the sky, and in mythic language springs from his forehead; but, according to the Greek conception, this imagery signifies that she shares, more than any other deity, in the boundless wisdom of Zeus. The knowledge of Apollo, on the other hand, is the peculiar privilege of the sun, who, from his lofty position, sees everything that takes place upon the earth. Even the secondary divinity Helios possesses this prerogative to a certain extent.

Next to a Hebrew, Mr. Gladstone prefers a Phœnician ancestry for the Greek divinities. But the same lack of acquaintance with the old Aryan mythology vitiates all his conclusions. No doubt the Greek mythology is in some particulars tinged with Phœnician conceptions. Aphrodite was originally a purely Greek divinity, but in course of time she acquired some of the attributes of the Semitic Astarte, and was hardly improved by the change. Adonis is simply a Semitic divinity, imported into Greece. But the same cannot be proved of Poseidon ; * far less of Hermes, who is identical with the Vedic Sarameyas, the rising wind, the son of Sarama the dawn, the lying, tricksome wind-god, who invented music, and conducts the souls of dead men to the house of Hades, even as his counterpart the Norse Odin rushes over the tree-tops leading the host of the departed. When one sees Iris, the messenger of Zeus, referred to a Hebrew original, because of Jehovah's promise to Noah, one is at a loss to understand the relationship between the two conceptions. Nothing could be more natural to the Greeks than to call

---

* I have no opinion as to the nationality of the Earth-shaker, and, regarding the etymology of his name, I believe we can hardly do better than acknowledge, with Mr. Cox, that it is unknown. It may well be doubted, however, whether much good is likely to come of comparisons between Poseidon, Dagon, Oannes, and Noah, or of distinctions between the children of Shem and the children of Ham. See Brown's Poseidon ; a Link between Semite, Hamite, and Aryan, London, 1872, — a book which is open to several of the criticisms here directed against Mr. Gladstone's manner of theorizing.

the rainbow the messenger of the sky-god to earth-dwell-
ing-men ; to call it a token set in the sky by Jehovah, as
the Hebrews did, was a very different thing. We may
admit the very close resemblance between the myth of
Bellerophon and Anteia, and that of Joseph and Zuleikha;
but the fact that the Greek story is explicable from Aryan
antecedents, while the Hebrew story is isolated, might
perhaps suggest the inference that the Hebrews were the
borrowers, as they undoubtedly were in the case of the
myth of Eden. Lastly, to conclude that Helios is an
Eastern deity, because he reigns in the East over Thrina-
kia, is wholly unwarranted. Is not *Helios* pure Greek for
the sun? and where should his sacred island be placed,
if not in the East ? As for his oxen, which wrought such
dire destruction to the comrades of Odysseus, and which
seem to Mr. Gladstone so anomalous, they are those very
same unhappy cattle, the clouds, which were stolen by
the storm-demon Cacus and the wind-deity Hermes, and
which furnished endless material for legends to the poets
of the Veda.

But the whole subject of comparative mythology seems
to be *terra incognita* to Mr. Gladstone. He pursues the
even tenour of his way in utter disregard of Grimm, and
Kuhn, and Breal, and Dasent, and Burnouf. He takes
no note of the Rig-Veda, nor does he seem to realize that
there was ever a time when the ancestors of the Greeks
and Hindus worshipped the same gods. Two or three
times he cites Max Müller, but makes no use of the
copious data which might be gathered from him. The
only work which seems really to have attracted his attention is M. Jacolliot's very discreditable performance
called "The Bible in India." Mr. Gladstone does not,
indeed, unreservedly approve of this book; but neither
does he appear to suspect that it is a disgraceful piece of

charlatanry, written by a man ignorant of the very rudiments of the subject which he professes to handle.

Mr. Gladstone is equally out of his depth when he comes to treat purely philological questions. Of the science of philology, as based upon established laws of phonetic change, he seems to have no knowledge whatever. He seems to think that two words are sufficiently proved to be connected when they are seen to resemble each other in spelling or in sound. Thus he quotes approvingly a derivation of the name *Themis* from an assumed verb *them,* " to speak," whereas it is notoriously derived from τίθημι, as *statute* comes ultimately from *stare.* His reference of *hieros,* "a priest," and *geron,* "an old man," to the same root, is utterly baseless; the one is the Sanskrit *ishiras,* "a powerful man," the other is the Sanskrit *jaran,* "an old man." The lists of words on pages 96 – 100 are disfigured by many such errors; and indeed the whole purpose for which they are given shows how sadly Mr. Gladstone's philology is in arrears. The theory of Niebuhr — that the words common to Greek and Latin, mostly descriptive of peaceful occupations, are Pelasgian — was serviceable enough in its day, but is now rendered wholly antiquated by the discovery that such words are Aryan, in the widest sense. The Pelasgian theory works very smoothly so long as we only compare the Greek with the Latin words, — as, for instance, ζυγόν with *jugum;* but when we add the English *yoke* and the Sanskrit *yugam,* it is evident that we have got far out of the range of the Pelasgoi. But what shall we say when we find Mr. Gladstone citing the Latin *thalamus* in support of this antiquated theory ? Doubtless the word *thalamus* is, or should be, significative of peaceful occupations; but it is not a Latin word at all, except by adoption. One might as well cite the word *ensemble* to prove the original identity or kinship between English and French.

When Mr. Gladstone, leaving the dangerous ground of pure and applied philology, confines himself to illustrating the contents of the Homeric poems, he is always excellent. His chapter on the " Outer Geography " of the Odyssey is exceedingly interesting; showing as it does how much may be obtained from the patient and attentive study of even a single author. Mr. Gladstone's knowledge of the *surface* of the Iliad and Odyssey, so, to speak, is extensive and accurate. It is when he attempts to penetrate beneath the surface and survey the treasures hidden in the bowels of the earth, that he shows himself unprovided with the talisman of the wise dervise, which alone can unlock those mysteries. But modern philology is an exacting science : to approach its higher problems requires an amount of preparation sufficient to terrify at the outset all but the boldest; and a man who has had to regulate taxation, and make out financial statements, and lead a political party in a great nation, may well be excused for ignorance of philology. It is difficult enough for those who have little else to do but to pore over treatises on phonetics, and thumb their lexicons, to keep fully abreast with the latest views in linguistics. In matters of detail one can hardly ever broach a new hypothesis without misgivings lest somebody, in some weekly journal published in Germany, may just have anticipated and refuted it. Yet while Mr. Gladstone may be excused for being unsound in philology, it is far less excusable that he should sit down to write a book about Homer, abounding in philological statements, without the slightest knowledge of what has been achieved in that science for several years past. In spite of all drawbacks, however, his book shows an abiding taste for scholarly pursuits, and therefore deserves a certain kind of praise. I hope, — though just now the idea savours of the ludicrous, — that the day may some time arrive when *our* Congressmen and Secretaries of the Treasury will spend their vacations in writing books about Greek antiquities, or in illustrating the meaning of Homeric phrases.

July, 1870.

VII.

THE PRIMEVAL GHOST-WORLD.

NO earnest student of human culture can as yet have forgotten or wholly outlived the feeling of delight awakened by the first perusal of Max Müller's brilliant "Essay on Comparative Mythology," — a work in which the scientific principles of myth-interpretation, though not newly announced, were at least brought home to the reader with such an amount of fresh and striking concrete illustration as they had not before received. Yet it must have occurred to more than one reader that, while the analyses of myths contained in this noble essay are in the main sound in principle and correct in detail, nevertheless the author's theory of the genesis of myth is expressed, and most likely conceived, in a way that is very suggestive of carelessness and fallacy. There are obvious reasons for doubting whether the existence of mythology can be due to any "disease," abnormity, or hypertrophy of metaphor in language; and the criticism at once arises, that with the myth-makers it was not so much the character of the expression which originated the thought, as it was the thought which gave character to the expression. It is not that the early Aryans were myth-makers because their language abounded in metaphor; it is that the Aryan mother-tongue abounded in metaphor because the men and women who spoke it were myth-makers. And they were myth-makers because they had nothing but the phenomena of human will and effort with which to compare objective phenomena. Therefore it was that they spoke of the sun as an unwearied voyager or a matchless archer, and classified inanimate no less than animate objects as masculine and feminine. Max Müller's way of stating his theory, both in this Essay and in his later Lectures, affords one among several instances of the curious manner in which he combines a marvellous penetration into the significance of details with a certain looseness of general conception.* The principles of philological interpretation are an indispensable aid to us in detecting the hidden meaning of many a legend in which the powers of nature are represented in the guise of living and thinking persons ; but before we can get at the secret of the myth-making tendency itself, we must leave philology and enter upon a psychological study. We must inquire into the characteristics of that primitive style of thinking to which it seemed quite natural that the sun should be an unerring archer, and the thunder-cloud a black demon or gigantic robber find-

---

* "The expression that the Erinys, Saranyu, the Dawn, finds out the criminal, was originally quite free from mythology ; *it meant no more than that crime would be brought to light some day or other*. It became mythological, however, as soon as the etymological meaning of Erinys was forgotten, and as soon as the Dawn, a portion of time, assumed the rank of a personal being." — Science of Language, 6th edition, II. 615. This paragraph, in which the italicizing is mine, contains Max Müller's theory in a nutshell. It seems to me wholly at variance with the facts of history. The facts concerning primitive culture which are to be cited in this paper will show that the case is just the other way. Instead of the expression " Erinys finds the criminal" being originally a metaphor, it was originally a literal statement of what was believed to be fact. The Dawn (not "a portion of time," (!) but the rosy flush of the morning sky) was originally regarded as a real person. Primitive men, strictly speaking, do not talk in metaphors ; they believe in the literal truth of their similes and personifications, from which, by survival in culture, our poetic metaphors are lineally descended. Homer's allusion to a rolling stone as ἐσσύμενος or " yearning" (to keep on rolling), is to us a mere figurative expression ; but to the savage it is the description of a fact.

ing his richly merited doom at the hands of the indignant Lord of Light.

Among recent treatises which have dealt with this interesting problem, we shall find it advantageous to give especial attention to Mr. Tylor's "Primitive Culture," * one of the few erudite works which are at once truly great and thoroughly entertaining. The learning displayed in it would do credit to a German specialist, both for extent and for minuteness, while the orderly arrangement of the arguments and the elegant lucidity of the style are such as we are accustomed to expect from French essay-writers. And what is still more admirable is the way in which the enthusiasm characteristic of a genial and original speculator is tempered by the patience and caution of a cool-headed critic. Patience and caution are nowhere more needed than in writers who deal with mythology and with primitive religious ideas; but these qualities are too seldom found in combination with the speculative boldness which is required when fresh theories are to be framed or new paths of investigation opened. The state of mind in which the explaining powers of a favourite theory are fondly contemplated is, to some extent, antagonistic to the state of mind in which facts are seen, with the eye of impartial criticism, in all their obstinate and uncompromising reality. To be able to preserve the balance between the two opposing tendencies is to give evidence of the most consummate scientific training. It is from the want of such a balance that the recent great work of Mr. Cox is at times so unsatisfactory. It may, I fear, seem ill-natured to say so, but the eagerness with which Mr. Cox waylays

* Primitive Culture : Researches into the Development of Mythology, Philosophy, Religion, Art, and Custom. By Edward B. Tylor. 2 vols. 8vo. London. 1871.

every available illustration of the physical theory of the
origin of myths has now and then the curious effect of
weakening the reader's conviction of the soundness of
the theory. For my own part, though by no means inclined to waver in adherence to a doctrine once adopted
on good grounds, I never felt so much like rebelling
against the mythologic supremacy of the Sun and the
Dawn as when reading Mr. Cox's volumes. That Mr.
Tylor, while defending the same fundamental theory,
awakens no such rebellious feelings, is due to his clear
perception and realization of the fact that it is impossible
to generalize in a single formula such many-sided corre-
spondences as those which primitive poetry and philosophy
have discerned between the life of man and the life of
outward nature. Whoso goes roaming up and down the
elf-land of popular fancies, with sole intent to resolve
each episode of myth into some answering physical event,
his only criterion being outward resemblance, cannot be
trusted in his conclusions, since wherever he turns for
evidence he is sure to find something that can be made
to serve as such. As Mr. Tylor observes, no household
legend or nursery rhyme is safe from his hermeneutics.
"Should he, for instance, demand as his property the
nursery 'Song of Sixpence,' his claim would be easily
established, — obviously the four-and-twenty blackbirds
are the four-and-twenty hours, and the pie that holds
them is the underlying earth covered with the overarching sky, — how true a touch of nature it is that when the
pie is opened, that is, when day breaks, the birds begin
to sing ; the King is the Sun, and his counting out his
money is pouring out the sunshine, the golden shower of
Danaë ; the Queen is the Moon, and her transparent
honey the moonlight ; the Maid is the 'rosy-fingered'
Dawn, who rises before the Sun, her master, and hangs

out the clouds, his clothes, across the sky ; the particular
blackbird, who so tragically ends the tale by snipping off
her nose, is the hour of sunrise." In all this interpretation there is no *a priori* improbability, save, perhaps, in
its unbroken symmetry and completeness. That some
points, at least, of the story are thus derived from antique
interpretations of physical events, is in harmony with all
that we know concerning nursery rhymes. In short, " the
time-honoured rhyme really wants but one thing to
prove it a sun-myth, that one thing being a proof by
some argument more valid than analogy." The character
of the argument which is lacking may be illustrated by
a reference to the rhyme about Jack and Jill, explained
some time since in the paper on "The Origins of Folk-
Lore." If the argument be thought valid which shows
these ill-fated children to be the spots on the moon, it is
because the proof consists, not in the analogy, which is
in this case not especially obvious, but in the fact that
in the Edda, and among ignorant Swedish peasants of
our own day, the story of Jack and Jill is actually given
as an explanation of the moon-spots. To the neglect of
this distinction between what is plausible and what is
supported by direct evidence, is due much of the crude
speculation which encumbers the study of myths.

It is when Mr. Tylor merges the study of mythology
into the wider inquiry into the characteristic features of
the mode of thinking in which myths originated, that we
can best appreciate the practical value of that union of
speculative boldness and critical sobriety which everywhere distinguishes him. It is pleasant to meet with a
writer who can treat of primitive religious ideas without
losing his head over allegory and symbolism, and who
duly realizes the fact that a savage is not a rabbinical
commentator, or a cabalist, or a Rosicrucian, but a plain

man who draws conclusions like ourselves, though with
feeble intelligence and scanty knowledge. The mystic
allegory with which such modern writers as Lord Bacon
have invested the myths of antiquity is no part of their
original clothing, but is rather the late product of a style
of reasoning from analogy quite similar to that which we
shall perceive to have guided the myth-makers in their
primitive constructions. The myths and customs and
beliefs which, in an advanced stage of culture, seem
meaningless save when characterized by some quaintly
wrought device of symbolic explanation, did not seem
meaningless in the lower culture which gave birth to
them. Myths, like words, survive their primitive meanings. In the early stage the myth is part and parcel of
the current mode of philosophizing; the explanation
which it offers is, for the time, the natural one, the one
which would most readily occur to any one thinking on
the theme with which the myth is concerned. But by
and by the mode of philosophizing has changed; explanations which formerly seemed quite obvious no longer
occur to any one, but the myth has acquired an independent substantive existence, and continues to be handed
down from parents to children as something true, though
no one can tell why it is true. Lastly, the myth itself
gradually fades from remembrance, often leaving behind
it some utterly unintelligible custom or seemingly absurd
superstitious notion. For example,—to recur to an illustration already cited in a previous paper,—it is still
believed here and there by some venerable granny that it
is wicked to kill robins; but he who should attribute
the belief to the old granny's refined sympathy with all
sentient existence, would be making one of the blun-
ders which are always committed by those who reason
a priori about historical matters without following the

historical method. At an earlier date the superstition existed in the shape of a belief that the killing of a robin portends some calamity; in a still earlier form the calamity is specified as death; and again, still earlier, as death by lightning. Another step backward reveals that the dread sanctity of the robin is owing to the fact that he is the bird of Thor, the lightning god; and finally we reach that primitive stage of philosophizing in which the lightning is explained as a red bird dropping from its beak a worm which cleaveth the rocks. Again, the belief that some harm is sure to come to him who saves the life of a drowning man, is unintelligible until it is regarded as a case of survival in culture. In the older form of the superstition it is held that the rescuer will sooner or later be drowned himself; and thus we pass to the fetichistic interpretation of drowning as the seizing of the unfortunate person by the water-spirit or nixy, who is naturally angry at being deprived of his victim, and henceforth bears a special grudge against the bold mortal who has thus dared to frustrate him.

The interpretation of the lightning as a red bird, and of drowning as the work of a smiling but treacherous fiend, are parts of that primitive philosophy of nature in which all forces objectively existing are conceived as identical with the force subjectively known as volition. It is this philosophy, currently known as fetichism, but treated by Mr. Tylor under the somewhat more comprehensive name of "animism," which we must now consider in a few of its most conspicuous exemplifications. When we have properly characterized some of the processes which the untrained mind habitually goes through, we shall have incidentally arrived at a fair solution of the genesis of mythology.

Let us first note the ease with which the barbaric or

uncultivated mind reaches all manner of apparently fanciful conclusions through reckless reasoning from analogy. It is through the operation of certain laws of ideal association that all human thinking, that of the highest as well as that of the lowest minds, is conducted : the discovery of the law of gravitation, as well as the invention of such a superstition as the Hand of Glory, is at bottom but a case of association of ideas. The difference between the scientific and the mythologic inference consists solely in the number of checks which in the former case combine to prevent any other than the true conclusion from being framed into a proposition to which the mind assents. Countless accumulated experiences have taught the modern that there are many associations of ideas which do not correspond to any actual connection of cause and effect in the world of phenomena ; and he has learned accordingly to apply to his newly framed notions the rigid test of verification. Besides which the same accumulation of experiences has built up an organized structure of ideal associations into which only the less extravagant newly framed notions have any chance of fitting. The primitive man, or the modern savage who is to some extent his counterpart, must reason without the aid of these multifarious checks. That immense mass of associations which answer to what are called physical laws, and which in the mind of the civilized modern have become almost organic, have not been formed in the mind of the savage ; nor has he learned the necessity of experimentally testing any of his newly framed notions, save perhaps a few of the commonest. Consequently there is nothing but superficial analogy to guide the course of his thought hither or thither, and the conclusions at which he arrives will be determined by associations of ideas occurring apparently at haphazard. Hence the quaint or grotesque fancies with which European and barbaric folk-lore is filled, in the framing of which the myth-maker was but reasoning according to the best methods at his command. To this simplest class, in which the association of ideas is determined by mere analogy, belong such cases as that of the Zulu, who chews a piece of wood in order to soften the heart of the man with whom he is about to trade for cows, or the Hessian lad who "thinks he may escape the conscription by carrying a baby-girl's cap in his pocket, — a symbolic way of repudiating manhood." * A similar style of thinking underlies the mediæval necromancer's practice of making a waxen image of his enemy and shooting at it with arrows, in order to bring about the enemy's death; as also the case of the magic rod, mentioned in a previous paper, by means of which a sound thrashing can be administered to an absent foe through the medium of an old coat which is imagined to cover him. The principle involved here is one which is doubtless familiar to most children, and is closely akin to that which Irving so amusingly illustrates in his doughty general who struts through a field of cabbages or cornstalks, smiting them to earth with his cane, and imagining himself a hero of chivalry conquering singlehanded a host of caitiff ruffians. Of like origin are the fancies that the breaking of a mirror heralds a death in the family, — probably because of the destruction of the reflected human image; that the "hair of the dog that bit you" will prevent hydrophobia if laid upon the wound; or that the tears shed by human victims, sacrificed to mother earth, will bring down showers upon the land. Mr. Tylor cites Lord Chesterfield's remark, "that the king had been ill, and that people generally expected the illness to be fatal, because the oldest lion in the

---

* Tylor, op. cit. I. 107.

10

Tower, about the king's age, had just died. 'So wild
and capricious is the human mind,'" observes the elegant
letter-writer.   But indeed, as Mr. Tylor justly remarks,
"the thought was neither wild nor capricious; it was
simply such an argument from analogy as the educated
world has at length painfully learned to be worthless, but
which, it is not too much to declare, would to this day
carry considerable weight to the minds of four fifths of the
human race."   Upon such symbolism are based most of
the practices of divination and the great pseudo-science
of astrology.   "It is an old story, that when two brothers
were once taken ill together, Hippokrates, the physician,
concluded from the coincidence that they were twins, but
Poseidonios, the astrologer, considered rather that they
were born under the same constellation; we may add
that either argument would be thought reasonable by a
savage."   So when a Maori fortress is attacked, the besiegers and besieged look to see if Venus is near the
moon.   The moon represents the fortress; and if it
appears below the companion planet, the besiegers will
carry the day, otherwise they will be repulsed.   Equally
primitive and childlike was Rousseau's train of thought
on the memorable day at Les Charmettes when, being
distressed with doubts as to the safety of his soul, he
sought to determine the point by throwing a stone at a
tree.   "Hit, sign of salvation; miss, sign of damnation!"
The tree being a large one and very near at hand, the
result of the experiment was reassuring, and the young
philosopher walked away without further misgivings concerning this momentous question.*

When the savage, whose highest intellectual efforts
result only in speculations of this childlike character, is

---

* Rousseau, Confessions, I. vi.   For further illustration, see especially
the note on the "doctrine of signatures," *supra*, p. 55.

confronted with the phenomena of dreams, it is easy to see what he will make of them. His practical knowledge of psychology is too limited to admit of his distinguishing between the solidity of waking experience and what we may call the unsubstantialness of the dream. He may, indeed, have learned that the dream is not to be relied on for telling the truth ; the Zulu, for example, has even reached the perverse triumph of critical logic achieved by our own Aryan ancestors in the saying that "dreams go by contraries." But the Zulu has not learned, nor had the primeval Aryan learned, to disregard the utterances of the dream as being purely subjective phenomena. To the mind as yet untouched by modern culture, the visions seen and the voices heard in sleep possess as much objective reality as the gestures and shouts of waking hours. When the savage relates his dream, he tells how he *saw* certain dogs, dead warriors, or demons last night, the implication being that the things seen were objects external to himself. As Mr. Spencer observes, "his rude language fails to state the difference between seeing and dreaming that he saw, doing and dreaming that he did. From this inadequacy of his language it not only results that he cannot truly represent this difference to others, but also that he cannot truly represent it to himself. Hence in the absence of an alternative interpretation, his belief, and that of those to whom he tells his adventures, is that his *other self* has been away and came back when he awoke. And this belief, which we find among various existing savage tribes, we equally find in the traditions of the early civilized races." *

Let us consider, for a moment, this assumption of the

* Spencer, Recent Discussions in Science, etc., p. 36, "The Origin of Animal Worship."

other self, for upon this is based the great mass of crude
inference which constitutes the primitive man's philosophy of nature. The hypothesis of the *other self,* which
serves to account for the savage's wanderings during
sleep in strange lands and among strange people, serves
also to account for the presence in his dreams of parents,
comrades, or enemies, known to be dead and buried. The
other self of the dreamer meets and converses with the
other selves of his dead brethren, joins with them in the
hunt, or sits down with them to the wild cannibal ban-
quet. Thus arises the belief in an ever-present world of
souls or ghosts, a belief which the entire experience of
uncivilized man goes to strengthen and expand. The
existence of some tribe or tribes of savages wholly desti-
tute of religious belief has often been hastily asserted
and as often called in question. But there is no question
that, while many savages are unable to frame a conception so general as that of godhood, on the other hand no
tribe has ever been found so low in the scale of intelligence as not to have framed the conception of ghosts or
spiritual personalities, capable of being angered, propitiated, or conjured with. Indeed it is not improbable
a priori that the original inference involved in the notion
of the other self may be sufficiently simple and obvious
to fall within the capacity of animals even less intelligent than uncivilized man. An authentic case is on
record of a Skye terrier who, being accustomed to obtain
favours from his master by sitting on his haunches, will
also sit before his pet india-rubber ball placed on the
chimney-piece, evidently beseeching it to jump down
and play with him.* Such a fact as this is quite in

---

* See Nature, Vol. VI. p. 262, August 1, 1872. The circumstances
narrated are such as to exclude the supposition that the sitting up is intended to attract the master's attention. The dog has frequently been

harmony with Auguste Comte's suggestion that such intelligent animals as dogs, apes, and elephants may be
capable of forming a few fetichistic notions. The be-
haviour of the terrier here rests upon the assumption
that the ball is open to the same sort of entreaty which
prevails with the master; which implies, not that the
wistful brute accredits the ball with a soul, but that in
his mind the distinction between life and inanimate
existence has never been thoroughly established. Just
this confusion between things living and things not living is present throughout the whole philosophy of fetichism; and the confusion between things seen and things
dreamed, which suggests the notion of another self, belongs to this same twilight stage of intelligence in which
primeval man has not yet clearly demonstrated his im-
measurable superiority to the brutes.[*]

seen trying to soften the heart of the ball, while observed unawares by
his master.

[*] "We would, however, commend to Mr. Fiske's attention Mr. Mark
Twain's dog, who 'could n't be depended on for a special providence,'
as being nearer to the actual dog of every-day life than is the Skye terrier mentioned by a certain correspondent of *Nature*, to whose letter
Mr. Fiske refers. The terrier is held to have had 'a few fetichistic notions,' because he was found standing up on his hind legs in front of a
mantel-piece, upon which lay an india-rubber ball with which he wished
to play, but which he could not reach, and which, says the letter-writer,
he was evidently beseeching to come down and play with him. We
consider it more reasonable to suppose that a dog who had been drilled
into a belief that standing upon his hind legs was very pleasing to his
master, and who, therefore, had accustomed himself to stand on his
hind legs whenever he desired anything, and whose usual way of getting what he desired was to induce somebody to get it for him, may
have stood up in front of the mantel-piece rather from force of habit and
eagerness of desire than because he had any fetichistic notions, or expected the india-rubber ball to listen to his supplications. We admit,
however, to avoid polemical controversy, that in matter of religion the
dog is capable of anything." The Nation, Vol. XV. p. 284, October
1, 1872. To be sure, I do not know for certain what was going on in

The conception of a soul or other self, capable of going away from the body and returning to it, receives decisive confirmation from the phenomena of fainting, trance, catalepsy, and ecstasy,* which occur less rarely among savages, owing to their irregular mode of life, than among civilized men. "Further verification," observes Mr. Spencer, "is afforded by every epileptic subject, into whose body, during the absence of the other self, some enemy has entered ; for how else does it happen that the other self on returning denies all knowledge of what his body has been doing? And this supposition, that the body has been 'possessed' by some other being, is confirmed by the phenomena of somnambulism and insan-

the dog's mind ; and so, letting both explanations stand, I will only add another fact of similar import. "The tendency in savages to imagine that natural objects and agencies are animated by spiritual or living essences is perhaps illustrated by a little fact which I once noticed : my dog, a full-grown and very sensible animal, was lying on the lawn during a hot and still day ; but at a little distance a slight breeze occasionally moved an open parasol, which would have been wholly disregarded by the dog, had any one stood near it. As it was, every time that the parasol slightly moved, the dog growled fiercely and barked. He must, I think, have reasoned to himself, in a rapid and unconscious manner, that movement without any apparent cause indicated the presence of some strange living agent, and no stranger had a right to be on his territory." Darwin, Descent of Man, Vol. I. p. 64. Without insisting upon all the details of this explanation, one may readily grant, I think, that in the dog, as in the savage, there is an undisturbed association between motion and a living motor agency ; and that out of a multitude of just such associations common to both, the savage, with his greater generalizing power, frames a truly fetichistic conception.

* Note the fetichism wrapped up in the etymologies of these Greek words. *Catalepsy, κατάληψις,* a seizing of the body by some spirit or demon, who holds it rigid. *Ecstasy, ἔκστασις,* a displacement or removal of the soul from the body, into which the demon enters and causes strange laughing, crying, or contortions. It is not metaphor, but the literal belief in a ghost-world, which has given rise to such words as these, and to such expressions as "a man *beside himself* or *transported.*"

ity." Still further, as Mr. Spencer points out, when we
recollect that savages are very generally unwilling to
have their portraits taken, lest a portion of themselves
should get carried off and be exposed to foul play,* we

* Something akin to the savage's belief in the animation of pictures
may be seen in young children. I have often been asked by my three-
year-old boy, whether the dog in a certain picture would bite him if he
were to go near it; and I can remember that, in my own childhood,
when reading a book about insects, which had the formidable likeness
of a spider stamped on the centre of the cover, I was always uneasy lest
my finger should come in contact with the dreaded thing as I held the
book.

With the savage's unwillingness to have his portrait taken, lest it fall
into the hands of some enemy who may injure him by conjuring with
it, may be compared the reluctance which he often shows toward telling
his name, or mentioning the name of his friend, or king, or tutelar
ghost-deity. In fetichistic thought, the name is an entity mysteriously
associated with its owner, and it is not well to run the risk of its getting into hostile hands. Along with this caution goes the similarly
originated fear that the person whose name is spoken may resent such
meddling with his personality. For the latter reason the Dayak will
not allude by name to the small-pox, but will call it "the chief" or
"jungle-leaves"; the Laplander speaks of the bear as the "old man
with the fur coat"; in Annam the tiger is called "grandfather" or
"Lord"; while in more civilized communities such sayings are current
as "talk of the Devil, and he will appear," with which we may also
compare such expressions as "Eumenides" or "gracious ones" for the
Furies, and other like euphemisms. Indeed, the maxim *nil mortuis
nisi bonum* had most likely at one time a fetichistic flavour.

In various islands of the Pacific, for both the reasons above specified, the
name of the reigning chief is so rigorously "tabu," that common words
and even syllables resembling that name in sound must be omitted from
the language. In New Zealand, where a chief's name was *Maripi*, or
"knife," it became necessary to call knives *nekra;* and in Tahiti, *fetu*,
"star," had to be changed into *fetia*, and *tui*, "to strike," became *tiai*,
etc., because the king's name was *Tu*. Curious freaks are played with
the languages of these islands by this ever-recurring necessity. Among
the Kafirs the women have come to speak a different dialect from the
men, because words resembling the names of their lords or male relatives are in like manner "tabu." The student of human culture will
trace among such primeval notions the origin of the Jew's unwillingness

must readily admit that the weird reflection of the person
and imitation of the gestures in rivers or still woodland
pools will go far to intensify the belief in the other self.
Less frequent but uniform confirmation is to be found in
echoes, which in Europe within two centuries have been
commonly interpreted as the voices of mocking fiends or
wood-nymphs, and which the savage might well regard
as the utterances of his other self.

Chamisso's well-known tale of Peter Schlemihl belongs
to a widely diffused family of legends, which show that a
man's shadow has been generally regarded not only as an
entity, but as a sort of spiritual attendant of the body,
which under certain circumstances it may permanently
forsake. It is in strict accordance with this idea that
not only in the classic languages, but in various barbaric
tongues, the word for "shadow" expresses also the soul
or other self. Tasmanians, Algonquins, Central-Ameri-
cans, Abipones, Basutos, and Zulus are cited by Mr. Tylor
as thus implicitly asserting the identity of the shadow
with the ghost or phantasm seen in dreams; the Basutos
going so far as to think "that if a man walks on the
river-bank, a crocodile may seize his shadow in the water
and draw him in." Among the Algonquins a sick person
is supposed to have his shadow or other self temporarily
detached from his body, and the convalescent is at times
"reproached for exposing himself before his shadow was
safely settled down in him." If the sick man has been

to pronounce the name of Jehovah; and hence we may perhaps have
before us the ultimate source of the horror with which the Hebraizing
Puritan regards such forms of light swearing — "Mon Dieu," etc. —
as are still tolerated on the continent of Europe, but have disappeared
from good society in Puritanic England and America. The reader interested in this group of ideas and customs may consult Tylor, Early
History of Mankind, pp. 142, 363; Max Müller, Science of Language,
6th edition, Vol. II. p. 37; Mackay, Religious Development of the
Greeks and Hebrews, Vol. I. p. 146.

plunged into stupor, it is because his other self has
travelled away as far as the brink of the river of death,
but not being allowed to cross has come back and re-
entered him. And acting upon a similar notion the ail-
ing Fiji will sometimes lie down and raise a hue and cry
for his soul to be brought back. Thus, continues Mr.
Tylor, "in various countries the bringing back of lost
souls becomes a regular part of the sorcerer's or priest's
profession." * On Aryan soil we find the notion of a
temporary departure of the soul surviving to a late date
in the theory that the witch may attend the infernal Sabbath while her earthly tabernacle is quietly sleeping at
home. The primeval conception reappears, clothed in
bitterest sarcasm, in Dante's reference to his living contemporaries whose souls he met with in the vaults of
hell, while their bodies were still walking about on the
earth, inhabited by devils.

The theory which identifies the soul with the shadow,
and supposes the shadow to depart with the sickness and
death of the body, would seem liable to be attended with
some difficulties in the way of verification, even to the
dim intelligence of the savage. But the propriety of
identifying soul and breath is borne out by all primeval
experience. The breath, which really quits the body at
its decease, has furnished the chief name for the soul,
not only to the Hebrew, the Sanskrit, and the classic
tongues; not only to German and English, where *geist*,
and *ghost*, according to Max Müller, have the meaning of
"breath," and are akin to such words as *gas, gust,* and
geyser; but also to numerous barbaric languages. Among

* Tylor, Primitive Culture, I. 394. "The Zulus hold that a dead
body can cast no shadow, because that appurtenance departed from it at
the close of life." Hardwick, Traditions, Superstitions, and Folk-Lore,
p. 123.

the natives of Nicaragua and California, in Java and in
West Australia, the soul is described as the air or breeze
which passes in and out through the nostrils and mouth ;
and the Greenlanders, according to Cranz, reckon two
separate souls, the breath and the shadow. "Among the
Seminoles of Florida, when a woman died in childbirth,
the infant was held over her face to receive her parting
spirit, and thus acquire strength and knowledge for its
future use. . . . . Their state of mind is kept up to this
day among Tyrolese peasants, who can still fancy a good
man's soul to issue from his mouth at death like a little
white cloud." *   It is kept up, too, in Lancashire, where a
well-known witch died a few years since ; "but before she
could 'shuffle off' this mortal coil' she must needs *trans-
fer her familiar spirit* to some trusty successor.   An in-
timate acquaintance from a neighbouring township was
consequently sent for in all haste, and on her arrival was
immediately closeted with her dying friend.   What
passed between them has never fully transpired, but it is
confidently affirmed that at the close of the interview
this associate *received the witch's last breath into her mouth
and with it her familiar spirit*.   The dreaded woman
thus ceased to exist, but her powers for good or evil were
transferred to her companion ; and on passing along the
road from Burnley to Blackburn we can point out a farm-
house at no great distance with whose thrifty matron no
neighbouring farmer will yet dare to quarrel." †

Of the theory of embodiment there will be occasion to
speak further on.   At present let us not pass over the
fact that the other self is not only conceived as shadow
or breath, which can at times quit the body during life,
but is also supposed to become temporarily embodied in

---

* Tylor, op. cit. I. 391.

† Harland and Wilkinson, Lancashire Folk-Lore, 1867, p. 210.

the visible form of some bird or beast. In discussing elsewhere the myth of Bishop Hatto, we saw that the soul is sometimes represented in the form of a rat or mouse; and in treating of werewolves we noticed the belief that the spirits of dead ancestors, borne along in the night-wind, have taken on the semblance of howling dogs or wolves. " Consistent with these quaint ideas are ceremonies in vogue in China of bringing home in a cock (live or artificial) the spirit of a man deceased in a distant place, and of enticing into a sick man's coat the departing spirit which has already left his body and so conveying it back." * In Castrén's great work on Finnish mythology, we find the story of the giant who could not be killed because he kept his soul hidden in a twelve-headed snake which he carried in a bag as he rode on horseback; only when the secret was discovered and the snake carefully killed, did the giant yield up his life. In this Finnish legend we have one of the thousand phases of the story of the " Giant who had no Heart in his Body," but whose heart was concealed, for safe keeping, in a duck's egg, or in a pigeon, carefully disposed in some belfry at the world's end a million miles away, or encased in a well-nigh infinite series of Chinese boxes.† Since, in spite of all these precautions, the poor giant's heart invariably came to grief, we need not wonder at the Karen superstition that the soul is in danger when it quits the body

* Tylor, op. cit. II. 139.
† In Russia the souls of the dead are supposed to be embodied in pigeons or crows. "Thus when the Deacon Theodore and his three schismatic brethren were burnt in 1681, the souls of the martyrs, as the 'Old Believers' affirm, appeared in the air as pigeons. In Volhynia dead children are supposed to come back in the spring to their native village under the semblance of swallows and other small birds, and to seek by soft twittering or song to console their sorrowing parents." Ralston, Songs of the Russian People, p. 118.

on its excursions, as exemplified in countless Indo-European stories of the accidental killing of the weird mouse or pigeon which embodies the wandering spirit. Conversely it is held that the detachment of the other self is fraught with danger to the self which remains. In the philosophy of "wraiths" and "fetches," the appearance of a double, like that which troubled Mistress Affery in her waking dreams of Mr. Flintwinch, has been from time out of mind a signal of alarm. "In New Zealand it is ominous to see the figure of an absent person, for if it be shadowy and the face not visible, his death may erelong be expected, but if the face be seen he is dead already. A party of Maoris (one of whom told the story) were seated round a fire in the open air, when there appeared, seen only by two of them, the figure of a relative, left ill at home ; they exclaimed, the figure vanished, and on the return of the party it appeared that the sick man had died about the time of the vision." * The belief in wraiths has survived into modern times, and now and then appears in the records of that remnant of primeval philosophy known as " spiritualism," as, for example, in the case of the lady who " thought she saw her own father look in at the church-window at the moment he was dying in his own house."

The belief in the " death-fetch," like the doctrine which identifies soul with shadow, is instructive as showing that in barbaric thought the other self is supposed to resemble the material self with which it has customarily been associated. In various savage superstitions the minute resemblance of soul to body is forcibly stated. The Australian, for instance, not content with slaying his enemy, cuts off the right thumb of the corpse, so that the departed soul may be incapacitated from throwing a spear.

* Tylor, op. cit. I. 404.

Even the half-civilized Chinese prefer crucifixion to decapitation, that their souls may not wander headless about the spirit-world.* Thus we see how far removed from the Christian doctrine of souls is the primeval theory of the soul or other self that figures in dreamland. So grossly materialistic is the primitive conception that the savage who cherishes it will bore holes in the coffin of his dead friend, so that the soul may again have a chance, if it likes, to revisit the body. To this day, among the peasants in some parts of Northern Europe, when Odin, the spectral hunter, rides by attended by his furious host, the windows in every sick-room are opened, in order that the soul, if it chooses to depart, may not be hindered from joining in the headlong chase. And so, adds Mr. Tylor, after the Indians of North America had spent a riotous night in singeing an unfortunate captive to death with firebrands, they would howl like the fiends they were, and beat the air with brushwood, to drive away the distressed and revengeful ghost. "With a kindlier feeling, the Congo negroes abstained for a whole year after a death from sweeping the house, lest the dust should injure the delicate substance of the ghost"; and even now, "it remains a German peasant saying that it is wrong to slam a door, lest one should pinch a soul in it."† Dante's experience with the ghosts in hell and purgatory, who were astonished at his weighing down the boat in which they were carried, is belied by the sweet German notion "that the dead mother's coming back in the night to suckle the

---

* Tylor, op. cit. I. 407.

† Tylor, op. cit. I. 410. In the next stage of survival this belief will take the shape that it is wrong to slam a door, no reason being assigned; and in the succeeding stage, when the child asks why it is naughty to slam a door, he will be told, because it is an evidence of bad temper. Thus do old-world fancies disappear before the inroads of the practical sense.

baby she has left on earth may be known by the hollow
pressed down in the bed where she lay." Almost universally ghosts, however impervious to thrust of sword or
shot of pistol, can eat and drink like Squire Westerns.
And lastly, we have the grotesque conception of souls
sufficiently material to be killed over again, as in the
case of the negro widows who, wishing to marry a second
time, will go and duck themselves in the pond, in order
to drown the souls of their departed husbands, which are
supposed to cling about their necks; while, according to
the Fiji theory, the ghost of every dead warrior must go
through a terrible fight with Samu and his brethren, in
which, if he succeeds, he will enter Paradise, but if he
fails he will be killed over again and finally eaten by the
dreaded Samu and his unearthly company.

From the conception of souls embodied in beast-forms,
as above illustrated, it is not a wide step to the conception of beast-souls which, like human souls, survive the
death of the tangible body. The wide-spread superstitions concerning werewolves and swan-maidens, and the
hardly less general belief in metempsychosis, show that
primitive culture has not arrived at the distinction attained by modern philosophy between the immortal man
and the soulless brute. Still more direct evidence is furnished by sundry savage customs. The Kafir who has
killed an elephant will cry that he did n't mean to do it,
and, lest the elephant's soul should still seek vengeance,
he will cut off and bury the trunk, so that the mighty
beast may go crippled to the spirit-land. In like manner,
the Samoyeds, after shooting a bear, will gather about
the body offering excuses and laying the blame on the
Russians; and the American redskin will even put the
pipe of peace into the dead animal's mouth, and beseech
him to forgive the deed. In Assam it is believed that

the ghosts of slain animals will become in the next world the property of the hunter who kills them; and the Kamtchadales expressly declare that all animals, even flies and bugs, will live after death, — a belief, which, in our own day, has been indorsed on philosophical grounds by an eminent living naturalist.* The Greenlanders, too, give evidence of the same belief by supposing that when after an exhausting fever the patient comes up in unprecedented health and vigour, it is because he has lost his former soul and had it replaced by that of a young child or a *reindeer*. In a recent work in which the crudest fancies of primeval savagery are thinly disguised in a jargon learned from the superficial reading of modern books of science, M. Figuier maintains that human souls are for the most part the surviving souls of deceased animals; in general, the souls of precocious musical children like Mozart come from nightingales, while the souls of great architects have passed into them from beavers, etc., etc. †

The practice of begging pardon of the animal one has just slain is in some parts of the world extended to the case of plants. When the Talein offers a prayer to the tree which he is about to cut down, it is obviously because he regards the tree as endowed with a soul or ghost which in the next life may need to be propitiated. And the doctrine of transmigration distinctly includes plants along with animals among the future existences into which the human soul may pass.

As plants, like animals, manifest phenomena of life, though to a much less conspicuous degree, it is not incomprehensible that the savage should attribute souls to them. But the primitive process of anthropomorphisa-

---

* Agassiz, Essay on Classification, pp. 97 – 99.

† Figuier, The To-morrow of Death, p. 247.

tion does not end here. Not only the horse and dog, the bamboo, and the oak-tree, but even lifeless objects, such as the hatchet, or bow and arrows, or food and drink of the dead man, possess other selves which pass into the world of ghosts. Fijis and other contemporary savages, when questioned, expressly declare that this is their belief. "If an axe or a chisel is worn out or broken up, away flies its soul for the service of the gods." The Algonquins told Charlevoix that since hatchets and kettles have shadows, no less than men and women, it follows, of course, that these shadows (or souls) must pass along with human shadows (or souls) into the spirit-land. In this we see how simple and consistent is the logic which guides the savage, and how inevitable is the genesis of the great mass of beliefs, to our minds so arbitrary and grotesque, which prevail throughout the barbaric world. However absurd the belief that pots and kettles have souls may seem to us, it is nevertheless the only belief which can be held consistently by the savage to whom pots and kettles, no less than human friends or enemies, may appear in his dreams; who sees them followed by shadows as they are moved about; who hears their voices, dull or ringing, when they are struck; and who watches their doubles fantastically dancing in the water as they are carried across the stream.* To minds, even in civilized countries, which are unused to the severe training of science, no stronger evidence can be alleged than what is called "the evidence of the senses"; for it is only long familiarity with science which teaches

* Here, as usually, the doctrine of metempsychosis comes in to complete the proof. "Mr. Darwin saw two Malay women in Keeling Island, who had a wooden spoon dressed in clothes like a doll; this spoon had been carried to the grave of a dead man, and becoming inspired at full moon, in fact lunatic, it danced about convulsively like a table or a hat at a modern spirit-*séance.*" Tylor, op. cit. II. 139.

us that the evidence of the senses is trustworthy only in so far as it is correctly interpreted by reason. For the truth of his belief in the ghosts of men and beasts, trees and axes, the savage has undeniably the evidence of his senses which have so often seen, heard, and handled these *other selves.*

The funeral ceremonies of uncultured races freshly illustrate this crude philosophy, and receive fresh illustration from it. On the primitive belief in the ghostly survival of persons and objects rests the almost universal custom of sacrificing the wives, servants, horses, and dogs of the departed chief of the tribe, as well as of presenting at his shrine sacred offerings of food, ornaments, weapons, and money. Among the Kayans the slaves who are killed at their master's tomb are enjoined to take great care of their master's ghost, to wash and shampoo it, and to nurse it when sick. Other savages think that " all whom they kill in this world shall attend them as slaves after death," and for this reason the thrifty Dayaks of Borneo until lately would not allow their young men to marry until they had acquired some *post mortem* property by procuring at least one human head. It is hardly necessary to do more than allude to the Fiji custom of strangling all the wives of the deceased at his funeral, or to the equally well-known Hindu rite of suttee. Though, as Wilson has shown, the latter rite is not supported by any genuine Vedic authority, but only by a shameless Brahmanic corruption of the sacred text, Mr. Tylor is nevertheless quite right in arguing that unless the horrible custom had received the sanction of a public opinion bequeathed from pre-Vedic times, the Brahmans would have had no motive for fraudulently reviving it ; and this opinion is virtually established by the fact of the prevalence of widow sacrifice among Gauls, Scandinavians, Slaves, and other Euro-

pean Aryans.* Though under English rule the rite has
been forcibly suppressed, yet the archaic sentiments
which so long maintained it are not yet extinct. Within
the present year there has appeared in the newspapers a
not improbable story of a beautiful and accomplished
Hindu lady who, having become the wife of a wealthy
Englishman, and after living several years in England
amid the influences of modern society, nevertheless went
off and privately burned herself to death soon after her
husband's decease.

The reader who thinks it far-fetched to interpret funeral
offerings of food, weapons, ornaments, or money, on the
theory of object-souls, will probably suggest that such
offerings may be mere memorials of affection or esteem
for the dead man. Such, indeed, they have come to be
in many countries after surviving the phase of culture in
which they originated ; but there is ample evidence to
show that at the outset they were presented in the belief
that their ghosts would be eaten or otherwise employed
by the ghost of the dead man. The stout club which is
buried with the dead Fiji sends its soul along with him
that he may be able to defend himself against the hostile
ghosts which will lie in ambush for him on the road to
Mbulu, seeking to kill and eat him. Sometimes the club
is afterwards removed from the grave as of no further use,
since its ghost is all that the dead man needs. In like
manner, "as the Greeks gave the dead man the obolus
for Charon's toll, and the old Prussians furnished him
with spending money, to buy refreshment on his weary
journey, so to this day German peasants bury a corpse
with money in his mouth or hand," and this is also said
to be one of the regular ceremonies of an Irish wake.
Of similar purport were the funeral feasts and oblations

* Tylor, op. cit. I. 414-422.

of food in Greece and Italy, the "rice-cakes made with ghee" destined for the Hindu sojourning in Yama's kingdom, and the meat and gruel offered by the Chinaman to the manes of his ancestors. " Many travellers have described the imagination with which the Chinese make such offerings. It is that the spirits of the dead consume the impalpable essence of the food, leaving behind its coarse material substance, wherefore the dutiful sacrificers, having set out sumptuous feasts for ancestral souls, allow them a proper time to satisfy their appetite, and then fall to themselves." * So in the Homeric sacrifice to the gods, after the deity has smelled the sweet savour and consumed the curling steam that rises ghost-like from the roasting viands, the assembled warriors devour the remains." †

Thus far the course of fetichistic thought which we have traced out, with Mr. Tylor's aid, is such as is not always obvious to the modern inquirer without considerable concrete illustration. The remainder of the process, resulting in that systematic and complete anthropomorphisation of nature which has given rise to mythology, may be more succinctly described. Gathering together the conclusions already obtained, we find that daily or frequent experience of the phenomena of shadows and dreams has combined with less frequent experience of the phenomena of trance, ecstasy, and insanity, to generate in the mind of uncultured man the notion of a twofold existence appertaining alike to all animate or inanimate objects : as all alike possess material bodies, so all alike possess ghosts or souls. Now when the theory of object-souls is expanded into a general doctrine of spirits, the

---

* Tylor, op. cit. I. 435, 446 ; II. 30, 36.

† According to the Karens, blindness occurs when the *soul of the eye* is eaten by demons. Id., II. 353.

philosophic scheme of animism is completed. Once ha-
bituated to the conception of souls of knives and tobacco-
pipes passing to the land of ghosts, the savage cannot avoid
carrying the interpretation still further, so that wind and
water, fire and storm, are accredited with indwelling
spirits akin by nature to the soul which inhabits the
human frame. That the mighty spirit or demon by whose
impelling will the trees are rooted up and the storm-
clouds driven across the sky should resemble a freed
human soul, is a natural inference, since uncultured man
has not attained to the conception of physical force acting in accordance with uniform methods, and hence all
events are to his mind the manifestations of capricious
volition. If the fire burns down his hut, it is because the
fire is a person with a soul, and is angry with him, and
needs to be coaxed into a kindlier mood by means of
prayer or sacrifice. Thus the savage has *a priori* no
alternative but to regard fire-soul as something akin to
human-soul; and in point of fact we find that savage
philosophy makes no distinction between the human
ghost and the elemental demon or deity. This is sufficiently proved by the universal prevalence of the worship
of ancestors. The essential principle of manes-worship
is that the tribal chief or patriarch, who has governed the
community during life, continues also to govern it after
death, assisting it in its warfare with hostile tribes,
rewarding brave warriors, and punishing traitors and
cowards. Thus from the conception of the living king
we pass to the notion of what Mr. Spencer calls "the
god-king," and thence to the rudimentary notion of deity.
Among such higher savages as the Zulus, the doctrine of
divine ancestors has been developed to the extent of recognizing a first ancestor, the Great Father, Unkulunkulu,
who made the world. But in the stratum of savage

thought in which barbaric or Aryan folk-lore is for the most part based, we find no such exalted speculation. The ancestors of the rude Veddas and of the Guinea negroes, the Hindu *pitris* (*patres*, "fathers"), and the Roman *manes* have become elemental deities which send rain or sunshine, health or sickness, plenty or famine, and to which their living offspring appeal for guidance amid the vicissitudes of life.* The theory of embodiment, already alluded to, shows how thoroughly the demons which cause disease are identified with human and object souls. In Australasia it is a dead man's ghost which creeps up into the liver of the impious wretch who has ventured to pronounce his name ; while conversely in the well-known European theory of demoniacal possession, it is a fairy from elf-land, or an imp from hell, which has entered the body of the sufferer. In the close kinship, moreover, between disease-possession and oracle-possession, where the body of the Pythia, or the medicine-man, is placed under the direct control of some great deity,†

---

* The following citation is interesting as an illustration of the directness of descent from heathen manes-worship to Christian saint-worship : "It is well known that Romulus, mindful of his own adventurous infancy, became after death a Roman deity, propitious to the health and safety of young children, so that nurses and mothers would carry sickly infants to present them in his little round temple at the foot of the Palatine. In after ages the temple was replaced by the church of St. Theodorus, and there Dr. Conyers Middleton, who drew public attention to its curious history, used to look in and see ten or a dozen women, each with a sick child in her lap, sitting in silent reverence before the altar of the saint. The ceremony of blessing children, especially after vaccination, may still be seen there on Thursday mornings." Op. cit. II. 111.

† Want of space prevents me from remarking at length upon Mr. Tylor's admirable treatment of the phenomena of oracular inspiration. Attention should be called, however, to the brilliant explanation of the importance accorded by all religions to the rite of *fasting*. Prolonged abstinence from food tends to bring on a mental state which is favourable to visions. The savage priest or medicine-man qualifies himself for

we may see how by insensible transitions the conception of the human ghost passes into the conception of the spiritual numen, or divinity.

To pursue this line of inquiry through the countless nymphs and dryads and nixies of the higher nature-worship up to the Olympian divinities of classic polytheism, would be to enter upon the history of religious belief, and in so doing to lose sight of our present purpose, which has merely been to show by what mental process the myth-maker can speak of natural objects in language which implies that they are animated persons. Brief as our account of this process has been, I believe that enough has been said, not only to reveal the inadequacy of purely philological solutions (like those contained in Max Müller's famous Essay) to explain the growth of myths, but also to exhibit the vast importance for this purpose of the kind of psychological inquiry into the mental habits of savages which Mr. Tylor has so ably conducted. Indeed, however lacking we may still be in points of detail, I think we have already reached a very satisfactory explanation of the genesis of mythology. Since the essential characteristic of a myth is that it is an attempt to explain some natural phenomenon by endowing with human feelings and capacities the senseless factors in the phenomenon, and since it has here been shown how un-cultured man, by the best use he can make of his rude common sense, must inevitably come, and has invariably come, to regard all objects as endowed with souls, and all nature as peopled with supra-human entities shaped after the general pattern of the human soul, I am inclined to suspect that we have got very near to the root of the

the performance of his duties by fasting, and where this is not sufficient, often uses intoxicating drugs ; whence the sacredness of the hasheesh, as also of the Vedic soma-juice. The practice of fasting among civilized peoples is an instance of survival.

whole matter. We can certainly find no difficulty in seeing why a water-spout should be described in the " Arabian Nights" as a living demon : " The sea became troubled before them, and there arose from it a black pillar, ascending towards the sky, and approaching the meadow, ... and behold it was a Jinni, of gigantic stature." We can see why the Moslem camel-driver should find it most natural to regard the whirling simoom as a malignant Jinni; we may understand how it is that the Persian sees in bodily shape the scarlet fever as " a blushing maid with locks of flame and cheeks all rosy red "; and we need not consider it strange that the primeval Aryan should have regarded the sun as a voyager, a climber, or an archer, and the clouds as cows driven by the wind-god Hermes to their milking. The identification of William Tell with the sun becomes thoroughly intelligible; nor can we be longer surprised at the conception of the howling night-wind as a ravenous wolf. When pots and kettles are thought to have souls that live hereafter, there is no difficulty in understanding how the blue sky can have been regarded as the sire of gods and men. And thus, as the elves and bogarts of popular lore are in many cases descended from ancient divinities of Olympos and Valhalla, so these in turn must acknowledge their ancestors in the shadowy denizens of the primeval ghost-world.

August, 1872.

NOTE.

THE following are some of the modern works most likely to be of use to the reader who is interested in the legend of William Tell.

HISELY, J. J.   Dissertatio historica inauguralis de Gulielmo Tellio, *etc.* Groningæ, 1824.

IDELER, J. L: Die Sage von dem Schuss des Tell. Berlin, 1836.

HÄUSSER, L. Die Sage vom Tell aufs Neue kritisch untersucht. Heidelberg, 1840.

HISELY, J. J.   Recherches critiques sur l'histoire de Guillaume Tell. Lausanne, 1843.

LIEBENAU, H.   Die Tell-Sage zu dem Jahre 1230 historisch nach neuesten Quellen. Aarau, 1864.

VISCHER, W.   Die Sage von der Befreiung der Waldstätte, *etc.* Nebst einer Beilage : das älteste Tellenschauspiel. Leipzig, 1867.

BORDIER, H. L.   Le Grütli et Guillaume Tell, ou défense de la tradition vulgaire sur les origines de la confédération suisse.   Genève et Bâle, 1869.

The same.   La querelle sur les traditions concernant l'origine de la confédération suisse. Genève et Bâle, 1869.

RILLIET, A.   Les origines de la confédération suisse : histoire et légende. 2ᵉ éd., revue et corrigée. Genève et Bâle, 1869.

The same.   Lettre à M. Henri Bordier à propos de sa défense de la tradition vulgaire sur les origines de la confédération suisse. Genève et Bâle, 1869.

HUNGERBÜHLER, H.   Étude critique sur les traditions relatives aux origines de la confédération suisse. Genève et Bâle, 1869.

MEYER, KARL.   Die Tellsage. [*In* Bartsch, Germanistische Studien, I. 159 – 170.] Wien, 1872.

See also the articles by M. Scherer, in *Le Temps*, 18 Feb., 1868 ; by M. Reuss, in the *Revue critique d'histoire*, 1868 ; by M. de Wiss, in the *Journal de Genève*, 7 July, 1868 ; also *Revue critique*, 17 July, 1869 ; *Journal de Genève*, 24 Oct., 1868 ; *Gazette de Lausanne*, feuilleton littéraire, 2 – 5 Nov., 1868, "Les origines de la confédération suisse," par M. Secrétan ; *Edinburgh Review*, Jan., 1869, "The Legend of Tell and Rütli."

INDEX.

THE END.